Sermons
from the
Bush

Sermons *from the* Bush

Ian Brickell

Sermons from the Bush
Published by Ian Brickell
New Zealand

© 2024 Ian Brickell

ISBN 978-0-473-72212-8 (Softcover)
ISBN 978-0-473-72213-5 (ePUB)
ISBN 978-0-473-72214-2 (Kindle)

Fourth updated edition 2024

Production & Typesetting:
Castle Publishing Services
www.castlepublishing.co.nz

Cover design:
Paul Smith

Unless otherwise indicated, all Scripture quotations are taken from
The Living Bible copyright © 1971.
Used by permission of Tyndale House Publishers, Inc.,
Carol Stream, Illinois 60188.
All rights reserved.

Copyright information for other versions used
appears at the back of this book.

ALL RIGHTS RESERVED

No part of this publication may be reproduced,
stored in a retrieval system, or transmitted
in any form or by any means, electronic, mechanical,
photocopying, recording or otherwise,
without prior written permission from the author.

Contents

Acknowledgements	9
Foreword by Bruce Cutler	11
A Fellow Traveller by Ros Rowe	13
One Solitary Life	17
Why I Believe in God by Winkie Pratney	19
The Sermons	23
The First Commandment	25
Self-worth	34
Ye Must Be Born Again	43
Seeking God	53
The Way	59
The Way of Fear	67
The Way of Humility	76
Wisdom	83
Faith	91
Revealing God's Glory	102
The Integrity of the Scriptures: Inspired by God	112
The Integrity of the Scriptures: The Way of Truth	118
Work Out Your Own Salvation	127
Salt – Light – Restraining	137
Listen and Obey	149
What Measure Ye Measure	160
Repent, for the Kingdom of Heaven is at Hand	168
Five Steps to Growing in Christ	181

Camels	193
Knowing the Faithfulness of God	201
Conquering Sin	208
Unravelling Some Mysteries	216
Faith for Today	226
Treasure-Hunting	231
Practical Christianity	238
Straining Out Gnats and Swallowing Camels	245
Standing Firm, Staying Grounded	255
Tested by the Word of God	264
Role of Women	276
Adamic Covenant	286
Left Behind	289
Communes: For Today or Not for Today?	297
All in a Month (Thessalonians, Message 1)	303
When Life Overflows (Thessalonians, Message 2)	309
Being a Christian (Thessalonians, Message 3)	314
Ready for Christ's Return (Thessalonians, Message 4)	320
Living as a Christian (Thessalonians, Message 5)	326
Rapture or Tribulation	333
Two Kingdoms – Two Days – Two Resurrections	343
Time to Get Serious	358
Staying Calm During Crises	368
Coming, Ready or Not	373
Two Faces of Evil	383
Understanding the Times	390
More on the Letters to the Churches (Revelation 2 & 3)	397
Global Warming is Not the Issue	415
The Bible: A Source of Guidance for the Future	423
Coincidence or Stark Warning?	426
Confidence in the Bible	429

Lessons from Past Revivals by Chris Strom	431
The Saint Must Walk Alone by A.W. Tozer	435
The Church and the World by Winkie Pratney	441
Cry Our Beloved Country – A Prayer	445
Epilogue	449
About the Author	451
Bible Versions Quoted	453

Acknowledgements

The Blessed Holy Spirit, my helper and teacher all these years, who alone is able to lead us into all truth.

My dear wife Carolyn, my faithful and loyal helpmate these past 58 years. So greatly loved by us all.

My granddaughter Bessie, who has worked so hard in the preparation of this book. She has certainly gone the extra mile for Granddad, and has provided all the photographs.

My daughter-in-law Bobbie, who has proofread the manuscript and corrected many mistakes.

My granddaughter Molly, who made time from her nursing studies to help with preparing the manuscript.

Last but not least, my granddaughter Ella, who does her best to keep Granddad on the straight and narrow path.

May God greatly bless you all.

Foreword
by Bruce Cutler

In life, sometimes your path will cross that of a person who will have an influence for the rest of your life.

I was a young farm adviser in the late 1960s, delegated the responsibility of supervising a government demonstration farm in the back-blocks of Northern Hawkes Bay. Naturally, I met with the adjoining ballot farm owners, one of whom was Ian Brickell.

That meeting was the birth of a friendship that continues to this day and which has influenced me in a way that has been positive, uplifting, challenging, supportive, generous, spiritual, and honouring to God. Wrap all this up in a bundle of passion, and that is who Ian Brickell is!

Read this book with a mind open to these influences. You will be challenged. You may not agree with all you read, but if you are honest with yourself and open your mind, your heart and your spirit, you will find pearls of great value.

Bruce Cutler

A Fellow Traveller
by Ros Rowe

Ian Brickell should not be a rarity, but he is becoming an increasingly endangered species. He has chosen to do what we all need to do, and that is to rely on the Word of God in our quest for the truth. His dedication to this shines from the pages of his book.

What drew me most to Ian was his close walk with the Lord and his adherence to the Scripture for guidance, obedience and hope. As a believer of some sixty years standing myself, I have witnessed, with dismay, the departure from the Bible as the inspired Word of God. It was refreshing to have conversations with someone whose steadfastness precluded him from falling into false doctrine. There is no room in his heart for the lukewarm Laodicean church, except as a mission field!

Ian has written many of his messages while in retreat at a basic hut on one of his farms, far from the reach of people and electronic devices. It is a perfect place to hear from God through the Word and the Holy Spirit. Not, I hasten to add, in the style of recent publications flooding the Christian bookshops by authors who claim to have conversations with God that only faintly pay homage to Scripture, or portray God the Father, the Son and the Holy Spirit as flawed humans who offer solace by watering down the truth.

He addresses the subjects of false teachers and New Age ideas creeping into the church in one of his sermons, a teaching all believers in these troubled times should delve into. Also, he tackles that one book in the Bible most preachers shy away from

– Revelation. He pays particular heed to the letters to the seven churches in Revelation chapters 2 and 3, which contain Christ's final messages to his church, where he emphasises the importance of listening to what the Spirit is saying.

I have listened to Ian's sermons at small gatherings made up of believers who want more than just the 'watered-down milk' served in so many churches today, and admit to having been challenged at times. Ian writes about contentious subjects such as the role of women in the church and the truth about global warming, and some may take issue with these, but they invite healthy discussion and debate. Proverbs 27:17 tells us that 'as iron sharpens iron, so a friend sharpens a friend'.

Anyone wanting 'happy-clappy' may have to look elsewhere, as Ian presents a less popular side of life for the true believer. For instance, the Christian walk can be a lonely one, as anyone who shuns the world's attraction knows, and Ian's inclusion of A.W. Tozer's sermon on the subject is inspired. Ian's sermon on 'The Way of Fear' doesn't portray God as the easy-going joker who doubles as a bellboy. What a foil for the 'pap' today's weak believers clamour for.

There is no doubt that the author of this book hears from God. But lest the readers imagine that he lives with his head in the clouds, piously above the reach of mere mortals like themselves, they should hop metaphorically on the back of his quad bike and head with him into the hills of his beloved Te Wae Wae. Until our Saviour blows the trumpet to call him home, Ian's at home out there in the bush. He's a totally down-to-earth man of the land, who rubs shoulders with all sorts, from church leaders to possum trappers. He gets on with most people, although he is fond of saying that he'd rather associate with 'rough diamonds' than 'polished glass'. Like most horses, he can spot a fake a mile away.

Ian Brickell is, above all, a person who is humble before his God.

What he has to say is worth reading – and heeding. Prepare to be challenged and inspired.

Ros Rowe
Founder of *Leg-Up Trust*, Hawke's Bay

One Solitary Life

There once was a man who was born in an obscure village, the child of a peasant woman. He grew to manhood in another obscure village – a despised one. The family was very poor; and when the father died, the boy took his father's place and supported his mother and family. He worked in a carpenter's shop until he was thirty, and then, for three years, was an itinerant minister. His short ministry was spent about the shores of one small lake. He never travelled more than two hundred miles from the place where he was born. He walked among men and women and touched their lives. His few intimate friends were lowly fishermen. He never wrote a book or won earthly fame. He never held office, owned a home or possessed material wealth. He never went to college or did any of the things that usually accompany greatness.

While he was still a young man, the tide of popular opinion turned against him. His friends ran away, and one of them denied him. His own people rejected him, turning him over to his enemies. He went through the mockery of a trial. Although guiltless, he was nailed to a cross between two thieves. His executioners gambled for the only piece of property he had on earth, his seamless robe. After he died, he was taken from the cross and laid in a borrowed grave, through the generosity of a friend.

Twenty centuries have come and gone, and I am well within the mark when I say that all the armies that ever marched, all the navies that were ever built, all the parliaments that ever sat, and all the kings that ever reigned, put together, have not affected the life of mankind upon this earth as powerfully as has that one solitary life.

Author unknown

Why I Believe in God
by Winkie Pratney

I believe in God
because I am a child of the age that asked life, 'why?'
So, I walked a road of honest reason, searching,
to find each answer pointing like light in his direction.
I needed a pathway,
I reached for reality
I hungered to live;
and he was closer than I dreamed.

I believe in God.
Each day this world declares him;
His wisdom stamps each snowflake 'made in Heaven!'
In the fresh chill of each new day
the air is alive with his closeness.
I feel his sky flare blue in praise above me,
watch a warm wind running ripples
as it blows across a field;
grip the good earth
and feel its rich black river cry,
'He lives!'
How can I help but believe?

I believe in God
when something deep within cries out

Sermons from the Bush

that I'm not a child of chance,
a lucky freak that grew unguided
from a mud without a mind.

I believe in God
for I am more than chemical change.
I am a man;
I know
I feel
I live
and love
and he who made me in his image
is worthy of my worship.
I have known God's nearness
for I have feet of clay and there are times
when no one could see if I should choose the wrong,
but when sin would be so simple
and I feel so strangely fascinated,
someone just seems to be there
someone puts me on my honour
someone dares me to do the difficult-
and no one is with me, my friend,
no one but God.

There is one book that speaks to me of God,
it struck within
a sacred flame that did not die.
This Bible tells of other men who felt as lost as I
who came with childlike trust
and found he did not lie.
Is it so hard to believe?
when we record the day he came

to cut our time in two?
Who else but Jesus showed us God made flesh,
the perfect Man who cannot be denied?
What other launched a life like his
to lift this world in love,
then cheated death to send us power from on
high?

And now
when earth-men walk among the stars
I know that the Creator walked my world.

I believe in God
for I have watched the men who do not care to own him;
I've seen, with sickness, little lives wrapped up in foolish pride,
with faces marked for all the world to see their sin,
who
just as I did
ran from Holy light
or tried to hide their selfish lives
beneath a shell of right.
Oh, stand them by a man who walks with God;
and see!

Yes,
I knew men who said there was no God,
but I listened as they died
and I knew that they had lied.

Say I am too young to be so sure,
but I am old enough to feel my age's agony,
its brokenness and barrenness,

to watch it waste with fear and war.
Yet I have seen from every tongue and tribe
like springing grain amid the sterile stone,
men come alive to live in love,
to share and care beneath Christ's cross...
and if you saw their smiles, you'd know
why I believe in God.

The day that I stopped running, this God found me.
Empty, trembling,
shaken with guilt and shame I came.
In a way I cannot draw with words.
He loved me,
forgave me,
restored
and gave me his own Name.
Say what you will,
but he met me then,
put in my heart
a homesickness for heaven.
I have heard the still, small Voice
and called him Friend
and I believe in God.

The Sermons

Rivers of living water shall flow from the inmost being of everyone who believes in me.
(John 7:38)

The First Commandment

This is a very old and well-known text:

> Hear O Israel, the Lord our God is one Lord. And thou shalt love the Lord your God with all your heart and with all your soul and with all your mind and with all your strength. (Mark 12:29-30 KJV)

Say slowly. God-wants-us-to-love-him. Sounds easy. God wants us to love him. But I believe he's asking us to love him in a way that we have not learnt to do so as yet. In a new way if you like. And in order to come into a new and deeper relationship with him, it is necessary to get to know him a little better.

Where do we start? It is not easy. God is so big, so wonderful, and the more we look, the greater he becomes. Can we ever get to know him fully? Perhaps not in this life but we can certainly make a start. Let's begin by looking at his love for us. Immediately we strike the first problem – we discover he loves us in so many ways.

To begin with, we are his creation. Remember the Creation story? God would create something new. At the end of each day, he would look at his handiwork and see that it was good. Six times it is recorded that he thought it was good. And at the end, after he had created mankind in his own image, after his creation was finished, it says,

> God saw everything that he had made, and behold, it was very good. (Genesis 1:31 KJV)

Very good! God loves his creation; every part of it is pleasing to him. But he especially loves man created in his own image. Can you imagine how God feels about the evolution lie?

> For everything created by God is good, and nothing is to be rejected if it is received with gratitude. (1 Timothy 4:4 ESV)

So, we are his creation. He is protective and jealous of his creation. He desires us to be grateful. But, as we all know, disaster struck and God's creation, which he had entrusted to mankind, became separated from him by sin.

Let us now look at the love of God our Saviour.

> The Lord thy God in the midst of thee is mighty. He will save, he will rejoice over thee with joy. He will rest in his love. He will joy over thee with singing. (Zephaniah 3:17 KJV)

> For God so loved the world, that he gave his only begotten son, that whoever believes in him should not perish, but have eternal life. For God did not send his Son to condemn the world but that the world should be saved through him. (John 3:16-17 KJV)

> God commended his love towards us, in that, while we were yet sinners, Christ died for us. (Romans 5:8 KJV)

Us all! All-encompassing love. Nobody left out. The most despised person in the world's eyes is precious to God. There's only one condition. Believe in the Lord Jesus Christ and you shall be saved. There is no other Saviour. No other way.

> Behold I have engraved thee on the palms of my hands. (Isaiah 49:16 KJV)

No wonder he commands us to love him. He has the right to, doesn't he?

Perhaps some of the following verses give us more insight into God's love and his feelings towards us. We see the love of God our Father in these verses.

> You have seen what I did to the Egyptians, and how I bore you on eagle's wings and brought you to myself. You shall be a special treasure to me, above all people. You shall be to me a kingdom of priests and a holy nation. (Exodus 19:4 KJV)

> I will walk among you and will be your God, and you shall be my people. (Leviticus 26:12 KJV)

> The Lord did not set his affection on you and choose you because you were more in number than any people, for you are the fewest of all people. But it was because the Lord loved you. He will love you and bless you. (Deuteronomy 7:7-8,13)

> For thus saith the Lord of hosts, I am jealous for Jerusalem and for Zion with a great jealousy. He that touches you touches the apple of my eye. (Zachariah 1:14 KJV)

> The beloved of the Lord shall dwell in safety by him, and the Lord shall cover him all the day long and he shall dwell between his shoulders. (Deuteronomy 33:12 KJV)

Between his shoulders. As a father carrying the little ones on his shoulders. And God carries us. Have you had a ride on his shoulders lately? Perhaps he's waiting for you to ask.

Let us look a little more at the love of God our Father. One of the better-known stories in the New Testament is the one our

Lord Jesus told of the prodigal son. We will just touch on a few verses.

Remember, the young man had actually got to the stage where he was eating pig food when he finally came to his senses and realised that things were a whole lot better for his father's servants than they were for him.

> And he arose and came to his father. But when he was yet a great way off, his father saw him and had compassion and ran, and fell on his neck and kissed him, and the son said to him, 'Father I have sinned against heaven and in thy sight, and I am not worthy to be called thy son.' But the father said to his servants, 'bring forth the best robe, and put it on him, and put a ring on his hand and shoes on his feet. And bring the fattened calf and kill it.' (Luke 15:20-23 KJV)

When did the father meet him? When he was yet a great way off. It is the same with us. Our Father has met us while we are still a great way off.

When did the father order his servants to clothe him with the best robe, the robe of righteousness? When he reached the point of honesty and humility, when he reached that place of true repentance, what did the father do? Showered him with gifts.

The robe of righteousness, a ring of betrothal and shoes of the gospel to spread the Good News. Not only that, he prepared a feast for him. Exactly as he does for us today. We don't necessarily have to eat pig food, but we do have to reach the same point of honesty and repentance that the prodigal son did.

> And because you are his sons, God has sent forth the spirit of adoption into our hearts, crying Abba Father. Therefore you are

no longer a slave but a son, and if a son, then an heir through Christ. (Galatians 4:6-7 KJV)

Intimate! And as if all these things were not enough;

The eye has not seen, nor ear heard, neither have entered into the heart of man, the things which God has prepared for them that love him.' (1 Corinthians 2:9 KJV)

No wonder he wants us to love him. It is for our sake, not his. Let us look deeper into God's amazing love for us.

For ye see your calling, brethren, how that not many wise men after the flesh, not many mighty, not many noble, are called: But God hath chosen the foolish things of the world to confound the wise; and God hath chosen the weak things of the world to confound the things which are mighty; And base things of the world, and things which are despised, hath God chosen, yea, and things which are not, to bring to naught things that are: That no flesh should glory in his presence. But of him are ye in Christ Jesus, who of God is made unto us wisdom, and righteousness, and sanctification, and redemption: That, according as it is written, He that glorieth, let him glory in the Lord. (1 Corinthians 1:26-31 KJV)

Do you understand the implications of the verse, 'But of him are ye in Christ Jesus, who of God is made unto us wisdom, and righteousness, and sanctification, and redemption'? I doubt if any of us fully do. By God's doing you are in Jesus Christ. In Jesus you have wisdom from God, righteousness, sanctification and redemption, and a whole lot of other things that we think we lack or do lack in the flesh.

Today I want to encourage you even further in God's love. Do you feel that you lack wisdom or education? Maybe it is just confidence you are lacking. Are you conscious of your social or ethnic background? Not much blue blood flowing in your veins? Or worse, from a family that has known shame or a family under spiritual bondage from some sin in the past? Perhaps you haven't got much personality. Not very charismatic. Not a natural leader. Don't seem to have much natural authority, not the best farmer, not the perfect mother?

Be of good cheer. You could be just the person God is looking for. Let's look at some examples in the scripture.

Ruth, a Moabite woman
Not accepted by the majority. Surviving on the gleanings of the harvest. But God raised her up in a wonderful way: Grandmother of Kings David and Solomon. The only Gentile blood in Jesus' ancestry. One of the books of the Bible named after her. A woman greatly honoured by God.

Gideon

> 'Oh Lord, how shall I ever deliver Israel? Behold my family is the least in Manasseh and I am the youngest.' (Judges 6:15 NASB)

> ...then Gideon took 10 men of his servant's and did as the Lord had spoken to him, and it came about because he was too afraid of his father's household and the men of the city to do it by day, that he did it by night. (Judges 6:27 KJV)

But he did do it; he did obey. Then there was all the business with the fleeces. First, he wanted it wet on top and dry on the bottom. Then he wanted it dry on top and wet on the bottom. You certainly couldn't describe Gideon as a bold, decisive person. But Gideon was precious to God and God raised him up and used him in a mighty way. First as a deliverer of Israel against incredible odds. Then as a keeper of the peace for 40 years.

Jephthah the Gileadean
Son of a harlot. Driven out of his father's house by his own brothers and sisters. He wasn't good enough. But he was precious in God's sight. God had his hand on Jephthah, and he raised up this despised man to be a deliverer and a leader of Israel. His name and Gideon's are both mentioned in the book of Hebrews amongst the mighty men of faith.

Saul of Tarsus
No question he was well educated. He was a student of the great teacher Gamaliel. He even had some breeding. But listen to the Jerusalem Bible:

> He writes powerful and strongly worded letters but when he's with you, you only see half a man and no preacher at all. (2 Corinthians 10:15)

The Living Bible is much more to the point. It says,

> ...you have never heard a worse preacher.

Some versions call him 'weak', 'feeble', 'an unimpressive person'. Reputed to be only four foot six, he was up against it right from the start. Murdering Christians. Hardly the best way to endear yourself to your future brother and sisters in Christ! He certainly wasn't a particularly nice character to start with.

Even after his conversion, he had no contact with the apostles for three years but went into Arabia. He never walked with Jesus in the flesh like the other apostles of his time. Not one of the twelve. Not even one of the 70. But in Jesus, he became the mighty apostle Paul. One of the truly great men of the New Testament.

And so many more. John the Baptist. The apostles themselves. Uneducated fishermen, a despised tax collector, Nathanial the cynic. Thomas the doubter. Peter, impetuous and then denying Jesus.

Yet in Jesus' Kingdom they will judge the twelve tribes of Israel. Mighty men of God. Leaders of great wisdom and great deeds. Through the saving grace of Jesus and the empowering of the blessed Holy Spirit. In their time they succeeded in turning the world upside down.

It was the same with John Wesley. They said of him: 'This man and his motley bunch of tinkers and tailors have all turned the country upside down.' For Jesus. Hallelujah! They were in Jesus. And by God's grace it is going to happen again. I've heard it said that when the blessed Holy Spirit moves in this nation it will not necessarily be prominent leaders of the church, but ordinary people, like little old ladies, faithful in prayer, who will be raising the dead.

C.T. Studd had it right. Any old turnip will do for a head. What God wants are hearts on fire for Jesus.

> For that which is highly esteemed among men is detestable in the sight of God. (Luke 16:15 KJV)

It is not ability God wants. It is love, gratitude, trust, obedience and availability. I want you to understand three things before you leave this morning:

1. You are incredibly precious and of infinite value to God – each one of you.
2. You are able to do all things through Christ who strengthens you.
3. Jesus said: 'You didn't choose me! I chose you! I appointed you to go and produce lovely fruit always, so that no matter what you ask for from the Father, using my name, he will give it to you'. (John 15:16)

Is it any wonder that God commands us to love him and love one another? When we begin to obey these commandments, we unleash a tidal wave of his love and his power into our lives, our church and our nation.

Self-worth

Now Jephthah was a great warrior from the land of Gilead, but his mother was a prostitute. His father (whose name was Gilead) had several other sons by his legitimate wife, and when these half brothers grew up, they chased Jephthah out of the country.

'You son of a whore!' they said. 'You'll not get any of our father's estate.'

So Jephthah fled from his father's home and lived in the land of Tob. Soon he had quite a band of malcontents as his followers, living off the land as bandits. It was about this time that the Ammonites began their war against Israel. The leaders of Gilead sent for Jephthah, begging him to come and lead their army against the Ammonites.

But Jephthah said to them, 'Why do you come to me when you hate me and have driven me out of my father's house? Why come now when you're in trouble?'

'Because we need you,' they replied. 'If you will be our commander-in-chief against the Ammonites, we will make you the king of Gilead.'

'Sure!' Jephthah exclaimed. 'Do you expect me to believe that?'

'We swear it,' they replied. 'We promise with a solemn oath.'

So Jephthah accepted the commission and was made commander-in-chief and king. The contract was ratified before the Lord in Mizpah at a general assembly of all the people. (Judges 11:1-11)

Self-worth

From time to time I hear people putting themselves down (and this is concerning) with remarks such as: 'I am fat', 'I have ugly legs', 'I am ugly', 'I have no friends' and 'I am dumb'. I am sure you have all heard these and worse. One hears people putting others down – for example, employers to their staff, parents to their children, husbands to their wives and vice-versa. These words can have a devastating effect, especially on children. I have seen two marriages destroyed because the husbands were constantly criticising and putting their wives down.

This talk is about self-worth and also about how utterly precious we are in God's sight. Perhaps we will gain a glimpse of just how much he loves us. I am sure this message is timely because after I began preparing it, I read in the newspaper that the late Billy Graham was speaking globally along similar lines. So, if you do not believe this message, then listen to the teaching of Billy Graham instead! We heard in the previous reading from Judges how Jephthah was despised by his brethren – his own family. And why? Because his mother was a harlot.

It didn't matter to them that he was a righteous man who spoke all his words before the Lord. Nor that he was also a man of great courage, a mighty man of valour and a natural leader. They ignored all these things and threw him out of the family because he was the son of another woman – same father, different mother.

But (praise God!) – God didn't despise Jephthah. He loved this man of valour and he raised him up to be a deliverer and a leader of his nation. You will find his name in the book of Hebrews, listed among those elite men and woman of faith found in the Old Testament.

It is high time we stopped looking at ourselves and others through our own eyes, and rather look as God does. Let us go right back to the book of Genesis – to the very beginning, when God created the world and all that is in it. At the end of each day, as

God completed another stage of his creation, he would stop and contemplate his handiwork and say, 'It is good.' And it *is* good! I marvel at the awesome splendour of God's creation – and I am sure we all do. It is just so incredibly magnificent, to say the least.

And when he had finished, he said:

> Let us make man in our image, after our likeness. (Genesis 1:26 KJV)

The point is, after God had created man in his image (or, if you like, the Godhead had created man in their image), he stood back, viewed his finished creation, and said: 'It is *very* good' (Genesis 1:31 KJV).

Mankind was the crowning glory of God's creation. Before man was created, he said it was good. After mankind was created, God said it was *very* good.

> For you have created all things [which includes all people], and for thy pleasure they are and were created. (Revelation 4:11 KJV)

This passage says it quite clearly. If you want further proof about how God feels about his creation, then read this:

> For everything created by God is good, and nothing [and I am sure that that means nobody] is to be rejected, if it is received with gratitude. (1 Timothy 4:4 AMP).

Every time we knock ourselves and knock other people, we are knocking God's creation. We are his handiwork, with which he is so pleased and which he loves so much. We are utterly precious to God – each one of us.

Jesus speaking to his disciples said the following:

Self-worth

> Are not five sparrows sold for two farthings and not one of them is forgotten before God? But even the very hairs of your head are all numbered. Fear not therefore, you are of more value than many sparrows. (Luke 12:6-7 KJV)

> And thy thoughts which are towards us, they cannot be reckoned up in order unto thee, they are more than can be numbered. (Psalm 40:5 KJV)

Or, as some Bible versions say: 'more than the grains of sand on the seashore'.

That is an indication of just how important we are to God. He thinks so highly about each one of us, as the following verse we all know so well tells us:

> For God so loved the world that he gave his only begotten Son, that whosoever believeth in him should not perish, but have everlasting life. For God did not send his Son to condemn the world, but that the world through him might be saved. (John 3:16-17 KJV)

Let us look at this verse carefully. God so loved you and me that he gave his only Son – Jesus, the only-begotten Son of God. The rest of us are created beings who, if we have been born again, have become adopted children of God. But Jesus is unique, the only-begotten Son of God.

God had nothing greater or more to give than Jesus – Jesus is the human manifestation of himself. He had to become a man in order to redeem man. Why? So that we would not perish through our own folly and sinfulness, but receive eternal life through him. This has to be the most powerful kind of love imaginable – especially when we relate it to Jesus' suffering and agonising on the cross on our behalf, paying the price for our sin and disobedience.

Let's look at the passage again. It says, in verse 17, that God did not send Jesus to condemn us, but rather to save us.

If Jesus does not condemn us, why then do we condemn ourselves and others? Are we greater than Christ? Can you see why it is so utterly wrong to do so?

> While we were yet sinners, Christ died for us all. (Romans 5:8)

Us all! All of us! Nobody is left out. The most despised person in the world's eyes is utterly precious to God. There are millions of Christians in the world today who can bear witness to the truth of this verse. The conditions are simple. Believe in the Lord Jesus Christ! Believe in the gospel! Believe in his love, his faithfulness, his goodness and his kindness. Oh, that we might start believing. Then we wouldn't have time for knocking and doubting.

> If God be for us, who can be against us. He that spared not his own Son, but delivered him up for us all, how shall he not with him also freely give us all things? (Romans 8:31-32 KJV)

Why, oh why, do we worry so much about what other people might think or say? If God be for us, who can be against us? If you want further confirmation of this, read God's promise to Joshua.

> There shall not any man be able to stand before thee all the days of thy life. As I was with Moses, so I will be with thee. (Joshua 1:5 KJV)

Praise God for his faithfulness. If those words applied only to Joshua, they wouldn't be recorded as they are. These words apply to all who walk with God in Christ Jesus. Let us read the promise again:

Self-worth

> If God be for us, who can ever be against us? He that spared not his own Son, but delivered him up for us all. (Romans 8:31-32 KJV)

Everyone. None left out. There is no one who approaches God with an honest and humble heart who is despised in his eyes. Look at the prodigal son:

> And while he was still a long distance away, his father saw him coming, and was filled with loving pity and ran and embraced him and kissed him. (Luke 15:20)

And look what he offers to those who come:

> How shall he not with him also [speaking of Jesus] freely give us all things? (Romans 8.32 KJV)

Jesus himself said,

> I came that you might have life and have it more abundantly. (John 10:10 KJV)

I have said it before and I will say it again. There are far too many Christians not walking in the fullness of their salvation. I am not seeking to condemn anyone in saying this, but I am rather trying to encourage you to reach out and grab hold of all that God is offering you. Do you fully understand what God is saying?

> But by his [God's] doing you are in Christ Jesus, who became for us wisdom from God, righteousness, sanctification and redemption. (1 Corinthians 1:30 NASB)

Do you ever feel foolish? Do you ever feel unrighteous? Do you ever feel unclean? Are you afraid of death? If we are really honest, I bet there are times when we all feel some or all of these things. And there is basically just one reason for this. We are not abiding in Christ Jesus as we ought to be. Look at the following verse. Many of you will know it by heart:

> There is therefore now no condemnation to them which are in Christ Jesus, who walk every day with the Lord.

Or as the King James version says,

> ...who walk not after the flesh but after the Spirit. (Romans 8:1 KJV)

I used to think there were quite a number of things that hindered our spiritual growth – unforgiveness, unbelief and our being born into bondage. It is true that all these things can hinder us, but as Jesus said to Martha:

> 'Martha, dear friend, you are so upset over all these details! There is really only one thing worth being concerned about. Mary has discovered it – and I won't take it away from her!' (Luke 10:41-42)

Abiding is what matters. Spending time with Jesus. All the rest will follow in due course. Look, it is good to come to church and be involved in church-related activities, but if you want to live and walk in victory in every area of your life (and walk by the Spirit, not the flesh, and become fruit-bearing disciples), you are going to have to learn to abide. Jesus said the following words:

> Abide in me, and I in you. As the branch cannot bear fruit of itself, except it abide in the vine, no more can you, except you abide in me. (John 15.4 KJV)

Self-worth

We must abide. Note the order: 'Abide in me, then I in you'. As we spend time with Jesus, as we abide in him, so he comes to us. We must spend time in fellowship with Jesus. This is meant to be a love affair. And I say that in all seriousness. Tell him what he really means to you. Thank him for all the blessings he has bestowed on you. Even when things seem bad, thank and praise him. Have you ever heard of the sacrifice of praise? Powerful stuff, I can tell you. It is not hard to think of things to praise him for – his creation, his love, his dying on the cross, the wonderful power of his resurrection that is available to all of us. Our wives, our children, our wider families(especially our parents), the good food we enjoy, the privilege of living in New Zealand. There is just so much to be grateful for. We need to spend time kneeling at his feet like Mary did.

If you don't feel spiritual, ask God for more of his Spirit.

> How much more will your Heavenly Father give the Holy Spirit to those who ask him. (Luke 11:13 KJV)

But get serious about it. Sometimes we have to get persistent. God likes that. Mean business when you pray, and ask for things. Don't be half-hearted or lukewarm like the Christians in the church at Laodicea. This is a scary verse:

> So then, because you are lukewarm, and neither cold nor hot, I will spew you out of my mouth. (Revelation 3:16 KJV)

I tell you that if the Presbyterian Church of New Zealand doesn't stand up and take a stand on the homosexual issue they are debating at Assembly this year, they are in grave danger of this very thing happening to them.

You can't 'sit on the fence' in issues like this. Jesus does not want us to be lukewarm followers. He desires us to walk in the very fullness of our salvation – living life abundantly in him. He desires that we abide in him and he in us, bearing much fruit. For it is by bearing fruit that we prove we are his disciples.

> That which is highly esteemed among men is detestable in the sight of God. (Luke 16:15 KJV)

It is not *ability* God wants, but *availability*.

I want to leave you with three thoughts. Firstly, you are incredibly precious and of infinite value to God. Each one of you. Secondly, you are able to do all things through Christ who strengthens you. Thirdly, the very words of Jesus himself:

> Ye have not chosen me, but I have chosen you, and ordained you, that ye should go and bring forth fruit, and that your fruit should remain: that whatsoever ye shall ask of the Father in my name, he may give it you. (John 15:16 KJV)

Let us pray. Father God, I pray that you will quicken these things in our hearts by your Spirit. Help us to hear and to respond.

Father, I ask you to forgive us for the times we have been lukewarm. Forgive us, I ask, Father.

Holy Spirit, help us to abide in Jesus so that he will be pleased to dwell in us also. And grant that we may indeed bear much fruit. Fruit which remains. In Jesus' name we ask and pray. Amen.

Ye Must Be Born Again

After dark one night, a Jewish religious leader named Nicodemus, a member of the sect of the Pharisees, came for an interview with Jesus. 'Sir' he said, 'we all know that God has sent you to teach us. Your miracles are proof enough of this.'

Jesus replied, 'With all the earnestness I possess, I tell you this, 'unless you are born again you can never get into the Kingdom of God.'

'Born again!' exclaimed Nicodemus. 'What do you mean? How can an old man go back into his mother's womb and be born again?'

Jesus replied, 'What I am telling you so earnestly is this; unless one is born of water and the Spirit, he cannot enter the Kingdom of God. Men can only reproduce human life, but the Holy Spirit gives new life from heaven; so, don't be surprised at my statement that you must be born again! That which is born of the flesh is flesh; and that which is born of the Spirit is Spirit. (John 3:1-7)

In Corinthians it says:

When someone becomes a Christian, he becomes a brand-new person inside. He is not the same any more. A new life has begun. (2 Corinthians 5:17)

As Jesus made clear, when we are 'born again' we become children of God.

> Haven't you yet learned that your body is the home of the Holy Spirit God gave to you, and he lives within you. Your own body does not belong to you. For God has bought you with a great price. So, use every part of your body to give glory back to God, because he owns it. (1 Corinthians 6:19-20)

Because he owns it, your own body does not belong to you. How we need to come to grips with this great truth. We belong to him, we are not our own. We have been purchased at a very great price.

Too many of us have a great big 'I' or 'me' on the throne of our lives. In so many ways, we want things our way and on our terms. We want all the benefits of God's love and promises, without being prepared to die to the flesh and self. We want it all on our terms, not his.

We want to remain in control, but where does that leave Jesus? Outside the door of our heart and church – knocking, wanting to come in and take his rightful place as Lord of this new life he purchased for us on the cross at Calvary.

> Behold I stand at the door and knock (Revelation 3:20, KJV)

This verse is often used as a call to salvation, but it is addressed to the members of the Laodicean church, who claimed they were rich and had everything they needed.

Obedience and submission do not come easily. There is a large amount of 'Cain' in all of us. Cain was willing to bring an offering to God, but he chose to do it on his terms, not God's. And what happened? God rejected Cain's offering.

It has to be on our Lord's terms. This is simply not negotiable. Either his terms or we remain as spiritual babies, as described in the book of Hebrews. The writer of Hebrews wrote to the group of Christian believers as follows:

> You have been Christians for a long time now, and you ought to be teaching others, but instead you have dropped back to the place where you need someone to teach you all over again the very first principles in God's Word. You are like babies who can drink only milk, not old enough for solid food. And when a person is still living on milk it shows he isn't very far along the Christian life, and doesn't know much about the difference between right and wrong. He is still a baby-Christian! You will never be able to eat solid spiritual food and understand the deeper things of God's Word until you become better Christians and learn right from wrong by practicing doing right. (Hebrews 5:12-14)

These were older, long-standing Christians still living on milk. Teat-sucking Christians, still sucking on the breast of dependence. Why was this? Verse 14 gives us a clue:

> You will never be able to eat solid spiritual food and understand the deeper things of God's Word until you become better Christians and learn right from wrong by practicing doing right.

Yes, we have to put it into practice. Perhaps the Phillips Translation puts it best:

> You have become a people who need a milk diet and cannot face solid food! For anyone who continues to live on milk is unable to digest what is right, he simply has not grown up yet. Their stomachs can't handle solid food.

This group had been believers a long time, and yet they had still not progressed to solid food. They were quite content with sucking away on the teat of dependence on others. And that is fine for young babies – they need nurturing and mothering. They need to be cleaned up when they get messy, and they yell when they get hurt, suffer pain or need attention. You know how it is with babies.

But babies are not meant to remain babies all their lives, cute and lovely as they are. They need to progress on to solid food, or they simply will not grow.

And we all need to grow in Jesus, also to the point where we stop yelling for help every time we fall over or mess ourselves. We are supposed to share one another's burdens. Babies still have to be carried.

I have known a number of people, both believers and unbelievers, who are still seeking counsel and help for the same problem or problems they have had for years. It makes them feel important to be the centre of attention. This is not how it should be. Why is this? Frankly, in some cases, they like it that way. This is why Jesus asked the blind man:

'What do you want me to do for you?' (Matthew 10:51)

So, whatever the problem may be, take it to the cross, to Jesus, and leave it there. Don't keep digging it up and talking about it. When we are born again, we die to the old life and are born or raised into a new life.

We walk by faith, not by sight. (2 Corinthians 5:7 KJV)

As we read before, When someone becomes a Christian, he (or she) becomes a brand-new person inside. He is not the same any more. A new life has begun. (2 Corinthians 5:17)

Paul explains clearly what happens when we are born into God's family and become Christians.

> Sin's power over us was broken when we became Christians and were baptized to become a part of Jesus Christ; through his death the power of your sinful nature was shattered. Your old sin-loving nature was buried with him by baptism when he died; and when God the Father, with glorious power, brought him back to life again, you were given his wonderful new life to enjoy. For you have become a part of him, and so you died with him, so to speak, when he died; and now you share his new life and shall rise as he did. Your old evil desires were nailed to the cross with him; that part of you that loves to sin was crushed and fatally wounded, so that your sin-loving body is no longer under sin's control, no longer needs to be a slave to sin; for when you are deadened to sin you are freed from all its allure and its power over you. And since your old sin-loving nature 'died' with Christ, we know that you will share his new life. Christ rose from the dead and will never die again. Death no longer has any power over him. He died once for all to end sin's power, but now he lives forever in unbroken fellowship with God. So look upon your old sin nature as dead and unresponsive to sin, and instead be alive to God, alert to him, through Jesus Christ our Lord. (Romans 6:3-11)

Look, our past is dead and buried. It was all part of the former sinful man or woman that we were.

> I have been crucified with Christ; and I myself no longer live, but Christ lives in me. And the real life I now have within this body is a result of my trusting in the Son of God who loved me and gave Himself for me. I am not one who treats Christ's death as meaningless. (Galatians 2:20-21)

Anyone who is wanting to keep living in the past, or is simply keeping a foot in both camps (the world and the church), or is only willing to serve God on his or her terms, not his (God's) is never going to grow into a mature man or woman of God.

Either we let go of the world and the old life in the flesh and grow in faith through obedience, or we keep clinging to it and remain spiritual babies. Let this message sink deeply into our ears and our hearts. It is simply our choice. If we want to mature and grow in Christ, we have to put all that behind us.

If our Heavenly Father has washed our past into the sea of his forgetfulness and removed it as far as the east is from the west, then we have absolutely no right to keep on hanging on to it. Because, as Paul says,

> We have been crucified with Christ, and we ourselves no longer live, but Christ lives in us. (Galatians 2:20)

Our past, our old life in the flesh, is dead and buried. Gone forever. That is the way it has to be. Every time we dig it up, we are like grave-robbers. Much worse, every time we dig it up, we are,

> One of those who treats Christ's death as meaningless. (Galatians 2:21)

Our whole focus in this new life in the Spirit is to grow up into the fullness of Christ himself. To become mature men and women of God. I quote from *The Word for Today*:

> Now, while effort has nothing to do with salvation, it has everything to do with growth. Eight times in the N.T. we are told to make every effort toward becoming like Christ. It doesn't just happen. It is conditional on our obedience.

When we don't obey, we don't grow. How can this happen?

> Beware of being like them and losing the prize that you and I have been working so hard to get. See to it that you win your full reward from the Lord. (2 John 8)

If we wander beyond the teaching of Christ, we leave God behind. It is just that simple. God tells us we need fear nothing but the Lord of the Armies of Heaven; if we fear him, we need fear nothing else. He will be our safety. (Tell that to the proponents of global warming.)

We have to start believing him. Somewhere along the way we have to start trusting him. Why?

> Because without faith it is impossible to please him. (Hebrews 11:6 KJV)

It is just that simple. It is not rocket science. All he wants us to do is believe him, trust him and obey him.

> You have been bought and paid for by Christ so you belong to him. Be free now from all these earthly prides and fears. (1 Corinthians 7:23)

Note the scriptures lump pride and fear together. Trouble is, we think we know better than God. Let us now take this growing in Christ further.

> Since we believe that Christ died for all of us, we should also believe that we have died to the old life we used to live. He died for us all; so that all who live, having received Eternal Life from him, might live no longer for themselves [to please themselves] but to spend their lives pleasing Christ who died and rose again for them. (2 Corinthians. 5:14-15)

Revelation reinforces this message:

> For thou hast created all things, and for thy pleasure they are and were created. (Revelation 4:11 KJV)

This should be our whole focus in this new life we have been given. To please him and to reveal his glory. His, not ours.

> You should have as little desire for this world as a dead person does. Your real life is in Heaven with Christ and God. (Colossians 3:3)

That does not mean that we are of no earthly use. It does mean that whatever we do, we do it as to the Lord.

> We should make plans – counting on God to direct us. (Proverbs 16:9)

Moses was speaking with God and he requested:

> Guide me clearly along the way you want me to travel so I will understand you and walk acceptably before you. (Exodus 33:13)

Abraham's faithful servant Eliezer was praying:

> Oh Jehovah the God of my master,' he prayed, 'show kindness to my master Abraham and help me to accomplish the purpose of my journey. (Genesis 24:12)

We too can pray these prayers. Our master is Jesus. In our daily life, whatever our occupation or calling, we are being trained, tested and evaluated in everything we do. We should do it as to the Lord, with our whole focus on obeying and pleasing him. Our obedience in these matters, even in small menial tasks, will determine our future in heaven. Remember our Lord's promise:

> Well done, good and faithful servant; thou hast been faithful over a few things, I will make thee ruler over many things: enter thou into the joy of thy lord. (Matthew 25:23 KJV)

Peter has some good advice for us too.

> Long to grow up in the fullness of your Salvation; cry for this as a baby cries for his milk. (1 Peter 2:2-3)

Peter is not telling us to cry for milk, but he is exhorting us to really grow into the fullness of our salvation. So, cry out to God like a hungry baby. Cry to experience the fullness of this great and wonderful salvation which God has granted to us in Jesus.

Paul instructs us:

> You must be an example of good deeds of every kind. Let everything you do reflect your love of the truth and the fact you are in dead earnest about it. (Titus 2:7)

> It isn't enough just to have faith; you must do good works to prove that you have it. (James 2:17)

> You yourselves are our witness – as is God – that we have been pure and honest and faultless towards every one of you. (1 Thessalonians 2:10)

I have said it before and I will say it again – it is by our fruits we are known. Look, our Christian witness is of little or no value or effect if non-Christians can see bad fruit in us. And boy, do they watch our every move and hold on to our every word.

We will let Paul have the last word today.

> But I don't want anyone to think more highly of me than he should from what he can actually see in my life and my message. (2 Corinthians 12:6)

That says it all, doesn't it?

Seeking God

The next question is an important one. Why seek God?

1. We are commanded to seek him

> Seek the Lord and His strength, seek His face continually. (1 Chronicles 16:11)

King David is speaking to God here:

> When thou said'st, 'Seek my face,' my heart said to thee, 'Thy face, O Lord, I shall seek.' (Psalm 27:8 KJV)

Jesus said:

> Seek ye first the Kingdom of God and his righteousness and all these things shall be added unto you. (Matthew 6:33 KJV)

2. We were created to seek him
Speaking of God's creation, the Bible says:

> 'His purpose in all this is that they (us) should seek after God. And perhaps feel their way towards him and find him, though he is not far from any one of us.' (Acts 17:27)

3. Seeking is a test of our faithfulness

> The Lord looked down from Heaven upon the children of men, to see if there were any that did understand, and seek God.' (Psalm 14:2 KJV)

> And ye shall seek me and find me when ye shall search for me with all your heart (Jeremiah. 29:13 KJV)

> But without faith it is impossible to please him: for he that cometh to God must believe that he is, and that he is a rewarder of them that diligently seek him. (Hebrews 11:6 KJV)

The Greek word for 'seek', is a very strong word – Ek-zay-teh'-o – which means, 'search out', 'crave' or 'demand'.

> Those that seek me early shall find me. (Proverbs 8:17 KJV)

> O God, thou art my God, early will I seek thee. (Psalm 63:1 KJV)

Hosea, speaking prophetically, said the following:

> Afterwards shall the children of Israel return and seek the Lord their God, and David their king; and shall fear the Lord and his goodness in the latter days. (Hosea 3:5 KJV)

4. God will bless those who seek him

> The Lord is with you, while you be with him, and if ye seek him, He will be found of you, but if you forsake him, he will forsake you. (2 Chronicles 15:2 KJV)

Speaking of King Uzziah:

And as long as he sought the Lord, God made him prosper. (2 Chronicles 26:5 KJV)

Speaking of King Hezekiah:

And in every good work which he began in the service of the House of God in law and commandment, seeking his God, he did with all his heart and prospered. (2 Chronicles 31:21 KJV)

The Psalmist:

I sought the Lord, and he heard me, and delivered me from all my fears. (Psalm 34:4 KJV)

Seek the Lord and his strength, seek his face forevermore. (Psalm 105:4 KJV)

Proverbs:

If thou criest after understanding. If thou seekest her as silver and searcheth for her as for hid treasures. Then shalt thou understand the fear of the Lord, and find knowledge of God. (Proverbs 2:3-5 KJV)

But they that seek the Lord, understand all things. (Proverbs 28:5 KJV)

Seek ye first the kingdom of God, and his righteousness; and all these things shall be added unto you. (Matthew 6:33 KJV)

Seek and ye shall find. (Luke 11:9 KJV)

Seeking entails keeping on seeking.

Blessed are they that keep his testimonies, and that seek him with a whole heart. (Psalm 119:2 KJV)

5. Seeking brings revival and healing

If my people who are called by my name, will humble themselves and pray, and seek my face, and turn from their wicked ways, then I will hear from Heaven and heal their land.' (2 Chronicles 7:14 KJV)

I set my face unto the Lord God, to seek by prayer and supplications, with fasting and sackcloth and ashes. (Daniel 9:3 KJV)

It is time to seek the Lord till he come and rain righteousness upon you. (Hosea 10:12 KJV)

He gives power to the tired and worn out, and strength to the weak. (Isaiah 40:29)

Did men of God get answers? They certainly did! Elijah was a man who sought God's face.

Elijah was as completely human as we are, and yet when he prayed earnestly that no rain would fall, none fell for the next three and a half years! Then he prayed again, this time that it would rain, and down it poured, and the grass turned green and the gardens began to grow again. (James 5:17-18)

In conclusion, let us look at how this commandment to seek God was fulfilled in the life of Jesus, as well as in Paul and other New Testament Christians. Firstly, and most obviously, Jesus himself taught us to seek God. It was he who taught us the following:

> But seek ye first the kingdom of God, and his righteousness; and all these things shall be added unto you. (Matthew 6:33 KJV)

> Seek and ye shall find. (Matthew 7:7 KJV)

Let us look at the example he himself set the night before he chose his disciples:

> And it was at this time that he went off to the mountain to pray, and he spent the whole night in prayer to God. (Luke 6:12 NASB)

Here are some more of Jesus' words:

> Truly, truly I say to you, the Son can do nothing of himself, unless it is something he sees the Father doing. (John 5:19 KJV)

> I can do nothing of my own initiative, As I hear I judge, and my judgment is just, because I do not seek my own will, but the will of him who sent me. (Matthew 5:30 KJV)

Jesus sought God's will in everything he did, but in some ways Paul's story is even more graphic.

> Dear friends, I solemnly swear that the way to heaven that I preach is not based on some mere human whim or dream. For my message comes from no less a person than Jesus Christ himself, who told me what to say. No one else has taught me. (Galatians 1:11)

Do you pick up the incredible implications of Paul's testimony? He kept away from all people, even the Apostles, for three years whilst he sought revelation from Jesus alone. And what a revelation he had!

It is good to come to church. It is good to go off to conventions and Summer School. It is good to read Christian books. It is good to listen to Christian music. It is good to go to house groups and prayer meetings.

But how God longs for those who will seek his face and his presence. Those who will take time off from life's busyness and just spend time alone with him, seeking his will and his purpose for their lives.

> Behold, I stand at the door and knock; if anyone hears my voice and opens the door, I will come into him, and will sup [dine] with him, and he with me. (Revelation 3:20 KJV)

The Way

Guide me clearly along the way you want me to travel (Exodus 33:13)

Why? Because God's way is different, and if we are not able to learn and accept God's way and understand him and what he requires and desires from us, he won't (indeed is not able to) travel with us. It has to be on his terms, not ours. And that truly is the key to the Christian life.

Moses latched on to this great truth and hence his words to God:

> If you aren't going with us, don't let us move a step from this place. If you don't go with us, who will ever know that I and my people have found favour with you, and that we are different from any other people upon the face of the earth. (Exodus 33:15)

That is powerful stuff. What makes us Christians different? What sets us apart from the rest of the world? Nothing less than the presence of God in our lives. That's what makes us different. And if we are not abiding – doing things his way – what happens?

> Beware of being like them and losing the prize that you and I have been working so hard to get. See to it that you win your full reward from the Lord. For if you wander beyond the teaching of Christ, you will leave God behind; while if you are loyal to Christ's

teachings, you will have God too. Then you will have both the Father and the Son. (2 John 1:8-9)

Remember we wrote previously about living in victory and Jesus' words.

Because I will only reveal myself to those who love and obey me. The Father will love them too, and we will come to them and live with them (John 14:23)

You can see the parallel between Moses' words to God in Exodus 33 and Jesus' words to his disciples in John 14. The message is simple: we need to have a real desire to learn his ways and do things his way – not the world's way – if we desire to have the Godhead dwelling in us. Yes, that's right, the whole Godhead – Father, Son and Holy Spirit – dwelling in us. Then the world will see the difference.

If this is really so, guide me clearly along the way you want me to travel so that I will understand you and walk acceptably before you. (Exodus 33:13)

What an awesome and wonderful God we have – but life has to be on his terms, not ours. His terms are good terms. He wants the very best for us. But oh, what a struggle it can be.

Those of you who read *The Word for Today*, published by Radio Rhema, might recollect once reading a wonderful little story about an old Indian: I presume he was a Red Indian who became a Christian. The minister came to visit the reservation where he lived and asked him how things were going.

'Sometimes good, sometimes not good,' he replied. 'It seems like there are two dogs inside me and they fight a lot.'

'Which one wins?' asked the minister.

'The one I feed the most,' he replied.

I think you get the message. The one I feed the most flourishes, either the 'flesh' or the 'spirit'.

Back to God's ways now. How do we know God's ways? Moses' request to God was, 'Let me know your ways so that I may know thee.' This is a good prayer because, if we ask God in faith, he will always faithfully answer us.

And remember, without faith it is impossible to please him. As he reveals his ways to us, so we come to know him. But we have to remember to put his ways into practice. And the more we do this, the more he reveals himself and his ways to us.

The first thing we learn is that his ways are higher than our ways and the ways of the world. Jesus was and is God's Way personified. Hence, he is the only one ever to have claimed:

> I am the way, the truth and the life. No one comes to the Father except through Me. (John 14:6 KJV)

There is no other way except through Jesus. That in itself makes us unique, special people. We are indeed different from any other people upon the face of the earth. Through our relationship with Jesus, we become children and co-heirs of our Heavenly Father, and we are granted so many privileges because of this. These include living more abundantly, freedom from the power of sin, victory over Satan and his horde of demons, and the help and empowering of the blessed Holy Spirit to enable us to walk every day with the Lord and to learn his ways and his truth.

Blessing upon blessing upon blessing. As Paul writes:

> He has brought us into this place of highest privilege where we now stand. (Romans 5:2)

Here we have God's covering and protection over our lives, and those of our children and grandchildren. We truly are privileged people. The privilege of direct access to the most powerful being in all of the universe, our Heavenly Father. But first we must do it God's way. We must come to the Cross of Calvary. The cross is unique. The cross is God's way. The cross symbolises love and wisdom in its highest form. The devil and the world simply have no answers to the cross. Through the cross, Satan was totally defeated and his power completely broken. And we are forgiven, set free and made acceptable to God, and he has become accessible to us.

Nothing will ever surpass or supplant the Cross of Calvary, on which Jesus, the Lamb of God, was slain on our behalf. Truly God's ways are higher than our ways. In the history of the universe and particularly in the history of mankind, the cross stands unique and supreme. Before the cross, man needed a priest to act as a mediator between himself/herself and God, and to offer sacrifices on his/her behalf.

The Levites were appointed for this task, so a man or woman only had contact with God through the priest. The cross changed that forever. After Jesus' death, the veil in the temple was split in two and ordinary individuals (you and me, Jew and Gentile) are able to come into the very presence of God. We are made acceptable, not just to walk in his presence but, as previously stated, to have the whole of the Godhead dwelling within us.

But much more was accomplished at Calvary. The power of the cross is far greater than any nuclear device invented. Nuclear devices can destroy material things and even human lives in great numbers, but the cross defeated the power of evil once and for all. Through the cross, eternal life is being granted to millions and millions of people; eternal life which can never be ended. Through the cross, we are granted unlimited authority in this world against the evil one and his fallen angels; their power is broken.

In the eyes of the world, the cross appears to be the ultimate defeat, but thanks be to God, whose ways are so much higher than our ways and the world's ways. The Cross of Calvary is the ultimate victory. You see, the cross allowed God to be reunited with mankind. Through sin, God became separated from mankind, and the devil became ruler of this world. Through the cross, the power of sin was broken, and the power of the devil was broken.

Jesus came preaching the message of the Kingdom of Heaven. Through the cross, we are born again as children of God. Through the cross, you and I are set free and reunited with our Creator. Oh, what an awesome God we have. But more – so much more. Jesus' death not only paid the price for our sins and broke Satan's hold over us, but his death set us free from the curse of sin.

Oh, the curses we place ourselves under through sin. The list goes on and on. False idols, dishonouring our parents, adultery, drugs and drunkenness, stealing, lying, murder, slander and unforgiveness. All these, and many more, place us under the curse of sin.

Dabbling in the occult, involvement with false religious sects, Freemasonry. Next thing we know, we are living under a curse. Often a curse on our family from a sin in the past. And none of us are exempt. The Bible says:

All have sinned and come short of the glory of God. (Romans 3:23 KJV)

But the cross sets us free.

But let us now move on from the cross to the empty tomb and our resurrected Lord. Oh, the awesome power of the risen Christ. No wonder he said:

I am come that you may have life and have it more abundantly. (John 10:10 KJV)

Nothing in this life can compare with walking and living in God's presence – made possible through the cross – and living life free and abundantly through the power of the risen Christ.

Because that same power of God which raised the dead Christ back to life from the tomb after his death will also raise us into a new life; not just when we reach the end of our days here on earth, but right now. When we too have been to the cross and have died to our past life, and have been born again into the living Christ. Praise God – what an awesome God he is! Truly, his ways are higher than our ways.

Let us pray. Father God, we remember Moses' prayer: 'If I have found grace in thy sight show me now thy way, that I might know thee, that I might find grace in thy sight.' Let this prayer be in our hearts, Lord, I pray. In Jesus' name. Amen.

I would like to finish this message with Paul's words:

> But all these things that I once thought very worthwhile – now I've thrown them all away so that I can put my trust and hope in Christ alone. Yes, everything else is worthless when compared with the priceless gain of knowing Christ Jesus my Lord. I have put aside all else, counting it worth less than nothing, in order that I can have Christ, and become one with him, no longer counting on being saved by being good enough or by obeying God's laws, but by trusting Christ to save me; for God's way of making us right with himself depends on faith – counting on Christ alone.
>
> Now I have given up everything else – I have found it to be the only way to really know Christ and to experience the mighty power that brought him back to life again, and to find out what it means to suffer and to die with him. Whatever it takes, I will be one who lives in the fresh newness of life of those who are alive from the dead. I don't mean to say I am perfect. I haven't learned

all I should even yet, but I keep working toward that day when I will finally be all that Christ saved me for and wants me to be.

No, dear brothers, I am still not all I should be, but I am bringing all my energies to bear on this one thing: Forgetting the past and looking forward to what lies ahead, I strain to reach the end of the race and receive the prize for which God is calling us up to heaven because of what Christ Jesus did for us. I hope all of you who are mature Christians will see eye-to-eye with me on these things, and if you disagree on some point, I believe that God will make it plain to you – if you fully obey the truth you have. (Philippians 3:7-16)

But when you pray,
go away by yourself all alone,
and shut the door behind you
and pray to your Father secretly,
and your Father, who knows your secrets
will reward you.
(Matthew 6:6)

The Way of Fear

We continue with the theme of knowing the ways of God in order that we might know him better. We have looked at the way of the cross, the amazing grace of God and the incredible love of God. We remember again the words of Moses:

> Now therefore, I pray thee, if I have found grace in thy sight, show me now thy way, that I may know thee, that I may find grace in thy sight; and consider that this nation is thy people.' (Exodus 33:13)

Now we will look at a new dimension – the *fear* of God.

> Teach me thy way, Oh Lord my God. I will walk in thy truth, unite my heart to fear thy name. (Psalm 86:11 KJV)

When I looked in my concordance and the Naves Topical Bible, I discovered pages of scriptures relating to the fear of God. The 'fear of the Lord' is an Old Testament expression meaning 'reverential trust', including the hatred of evil. But there are examples in scripture in both the Old and New Testaments where fear of the Lord bordered on terror. We will consider those later.

Now we will look at some of the many scriptures pertaining to the fear of the Lord.

> The fear of the Lord is the beginning of wisdom. (Proverbs 9:10 and Psalm 111:10 KJV)

The fear of the Lord is a basic truth on which to build our faith and our whole values system. Oh, that there was fear of the Lord in our nation today!

> The Lord takes pleasure in them that fear him. (Psalm 147:11 KJV)

I know of no greater purpose in life, no better reason for living than to bring pleasure to our Heavenly Father, who created us to have fellowship with him.

> The fear of the Lord prolongeth days. (Proverbs 10:27 KJV)

How can this be? Because by the fear of the Lord men turn from evil.

> But by the fear of the Lord, men depart from evil. (Proverbs 16:6 KJV)

> The fear of the Lord gives life, happiness and protection from harm. (Proverbs 19:23)

> Do not fear anything except the Lord of the Armies of Heaven! If you fear him, you need fear nothing else. He will be your safety. (Isaiah 8:13)

In all of life, he alone is worthy to be feared, honoured, respected, held in awe and worshipped. No one or nothing else in life has the status to be feared. In a sense, if we fear anything above God, we are making an idol of it, and a false idol at that.

Some of you may have heard of Smith Wigglesworth, a plumber raised up by God to be a mighty man of faith. He woke up one night to discover the devil sitting on the end of his bed. He said,

The Way of Fear

'Oh, just you,' and went back to sleep. The way it is meant to be!

God alone is worthy of our fear. One of the real dangers of not fearing God – and this can happen to us as individuals, as the church or as a nation – is that we start to question and rebel against the ways and instructions of God, especially those instructions we find less palatable. And we alone are the losers.

To whom does God extend his love mercy, forgiveness and blessings? To whom does he reveal his ways and, yes, his secrets? That's right – to those who fear and honour him.

> Blessings on all who fear and trust the Lord – on all who obey Him!
> Their reward shall be prosperity and happiness.
> Your wife shall be contented in your home. And look at all those children! There they sit around the dinner table as vigorous and healthy as young olive trees.
> That is God's reward to those who reverence and trust Him. May the Lord continually bless you with heaven's blessings, as well as human joys. May you live to enjoy your grandchildren! And may God bless Israel. (Psalm 128)

Are you starting to get the picture? There are just so many blessings of God, conditional on just one thing, that we fear and reverence him alone.

> By humility and fear of the Lord, are riches and honour and life. (Proverbs 22:4 KJV)

> The fear of the Lord is clean, enduring forever. (Psalm 19:9 KJV)

The Hebrew word for clean, Taw-Lorē, means fair and pure. It is right and fair that we fear God. He has the right to expect our fear and reverence. No one else is our Creator. No one else loves us as he does; no one else can save us or redeem us, forgive us, wash us clean, or set us free. No one else has the power of life and death, heaven or hell. No one else is sovereign over the whole of the universe and the affairs of men. He alone is the Lord of the Armies of Heaven.

And we do well to remember that at this important time in human history.

> Where is the man who fears the Lord? God will teach him how to choose the best.
> His soul shall dwell at ease, and his seed shall inherit the earth. The secret of the Lord is upon them that fear him; and he will show them his covenant. (Psalm 25:12-14)

Friendship with God is reserved for those who reverence him. With them alone God shares the secrets of his promises. We would do well to spend time meditating on this verse alone. So very much is conditional on this simple and yet profound instruction from God's word.

Speaking of Jesus, it says,

> So also Christ was heard in that he feared. (Hebrews 5:7 KJV)

God heard his Son because he, Jesus, respected and feared his Father.

Now we will look at seven other translations of this verse:

> TLB: God heard his prayers because of his strong desire to obey his Father at all times.

> GNT: Because he was humble and devoted God heard him.

NIV: He was heard because of his reverent submission.

Phillips: His prayers were heard because of his willingness to obey.

RSV: He was heard because of his Godly fear.

Jerusalem Bible: Because he submitted so humbly his prayer was heard.

NEB: Because of his humble submission his prayer was heard; Son though he was.

We are told:

> One shall come who rules righteously, who rules in the fear of God. (2 Samuel 23:3)

Let's now see what happened when the fear of the Lord came upon the people. It begins with Uzziah steadying the Ark.

> But when they arrived at the threshing floor of Nacon, the oxen stumbled and Uzzah put out his hand to steady the Ark. Then the anger of the Lord flared out against Uzzah and he killed him for doing this, so he died there beside the Ark. David was angry at what the Lord had done, and named the spot 'The Place of Wrath upon Uzzah' (which it is still called to this day). David was now afraid of the Lord and asked, 'How can I ever bring the Ark home?' So he decided against taking it into the City of David, but carried it instead to the home of Obed-edom, who had come from Gath. It remained there for three months, and the Lord blessed Obed. (2 Samuel 6:6-11)

Why did this happen? God had given explicit instructions regarding how the Ark should be carried. Already a number of people had died after disobeying those instructions.

A note in the Schofield Bible (page 364) sheds some light on this:

> The story of David's new cart and its results is a striking illustration of the Spiritual truth that blessing does not follow even the best intentions in the service of God, except as that service is rendered in God's way. God had given explicit directions how the Ark should be borne (Numbers 4:1-15) but David adopted a Philistine expedient (1 Samuel 6:7-8).

Remember Cain and Abel? They both brought a sin-offering to God.

Abel on God's terms, Cain's on his own terms. Cain's offering was rejected. Nothing has changed. How can we claim Jesus is Lord and at the same time follow the ways of the world?

In both these incidents and also in the story of Ananias and Sapphira in the book of Acts, God moved fast and decisively to stop error in its tracks. And see what happened – error was stopped alright!

> Terror gripped the entire church and all others who heard what had happened. And more and more believers were added to the Lord, crowds both of men and women. (Acts 5:11&15)

Today, as never before, we need a mighty outpouring of the fear of the Lord.

There is a great deal of clamouring going on in the world at present regarding the situation in the Middle East. Regarding Israel and the so-called Palestinians. The church also is extremely vocal.

I wonder how many Christians have really sought God's will in this matter. We read:

> Those who are wise will not try to interfere with the Lord in the dread day of punishment. (Amos 5:13)

As we look at what is happening in the world today it is obvious that the dread day of punishment is at hand and we would do well to study the scriptures and earnestly seek to discern God's will in this matter.

> The Lord, the God of Battle has spoken – who can change His plans? When his hand moves, who can stop him? (Isaiah 14:27)

That's right – our God is the God of Battle. We would do well to remember this.

> The Lord has opened his armoury and brought out weapons to explode his wrath upon his enemies. The terror that befalls Babylon will be the work of the Lord, the God of Hosts. Yes, come against her from distant lands, break open her granaries, knock down her walls and houses into heaps of ruins, and utterly destroy her; let nothing be left. Not even her cattle, woe to them! Kill them all! For the time has come for Babylon to be devastated. (Jeremiah 50:25-27)

You may well ask, what has Babylon to do with us today? The note in the Schofield Bible (Page 1369) on Revelation 18:2 gives understanding on this:

> There are two forms which Babylon is to have in the end-time. Political Babylon, Revelation 17:8-17 and the ecclesiastical

Babylon, Revelation 17:1-7, 18 and 18:1-24. Political Babylon is the Anti-Christ's Confederated Empire, the last form of Gentile world dominion. Ecclesiastical Babylon is all Apostate Christendom, the end-time false church, in which the Papacy will undoubtedly be prominent. It may well be that this union will embrace all the religions of the world.

Perhaps we can glimpse from the following verses how utterly important it is that we learn to fear God and live.

'Watch now,' the Lord Almighty declares, 'the day of judgment is coming, burning like a furnace. The proud and wicked will be burned up like straw; like a tree, they will be consumed, roots and all. But for you who fear my name, the Sun of Righteousness will rise with healing in his wings. And you will go free, leaping with joy like calves let out to pasture. Then you will tread upon the wicked as ashes underfoot,' says the Lord Almighty... 'See, I will send you another prophet like Elijah before the coming of the great and dreadful judgment day of God. His preaching will bring fathers and children together again, to be of one mind and heart, for they will know that if they do not repent, I will come and utterly destroy their land.' (Malachi 4:1-6).

One final verse:

The believers learnt how to walk in the fear of the Lord and in the comfort of the Holy Spirit. (Acts 9:31)

Let us pray. Father God, in this time of great clamour throughout the world, may we simply learn how to walk in the fear of the Lord and the comfort of the Holy Spirit.

Father God, speak to us, I ask. Help us to rightly discern the truth – to hear your voice and not the clamour of the world. And may we with humble hearts continue in loving service to you in your Kingdom.

Father, we love you, we respect you, and we fear you – for you alone are worthy of our fear.

And Father, in the mighty name of Jesus, we ask that there will be a great outpouring of the fear of God upon our land. That this beautiful nation of Aotearoa New Zealand will come to fear you and turn away from all evil – for we are a sinful and rebellious people, Father.

Please forgive us, please cause us to turn back to you as a nation and be healed.

In Jesus' name we worship you. In Jesus' name we bring our petition to your throne of grace.

The Way of Humility

We have been looking at the ways of God in response to Moses' question to him,

> Let me know Thy ways that I might know thee. (Exodus 33:13 KLV)

So far we have looked at the way of the cross, the way of grace and the way of fear. One of the scriptures we read was,

> Do not fear anything except the Lord of the armies of Heaven. If you fear him you need fear nothing else. He will be your safety. (Isaiah 8:13)

I had good reason to remember that scripture when I happened to be a passenger in a helicopter and the motor stopped. At the time we were not all that high above the ground – maybe 50 feet – and there were not a lot of options open to us. As we plummeted to the ground, I recall saying in my spirit, 'I'm safe in you, Lord.' And we were. We literally missed death by a millisecond.

The question today is why did Paul work so hard to reach others? We find the answer in the following scriptures:

> It is because of this solemn fear of the Lord, which is ever present in our minds, that we work so hard to win others. (2 Corinthians 5:11)

> Whatever we do, it is certainly not for our own profit, but because Christ's love controls us now. Since we believe that Christ died for us all, we should also believe that we have died to the old life we used to live. He died for all, so that all who live – having received eternal life from him – might no longer live for themselves, to please themselves, but to spend their lives pleasing Christ, who died and rose again for them. (2 Corinthian. 5:14-15)

Let us personalise these verses. He died for us all, so that all of us who live, having received Eternal Life from him – might no longer live for ourselves – to please ourselves, but rather spend our lives pleasing Christ, who died and rose again for us. It is that dying to the old life that is the hard part, isn't it?

We now move on a verse:

> When someone becomes a Christian, he becomes a brand-new person inside. He is not the same anymore. A new life has begun. (2 Corinthians 5:17)

A new life has begun; we have been born again – not yet as mature men and women of God. Yes, a new life has begun, we have been born as spiritual babies of the Kingdom of God. No longer to live for ourselves and pleasing others, but to spend our lives pleasing Christ. We sing the words, 'And for Thy pleasure we are created – Thou art worthy, Oh Lord.' Not quite the world's way, is it? Truly God's ways are different, as we have seen.

In 1 Corinthians, Paul talks about how we build our lives and the materials we use to build with.

> God, in his kindness, has taught me how to be an expert builder. I have laid the foundation and Apollos has built on it. But he who builds on the foundation must be very careful. And no one can

ever lay any other real foundation than that one we already have, Jesus Christ. But there are various kinds of materials that can be used to build on that foundation. Some use gold and silver and jewels; and some build with sticks and hay or even straw! There is going to come a time of testing at Christ's Judgment Day to see what kind of material each builder has used. Everyone's work will be put through the fire so that all can see whether or not it keeps its value, and what was really accomplished. Then every workman who has built on the foundation with the right materials, and whose work still stands, will get his pay. But if the house he has built burns up, he will have a great loss. He himself will be saved, but like a man escaping through a wall of flames. (1 Corinthians 3:10-15)

Will our building materials stand the test of fire? What happens to gold and silver in fire? They get purified. What happens to sticks, hay and straw? There is nothing left, just a few ashes. Please note – salvation is not the issue here because it says, 'He himself will be saved, but as by fire, or like a person escaping through a wall of flames.' The question we need to ask is, 'Will our work stand the test of fire?' The answer to this depends on what we build with.

Let us consider again the ways of God. Jesus said,

'I am the way, the truth and the life.' (John 14:6)

I believe here Jesus was picking up on Moses' discussion with God when Moses requested, 'Guide me clearly along the way you want me to travel.' Hence Jesus' words, 'I am the way...' (John 14:6 KJV).

Let us now look at some of Jesus' teaching. I guess the best place to start with is what we call the Beatitudes. What was the first thing taught? Humility.

The Way of Humility

> How blest are those who know their need of God. (Matthew 5:3 NEB)

> The Kingdom of Heaven is theirs and blessed are the meek for they shall inherit the earth. (Matthew 5:5 NIV)

The ways of God are not the ways of the world. The world is into assertiveness, rights of the individual, women's rights, gay rights and children's rights. What about God's rights?

The towering leader of the Old Testament was Moses. The Bible says,

> Now the man Moses was very meek. (Numbers 12:3-4 KJV)

The Living Bible puts it like this, 'Now Moses was the humblest man on earth.'

In the Psalms it says,

> The meek will teach his way. (Psalm 25:9 KJV)

If we want God to guide us clearly along the way he wants us to travel and if we want Jesus to be our guide, then we must choose the way of meekness and humility, trusting and depending on him all the way, casting our cares on him and following his example. Jesus said,

> 'For I am meek and lowly in heart.' (Matthew 11:29 KJV)

> Run from all these evil things, and work instead at what is right and good, learning to trust him and love others and to be patient and gentle. (1 Timothy 6:11)

We are instructed to follow after meekness. The following is one of many other references to humility and meekness in scripture.

> If My people who are called by my name, shall humble themselves and pray, and seek my face and turn from their wicked ways, then I will hear from heaven and forgive their sin and will heal their land. (2 Chronicles 7:14 KJV)

Do we want our land healed? If so, this starts with humbling ourselves. How blessed are those who know their need of God. The Kingdom of Heaven is theirs.

> Blessed are the meek, for they shall inherit the earth. (Matthew 5:5 KJV)

> My strength is made perfect in [our] weakness. (2 Corinthians 12:9 KJV)

Another example from scripture which most of you know:

> About that time the disciples came to Jesus to ask which of them would be greatest in the Kingdom of Heaven! Jesus called a small child over to him and set the little fellow down among them, and said, 'Unless you turn to God from your sins and become as little children, you will never get into the Kingdom of Heaven. Therefore anyone who humbles himself as this little child is the greatest in the Kingdom of Heaven. (Matthew 18:1-4)

What did Jesus mean? It is simple – a small child is totally dependent on its parents for all its needs, and so must we be dependent on our Heavenly Father. When we start trusting our Heavenly

Father in all things, we start making spiritual progress. Faith is a good building material.

The following is a quote from the *In Touch* magazine:

> We have qualified as saints of God because, and only because, he has qualified us. He chose us. He sent his son to die for us. He gave us the gift of faith. He forgave us. He redeemed us. He reconciled us. He justifies us. He is sanctifying us and he will glorify us.

On top of that, he offers us the gift of the Holy Spirit to help us along the way. You may well ask, what does that leave us to do? To start with, we have to believe him and believe his Word – all of it. We have to trust him, obey him, love him, fear him, humble ourselves before him and bear fruit in service to him.

We show that we are his disciples when we bear much fruit. Fruit which remains. We have received eternal life from him – that we might no longer live for ourselves, pleasing ourselves, but to spend our lives pleasing Christ who died and rose again for us. We are not our own. We have been bought with a price.

One final scripture:

> Gather together and pray, you shameless nation, while there still is time before judgment begins and your opportunity is blown away like chaff; before the fierce anger of the Lord falls and the terrible day of his wrath begins. Beg him to save you, all who are humble, all who have tried to obey. Walk humbly and do what is right; perhaps even yet the Lord will protect you from his wrath in that day of doom. (Zephaniah 2:1-3)

Let us pray. Father God, it is with humble hearts that we kneel before you tonight and confess our great need for you in every area of our lives. Father, we are so incredibly grateful for all that you have done and are doing for us.

We thank you for your Word and your faithfulness at all times – even when we are not faithful, you always are.

We thank you for Jesus, our Saviour, our Redeemer, our Lord, our coming King.

Father, please forgive us for the many times we have fallen short and tried to do things in our strength instead of yours.

Forgive us the many times we have trusted in the world rather than in you, for the many times we have sought to please ourselves rather than bring pleasure to you. Lord, we do believe. Help thou our unbelief.

Father, we ask for fruit, for we know that without you we can do nothing.

Help us in our abiding Lord, that as we abide in you, the True Vine, we will bear much fruit. And sanctify us in the truth, Lord. Thy Word is truth. Forgive us, we ask Lord. Heal us, we ask Lord. Heal our land, Lord.

Bless this beautiful nation of Aotearoa New Zealand. Pour out your Spirit upon us, Lord, your blessed Holy Spirit.

Father, we come to you and bring our petition to you in the only way possible. In Jesus' name we ask. Amen.

Wisdom

I have asked this question in the past, but I will ask it again. What is the most important quality anyone can possess? I will give you a clue: it is a very rare quality. You will find the answer in Proverbs – wisdom.

> Determination to be wise is the first step to becoming wise. (Proverbs 4:7)

> One tenth of one percent of the men I interviewed could be said to be wise, but not one woman. (Ecclesiastes 7:28)

I thought that would get your attention, ladies. Don't worry, we will return to this shortly. Can you tell me the important point to come out of that verse? Just one person in 2000 can be said to be wise. It just so happens to be a man. That means there are 999 men and 1000 woman who lack true wisdom.

It is a good thing Ecclesiastes was written about the natural rather than about the spiritual man. Do you know, in the Naves Topical Bible there are nine pages of verses about love and thirteen pages of verses about wisdom? That is why we must seek wisdom.

There are so many areas in our lives where wisdom is required, especially these days when there is so much false teaching and so many false values both in the society we live in and, sadly, the church. False teaching is rampant. The church has allowed herself to be caught up in New Age teaching and political correctness. 'Inclusiveness' and 'tolerance' are the 'in' words.

There are divisions over issues such as gender roles in the Christian Church, homosexual ministers, abortion and euthanasia, disciplining children, Maori claims, global warming and the problem of the Palestinians and the Jews both claiming Jerusalem.

These issues require real discernment, real wisdom and, above all else, a clear understanding of God's will in these matters.

No wonder Paul wrote:

> My prayer for you is that you will overflow more and more with love for others, and at the same time keep on growing in Spiritual knowledge and insight [or discernment, if you like]. For I want you always to see clearly the difference between right and wrong so that you will always recognize what is best. This will help you to become pure and blameless, and prepare you for the Day of Christ.' (Philippians 1:9-10)

There is a whole message in that text alone. Paul is praying that his converts at Philippi (and us too) will overflow more and more with love for others. But he knows the danger of love that is not tempered by wisdom; hence his words: 'at the same time keep on growing in Spiritual knowledge and insight' [discernment].

The last words in this passage are also interesting: 'and prepare you for the Day of Christ'. The Day of Christ is for those who are pure and blameless in their doctrine, not for those who have fallen into error. The Day of the Lord awaits these people.

Yes, there is a clear distinction in Scripture between the 'Day of Christ' and the 'Day of the Lord.' This is the reason wisdom is so important, for without wisdom and understanding, God's people will fall into error, and then under judgment.

Wisdom

> My people perish through lack of knowledge. (Hosea 4:6. KJV)

Jesus came at a time in history when a great deal of error and false teaching had crept into the religious community. He said:

> To this end was I born and for this cause I came into the world, that I should bear witness unto the truth. Everyone that is of the truth hears my voice. (John 18:37 KJV)

One of the great problems in the church today is this same thing, lack of knowledge of God and his ways. This is patently obvious when you consider the incredible amount of time that has been wasted debating the very issues I previously mentioned, along with a whole heap of other things that get the church side-tracked from the real reason we are here on earth – to preach the Good News of the gospel of salvation through Jesus Christ paying the price for our sins on the cross at Calvary.

The Good News that he came to set us free in every area of our lives, from every sin, curse and bondage and to grant us eternal life with him in his Kingdom. Now that really is Good News.

However, getting back to the issues which have side-tracked the church so badly down through the ages, it is not because the church lacks love. There has been plenty of loving concern demonstrated by people on both sides of these issues. No, it is not lack of love for one another. It is lack of discernment, lack of understanding of God and his ways, and lack of wisdom.

Sadly, love which is not tempered with wisdom and understanding of God and his ways quickly leads to error and apostasy. That is why it says:

> Therefore, be ye not unwise but understanding what the will of the Lord is. (Ephesians 5:17 KJV)

> Let the word of Christ dwell in you richly, in all wisdom, teaching and admonishing one another. (Colossians. 3:16 KJV)

The truth is we would rather be indulged than admonished. That's why there is so much error in the church today. There are so many areas in which the church is not giving, indeed cannot give, clear direction. When the church itself is divided, it is unable to fulfil its role as a light to the nations showing God's way to people.

It is no wonder that Moses prayed this great prayer. Actually, it was more a discussion between Moses and the Lord. Moses talked with the Lord and said to him:

> You have been telling me; take these people to the Promised Land, but you haven't told me whom you will send with me. You say, You are my friend, and that I have found favour before you. Please, if this is really so, guide me clearly along the way you want me to travel so that I will understand you and walk acceptably before you.
>
> And the Lord replied, 'I myself will go with you and give you success.'
>
> For Moses had said, 'If you aren't going with us, don't let us move a step from this place. If you don't go with us, who will ever know that we have found favour with you, and therefore are different from any other people on the face of the earth?' (Exodus 33:12-15)

You see, Moses was a wise man. He walked in the fear of the Lord. He knew that God wanted him to take his people to the Promised Land, and that the only way he could succeed in doing so was through God guiding him clearly in the way he wanted him to travel.

Why did he want that guidance? So that he could understand God and his ways and walk acceptably before him. Most importantly, so the world would clearly see the difference between God's people and all the other people on the face of the earth.

Nothing has changed. Well, nothing is meant to have changed. The world is still meant to be able to clearly see the difference between us Christians and those who are not.

And our Heavenly Father, through our Lord Jesus, has done his best to make it easier for us.

> But of him [God the Father] are you in Christ Jesus, who of God is made unto us Wisdom and Righteousness and Sanctification and Redemption. (1 Corinthians 1:30 KJV)

There you are, ladies; Christ's wisdom is available to you in the same way as to us males. No worries – we all have equal opportunities in Christ, but different roles to play. The Bible says:

> But you have received the Holy Spirit and he lives within you, in your hearts, so that you don't need anyone to teach you what is right. For he teaches you all things, and he is the Truth, and no liar, and so just as he has said, you must live in Christ, never to depart from Him. (1 John 2:27)

You know, it seems to me that every message we receive from the Lord always seems to end up saying the same thing, and we pick it up again in this verse, that we 'must live in Christ, never to depart from him.' Once again we get back to the idea of abiding. Abiding is absolutely central. If we want wisdom, we need to abide in him, and then his wisdom will flow through us.

> But the people that do know their God shall be strong and do exploits. They that understand among the people shall instruct many. (Daniel 11:32-33 KJV)

This is borne out in life of Stephen:

> And Stephen, full of faith and power, did great wonders and miracles among the people. And they were not able to resist the Wisdom and Spirit by which he spoke. (Acts 6:8,10 KJV)

Stephen had been abiding. He knew God. And more importantly, God knew him. And so must we, if we desire to stand strong and walk in the truth in these last days of this present age. Abiding is the key to wisdom. Of course love is important, but love which is not tempered by wisdom can quickly become misguided love which focuses on man and not on God. That brings us to the top of a slippery downhill doctrinal slope which at best leads straight into the Tribulation and the wrath of God, where our faith has to be tested by fire, and in most cases ends in martyrdom or, at worst, hell and eternal damnation.

That is why Jesus warned us:

> Watch and pray always that you might be accounted worthy to escape these things which shall come to pass, and to stand before the Son of Man. (Luke 21:36 KJV)

As we read before, we need to heed these words:

> Prepare us for the Day of Christ (Philippians 1:10 Jerusalem Bible)

Our Christianity must be God-centred, focused on Christ and his commandments, not man-centred. Jesus said that if we loved him, we would obey him. He commanded us:

> Go ye therefore, and teach all nations, baptising them in the name of the Father, and of the Son, and of the Holy Ghost: teach-

ing them to observe all things whatsoever I have commanded you. (Matthew 28:19-20 KJV)

We have got the first part right. The problem lies with the second part. In both Psalms and Proverbs we read:

The fear of the Lord is the beginning of Wisdom. (Psalm 111:10; Proverbs 9:10 KJV)

Pray to God for wisdom.

*A knotty problem.
Cast your cares upon him,
for he cares for you.
(1 Peter 5:7)*

Faith

Let us now look briefly at some aspects of what the Bible teaches us about faith. It says:

> Thou art worthy, Oh Lord, to receive glory and honour and power, for thou hast created all things, and for thy pleasure they are and were created. (Revelation 4:11 KJV)

Everything has been created for God's pleasure, including and especially mankind – us. You and me. We have been created for God's pleasure.

The Bible says:

> Now the just shall live by faith, but if any man draws back, my soul shall have no pleasure in him. (Hebrews 10:38 KJV)

> But without faith it is impossible to please God. For he who comes to God must believe that he is, that he is a rewarder of them that diligently seek him. (Hebrews 11:6 KJV)

Note that word *diligently*. There are times when you have to get really serious about seeking God for an answer. Are you getting the picture? We have been created for God's pleasure, and in order to bring him pleasure, which we know from the scriptures we have just read, we need to exercise faith. Without faith it is impossible to please him.

But what is faith?

What is faith? It is a confident assurance something we want is going to happen. It is the certainty that what we hope for is waiting for us even though we cannot see it up ahead. (Hebrews 11:1)

It was by faith that men of ancient times won God's approval. (Hebrews 11:2 NEB)

So, you can see how important faith is in our daily life. We can't please God without it, and indeed we need it to win his approval. By faith – by believing God – we know that the world and the stars, in fact all things, were created at God's command, and that they were all made from things that cannot be seen.

It is no wonder that the devil, working through evil men, has pushed the evolution theory so hard. By sowing even a small seed of doubt in people's minds, he is able to discredit God's Word and ultimately God himself. It is no wonder that there is so much unbelief in the world today when nearly all our children are taught this lie. And make no mistake, the whole theory of evolution is just that – a lie from the devil, the father of lies. Evolution is science fiction. Even Charles Darwin, the father of the evolution theory, changed his mind before he died, realising it was an impossible theory. He concluded there had to be a creator.

I have been digressing, but never the less, this is a foundational belief, and if people can be deceived into believing the world evolved and was not created, then it becomes more difficult for them to accept God and their need for salvation through Jesus Christ.

How do we get faith? Faith to confidently believe that something we want is going to happen. Romans teaches us:

Faith

> Faith comes from hearing, and hearing from the word of God. (Romans 10:17 KJV)

The Revised Standard Version says, '...by the teaching of Christ'. Jesus taught us:

> Repent and believe in the gospel. (Mark 1:15 NKJV)

If there is anything, the church needs to do today it is to repent and believe the gospel. The universal church of today is rife with unbelief and false teaching. Jesus said:

> ...if you canst believe – all things are possible to them that believe. (Mark 9:23 KJV)

The Greek word for 'believe' in Mark 1:15 is 'even', meaning 'fixed in place', 'time' or state', a relation of rest. This is very significant. It implies that the gospel does not just apply to the era or time in which the writer lived. It is true that God has instituted various covenants down through the ages. Christians are no longer subject to the Old Testament laws of Moses but are nevertheless still subject to the Genesis 3 (or Adamic) covenant, and will continue to be so until Jesus returns and establishes his Millennium Kingdom. We would do well to heed Jude's admonition:

> Stoutly defend the truth that God gave once for all to his people to keep without change through the years. (Jude 1:3)

Jesus himself said:

> Heaven and earth will disappear, but my words remain forever. (Matthew 24:35)

How often do you hear the excuse, especially regarding Paul's teaching on the role of women in the church, that this teaching applied only to that time and culture in which he lived? Rubbish! It applies today just the same as it did then. God's Word is fixed, unshakable, like silver refined seven times.

> The words of the Lord are pure words, like silver tested in a furnace of earth, purified seven times. Thou shalt keep them oh Lord, thou shalt preserve them from this generation forever. (Psalm 12:6-7 KJV)

Oh, that the church might start to believe God and his Word. Then we might start getting somewhere. How can you exercise faith in God and his Word if you do not believe what he says, or if you pick out the juicy morsels that taste sweet and reject the parts that aren't so appetising? Take this passage, for instance:

> Bless the Lord, O my soul: and all that is within me, bless his holy name. Bless the Lord, O my soul, and forget not all his benefits: who forgiveth all thine iniquities; who healeth all thy diseases; who redeemeth thy life from destruction; who crowneth thee with lovingkindness and tender mercies; who satisfieth thy mouth with good things; so that thy youth is renewed like the eagle's. (Psalm 103:1-5 KJV)

This psalm really tests our faith. We sing, 'Bless the Lord, oh my soul!' We preach forgiveness of sins in Jesus' name, and so we should. We preach redemption from hell through the blood of our Saviour, and so we should. We preach God's love and compassion, and so we should. But it takes a little more faith to believe that God will fill our lives with good things so that our youth is renewed like the eagle's.

As far as the east is from the west, so far he has removed our transgressions from us. (Psalm 103:12 KJV)

We love this verse, and it is all true. For this we can be truly grateful. Praise God my sins are forgiven. I am set free. I am on my way to heaven. And we have no problem with the first half of verse 3, 'who forgiveth all thine iniquities'. But what about the second part of the verse, 'who healeth all thy diseases?' There is only a comma between them. Boy, does this causes problems! If we believe all the rest, why do we have trouble with this? And yet healing was obviously an important part of Jesus' ministry, as it was for his disciples and the early church.

At the end of his ministry, just before he returned to heaven, he blessed his disciples and instructed them:

Go into all the world and preach the gospel. Whoever believes and is baptised shall be saved... These signs shall follow those who believe. In my name they shall cast out demons; they shall speak with new tongues; they shall take up serpents; if they drink any deadly thing, it shall not hurt them; they shall lay hands on the sick, and they shall recover. (Mark 16:15-18 KJV)

That is about as far as the church goes nowadays. Actually, that is not strictly correct, we baptise them before they believe, but that is another issue. The point is, we make a big issue of going into all the world and preaching the gospel to all creation. That is good. No problem. But what about the rest of (and even more important part of) the Great Commission?

Teaching them to obey everything I have commanded you. (Matthew 28:20 NIV)

> Whoever does not believe will be condemned. (Mark 16:16 KJV)

This does not *just* mean belief in Jesus for salvation. It means believing in Jesus, believing in the gospel, believing in his Word. All of these.

When the church goes out into the world preaching a New Age, social gospel based on man's ideas rather than on Jesus' commandments, we are condemned through our unbelief. We end up in the very situation Jesus warned against:

> You have never been mine. Go away, for your deeds are evil. (Matthew 7:23)

> But he answered and said, 'Verily I say unto you, I know you not.' (Matthew 25:12 KJV)

> So then, because thou art lukewarm, and neither cold nor hot, I will spew thee out of my mouth. (Revelation 3:16 KJV)

And indeed, there are a great number of other warnings in both the Old and New Testaments, besides these ones. According to the way I understand the Great Commission, we are to go into all the world and make disciples, not milk-dependent, spiritual babies sucking on the teat of dependence, as referred to in Hebrews.

> And when a person is still living on milk it shows he isn't very far along in the Christian life, and doesn't know much about the difference between right and wrong. He is still a baby Christian! (Hebrews 5:13)

In Mark it says:

> These signs shall accompany those who believe. In my name they will cast out demons, they will speak with new tongues, they will pick up snakes in their hands, and when they drink poison it will not hurt them at all, they will lay hands on the sick and they will recover.' (Mark 16:17)

Here is the interesting thing. Read the following two verses that follow the Great Commission:

> After the Lord Jesus had spoken to them, he was taken to Heaven and he sat at the right hand of God. Then the disciples went out and preached everywhere, and the Lord worked with them and confirmed his Word by the signs that accompanied it. (Mark 16:19-20 ASV)

It is my firm conviction that when we start to believe in God's Word and obey it – all of it – not just the bits that suit us and preach it in spirit and in truth, then God will be pleased to work with us, confirming his Word with signs and wonders.

Where do we begin? By repenting of our unbelief and disobedience. Look at this verse:

> Is any sick among you? Let him [or her] call for the elders of the church and let them pray over them, anointing them with oil in the name of the Lord. (James 5:14 ASV)

What happens when we get sick? Do we call for the elders? No! We go to the doctor. We choose to put our trust in men rather than God. Don't get me wrong, we do need doctors and hospitals, but there are many times when we should be exercising faith before going to the doctor. It has been so easy. Why do you think God is starting to shake the whole medical system? In order that people turn back to him and start trusting him again.

> I want you to trust me in your times of trouble, so I can rescue you, and you can give me glory. (Psalm 50:15)

There is such a need for repentance and turning back to God in the church today, in so many areas. We need to start believing the gospel – all of it, and not just the parts that suit us. Paul talks of this very thing:

> Having a form of godliness but denying the power of God; (2 Timothy 3:5 KJV)

The Living Bible puts it this way:

> They will go to church, but they won't really believe. Don't be fooled by people like that.

> For the time will come [and it has] when they will not endure sound doctrine, they shall turn away their ears from the truth. (2 Timothy 4:3-4 KJV)

It is high time we got in tune with what our Lord is saying and doing. It is no coincidence that in every letter to the churches in Revelation (these are Jesus' final instructions to his church) he warns, 'Listen to what the Spirit is saying.'

One of the signs which was to precede the return of Jesus is the outpouring of the Holy Spirit as described by the prophet Joel.

> And It shall come to pass afterward that I will pour out my Spirit on all flesh and your sons and your daughters shall prophesy,

Faith

your old men shall dream dreams, your young men shall see visions. (Joel 2:28 KJV)

The Prophet Joel speaks of the 'former rain and the latter rain'. It is said, the former rain fell at Pentecost and the late Dr. Derek Prince said that the latter rain began falling at the beginning of the 20th century. The point is, God is pouring out his Spirit on all of mankind today. Today is the time of the latter rain. Do you want a refreshing? Do you want to be sanctified in truth? Do you want faith?

Jesus says,

If we, being evil, know how to give good gifts to our children, how much more shall your Heavenly Father give the Holy Spirit to them that ask? (Luke 11:13 KJV)

The Holy Spirit is given to believers – to lead them into all truth, to equip them for service and to prepare the Bride for her coming Bridegroom.

When he, the Spirit of Truth is come, he will guide you into all truth. (John 16:13 KJV)

And they chose Stephen, a man unusually full of faith and the Holy Spirit. (Acts 6:5)

Why did they choose Stephen? Because he was full of faith and the Holy Spirit. They go together. The sad thing is that there are so many today who either deny or ignore this truth. How can God bless any church or any 'believer' which scorns or ignores his good gift of the Holy Spirit? How can Jesus work with so-called disciples and confirm his Word with signs and wonders when the message being taught is not the whole truth and where there is so much unbelief and error? God cannot dwell where there is error.

> Whosoever transgresseth, and abideth not in the doctrine of Christ, hath not God. (2 John 1:9 KJV)

We need the Holy Spirit. That is why God offers him to us as a gift. We need him to keep us on track and to lead us into all truth. We need him to enable us to witness with boldness. We need Jesus to work in us with his power and boldness, confirming his Word with signs and wonders.

It is interesting to note in Acts that these believers were mature Christians. They had already experienced Pentecost when they were all filled with the Holy Spirit, but they needed an extra top-up of the Holy Spirit when the going got tough.

> Now, O Lord, hear their threats, and grant to your servants great boldness in their preaching, and send your healing power, and may miracles and wonders be done by the name of your holy servant Jesus.' After this prayer, the building where they were meeting shook, and they were all filled with the Holy Spirit and boldly preached God's message. (Acts 4:29-31)

Look at the result:

> With great power the apostles gave witness of the resurrection of the Lord Jesus and great grace was upon them all. (Acts 4:33)

We must not let unbelief rob us of the precious gifts God is offering us – his Spirit, faith and power. We simply need to seek him, ask in faith, and believe. We might need to be like Jacob, who wrestled with God all night till he received the answer he was after.

And let us never forget it was unbelief that provoked God's anger and prevented the vast majority of the Children of Israel from entering into the Promised Land. Nothing has changed. When the Day of Christ comes, and our Lord Jesus comes to claim his Bride, once again it will be unbelief that causes many to be left behind to have their faith tested and purified by the fire of the Tribulation. Hence Jesus' solemn warning in the parable of the ten virgins recorded in Matthew 25, along with a number of other warnings in Scripture, in both the Old and New Testaments.

Let us pray. Father God, for your pleasure we are created. Father, without faith it is impossible to please you. Lord, we believe – the parts of your Word we like the sound of. Forgive us, Lord. Forgive us our unbelief. Father, we have all been guilty of unbelief at some stage. Help us in our unbelief. Empower us afresh with your Holy Spirit that we might be led into all truth – not just part-truth. Have mercy on us Father. In your graciousness and kindness, have mercy we pray.

In Jesus' name we ask. Amen.

Revealing God's Glory

When Jesus had finished saying all these things he looked up to heaven and said, 'Father, the time has come. Reveal the glory of your Son so that he can give the glory back to you. For you have given him authority over every man and woman in all the earth. He gives eternal life to each one you have given him. And this is the way to have eternal life – by knowing you, the only true God, and Jesus Christ, the one you sent to earth! I brought glory to you here on earth by doing everything you told me to. And now, Father, reveal my glory as I stand in your presence, the glory we shared before the world began.

I have told these men all about you. They were in the world, but then you gave them to me. Actually, they were always yours, and you gave them to me; and they have obeyed you. Now they know that everything I have is a gift from you, for I have passed on to them the commands you gave me; and they accepted them and know of a certainty that I came down to earth from you, and they believe you sent me.

My plea is not for the world but for those you have given me because they belong to you. And all of them, since they are mine, belong to you; and you have given them back to me with everything else of yours, and so they are my glory! Now I am leaving the world, and leaving them behind, and coming to you. Holy Father, keep them in your own care – all those you have given me – so that they will be united just as we are, with none missing.

Revealing God's Glory

During my time here I have kept safe within your family all of these you gave me. I guarded them so that not one perished, except the son of hell, as the Scriptures foretold.

And now I am coming to you. I have told them many things while I was with them so that they would be filled with my joy. I have given them your commands. And the world hates them because they don't fit in with it, just as I don't. I'm not asking you to take them out of the world, but to keep them safe from Satan's power. They are not part of this world any more than I am. Make them pure and holy through teaching them your words of truth. As you sent me into the world, I am sending them into the world, and I consecrate myself to meet their need for growth in truth and holiness.

I am not praying for these alone but also for the future believers who will come to me because of the testimony of these. My prayer for all of them is that they will be of one heart and mind, just as you and I are, Father – that just as you are in me and I am in you, so they will be in us, and the world will believe you sent me.

I have given them the glory you gave me – the glorious unity of being one, as we are – I in them and you in me, all being perfected into one – so that the world will know you sent me and will understand that you love them as much as you love me. Father, I want them with me – these you've given me – so that they can see my glory. You gave me the glory because you loved me before the world began!

O righteous Father, the world doesn't know you, but I do; and these disciples know you sent me. And I have revealed you to them and will keep on revealing you so that the mighty love you have for me may be in them, and I in them. (John 17:1-26)

God wants to reveal his glory through us, his people, who are called by his name – Christians. This building we are in, this church or this house, has no eternal value whatever. God's glory will never be revealed through a building.

We believers are his temple, and it is through us that he will be revealed. In fact, he commands us to give him glory.

> Give unto the Lord the glory due to his name. (1 Chronicles 16:2 KJV)

> All ye the seed of Jacob, glorify him. (Psalm 22:23 KJV)

> You must do everything for the glory of God, even your eating and drinking. (1 Corinthians 10:31)

> We give glory to God when our deeds are as good as our doctrine. (2 Corinthians 9:13)

Perhaps this verse says it all:

> For God has purchased you with a great price. So, use every part of your body to give glory back to God, because he owns it. (1 Corinthians 6:20)

Because he has purchased us, he owns us. That means we are his servants. Now the most important thing about a servant is that he does just what his master tells him to do. If a servant is not willing to obey his master, he is not much use.

> Since we believe that Christ died for all of us, we should also believe that we have died to the old life we used to live. He died for all of us so that all who live – having received eternal life from him – might no longer live for themselves, to please themselves,

but to spend their lives pleasing Christ who died and rose again.
(2 Corinthians 5:14)

When someone becomes a Christian, he becomes a brand-new person inside. He is not the same any more. A new life has begun. (2 Corinthians 2:17)

In 2003 I set out to seek God's face and direction for our church, our town and our nation. So I started to study the Scriptures, particularly Paul's instructions to the Gentile Christians. In part, this was in response to the verse which says:

If my people who are called by my name will humble themselves and pray, and seek my face, and turn from their wicked ways, then I will hear from heaven and heal their land. (2 Chronicles 7:14 KJV)

As a consequence of this, there are some things I would like to share with you. I sincerely believe God wants to make Wairoa a lighthouse to our nation. When Muri Thompson, a well-known Maori evangelist, came to Wairoa, he told us, 'Wairoa was a key town in God's eternal purposes'. And he wants to reveal his glory through us, the believers. For our part, we need to re-read the Scriptures and seek the wisdom of the Holy Spirit to show us where we need to make changes in our lives. And we will be greatly blessed when we do this.

But anyone who keeps looking steadily into God's law [not glancing briefly] he will not only remember it, but do what it says, and God will greatly bless him in everything he does. (James 1:25)

Do you see the connection? When we look steadily into his Word and obey it, he will greatly bless us. Remember, it is a message to obey, not just to listen to – God's words, not mine. For it isn't enough to just have faith; you must also do good to prove that you have it. Faith that does not result in good deeds is not real faith.

The apostle John wrote:

> Dear brothers I am not writing out a new rule for you to obey, for it is an old one you have always had right from the start. You have heard it all before. Yet it is always new and works for you just as it did for Christ, and as we obey his commandment to love one another, the darkness in our lives disappears and the new life in Christ shines in. (1 John 3:7-8)

> Little children, let us stop just saying we love people; let us really love them, and show it by our actions. (1 John 3:18)

> For though we have never yet seen God, when we love each other, God lives in us, and his love within us grows even stronger. (1 John 4:12)

> If we love God, we will do whatever he tells us to do. And he's told us from the very first to love each other. (1 John 1:6)

Romans further instructs us:

> And so dear brothers and sisters, I plead with you to give your bodies to God; Let them be a living sacrifice, holy, the kind he can accept. When you think of what he's done for you, is it too much to ask? (Romans 12:1)

We are all parts of Christ's body, and each needs all the others; really love them. As Paul says:

> When God's children are in need, you be the one to help them out. And get into the habit of inviting guests home for dinner, or if they need lodging, for the night! ...When others are happy, be happy with them. If they are sad, share their sorrow. Work happily together ... enjoy the company of ordinary folks. (Romans 12:13-15)

> Talk with each other much about the Lord. Always give thanks for everything. Is there any such thing as Christians cheering each other up? Do you love me enough to want to help me? Does it mean anything to you that we are brothers in the Lord, sharing the same Spirit. Are you hearts tender and compassionate at all? Then make me truly happy by loving each other and agreeing wholeheartedly with each other, working together with one heart, and mind and purpose. Don't be selfish; don't live to make a good impression on others. Be humble, thinking of others as better than yourself. Don't just think about your own affairs, but be interested in others too, in what they are doing. (Philippians 2:1-4)

> There is no one like Timothy for having a real interest in you, everyone else seems to be worrying about his own plans and not those of Jesus Christ. But you know Timothy. (Philippians 2:20-21)

Timothy cared about and was really interested in others. In Hebrews we read:

> In response to all that he has done for us, let us outdo each other in being helpful and kind to each other, especially now that the day of his coming is drawing near. (Hebrews 10:24-25)

Look after each other so that no one will fail to find God's blessings. That means a great deal more than just greeting each other once a week. Peter says:

> You should be like one big happy family loving one another with tender hearts and humble minds. (1 Peter 3:8)

> Most important of all, continue to show deep love for each other, for love makes up for many of your faults. Cheerfully share your home with those who need a meal or a bed for the night. God has given each one of you some special abilities; be sure to use them to help each other. (1 Peter 4:8-10)

This is not once a week on Sunday stuff, this is much deeper than that. Hebrews tells us:

> Speak to each other about these things every day while there is still time. (Hebrews 3:13)

The Scriptures are talking about deep relationships here. We should be speaking to each other about these deep things each day. We have settled for so much less than what God desires us to enter into. Pray that this will change. Let us become a real church. A real family.

Now some of you are going to be puzzled by the following passage. I know I was.

> As Jesus was speaking in a crowded house, his mother and his brothers were outside, wanting to talk with him. When someone told him they were there he remarked, 'Who is my mother? Who are my brothers?' He pointed to his disciples, 'Look,' he said, 'these are my mother and brothers. Anyone who obeys my Father in Heaven is my brother, sister and mother.' (Matthew 12:46-50)

Jesus was saying that his Christian family was of even more importance than his natural family. He clearly demonstrated this when, as he was dying on the cross, he removed his mother (who at that stage was the only one of his family who believed in him) from his natural brothers and sisters and entrusted her to his disciple John.

> When Jesus therefore saw his mother, and the disciple standing by, whom he loved, he saith unto his mother, Woman, behold thy son! Then saith he to the disciple, Behold thy mother! And from that hour that disciple took her unto his own home. (John 19:26-27 KJV)

Jesus had four natural brothers, all named in Scripture, and at least two sisters. Can you imagine the upheaval that would have caused in the family at the time? After his resurrection, he appeared to his brother James, so it is likely some or all of his family did come to believe. James and Jude certainly did, and both wrote important books in the Bible. So, let us start being committed to one another and really become a family of believers. A word of caution: I am not talking here about a Christian community or communities.

Another example is that of Jonathan and David. Jonathan was a king's son, heir to the throne. But his love and loyalty to David, his brother in the Lord, was of more importance to him than his own well-being. Actually, the story of Jonathan and David is a remarkable story. All the more so when you consider that Jonathan, the king's son and heir to the throne, formed a friendship with David, who came from a despised family, one of the least in Israel. That is certainly understandable when you study David's family line. Ruth the Moabitess and Rahab the harlot were only back a few generations.

Imagine how the upper-crust Jews and Pharisees viewed King David. He was not exactly bred in the purple. The point is, Jonathan was a remarkable man. I am sure he will be greatly honoured in the Kingdom to come. He had to make a choice between standing by David or yielding to his father, the king. Even though he knew it would cost him the throne (and eventually his life), he never wavered in his loyalty and brotherly love for David. We can learn much from the story of Jonathan and David. In fact, Johnathan also remained loyal to this father, but did not yield to the evil spirit which was controlling him.

> So, let us continue to love each other with true brotherly love. Don't forget to be kind to strangers. Don't forget about those in jail... Stay away from the love of money. (Hebrews 13:1-5)

> Don't forget to do good and share what you have with those in need, for such sacrifices are very pleasing to him [our Heavenly Father]. (Hebrews 13:16)

Work hard and cheerfully without complaining. Never let it be said that Christ's people are poor workers.

> And whatever you do, do it heartily, as to the Lord. (Colossians 3:23 NLT)

We must come to terms with the fact that we are not our own. We have been bought with a price. The precious blood of Jesus. We live in the world, but we are no longer a part of the world. We are no longer to live for ourselves. A new life has begun. The question is, do we want to enter heaven as spiritual babies – still sucking on the teat of dependence, still living on a milk diet – or as mature men and woman of God, bearing much fruit and giving glory to God with our new lives in Christ?

Let us pray. Lord Jesus, you lived among us and spoke the words of God to us over 2000 years ago, either directly or through your apostles. And now, in the last days of this present age, we are seeing the Scriptures being fulfilled in so many ways.

Lord, we worship you, we praise you and thank you for your great love and the integrity of your Word.

Lord, as things begin to fall apart in the world around us, I ask that you sanctify us in truth. Thy Word is truth. There is so much evil and deception in the world, and even in your church, Lord. Father God, pour out your Spirit upon us, the blessed Holy Spirit – the Spirit of Truth. Sanctify us in truth, Lord. Lead us not into temptation and deception, but deliver us from evil.

Lord Jesus, we read your words:

Watch ye, therefore, and pray always that ye may be accounted worthy to escape all these things that shall come to pass, and to stand before the Son of Man. (Luke 21:36 KJV)

Lord, we can never be worthy in our own right. We are not worthy to receive so great a salvation as you have granted us by your grace. We worship and thank you, Lord. We are not worthy to receive the gift of your Spirit. The Blessed Holy Spirit. The Spirit of Truth. This also you granted us in your love and graciousness.

We thank you, Father God, and we worship you. And now Father, we come in Jesus' name and we ask, Lord, that we might be accounted worthy to escape all these things which shall come to pass, and to stand before the Son of Man, our Saviour and King, Jesus. Pour out your Spirit upon us, Lord, pour out your Spirit upon this little district of Putere. Pour out your Spirit upon Wairoa, a key town in your eternal purpose. Pour out your Spirit upon this nation of Aotearoa New Zealand. The faraway place. Your Word tells us the faraway places have heard and have turned back. Cause us to hear, Lord. Cause us to turn back, Lord. Cause us to stand firm in truth and in love. May we truly reveal your glory. In Jesus' name we ask and pray, amen.

The Integrity of the Scriptures: Inspired by God

> For we speak as messengers from God, trusted by him, to tell the truth. We change his message not one bit to suit the taste of those who hear it, for we serve God alone, who examines our heart's deepest thoughts. (1 Thessalonians 2:4)

Perhaps the biggest question for the church, and indeed the individual Christian today, is simply this: Is the gospel which Paul preached, and his instructions to the fledgling Christian church, completely relevant today – or are his instructions outdated?

It is important at this point to shift our focus from Paul to the Godhead, and listen to what our God has to say about the Scriptures:

> The words of the Lord are pure words, as silver tried in a furnace of earth, purified seven times. (Psalms 12:6)

> All his commandments are sure. They stand fast forever and ever and are done and truth and righteousness. (Psalm 111:7-8 KJV)

> All Scripture is given by inspiration of God and is profitable for doctrine, for reproof, for correction, for instruction and righteousness. That the man of God may be perfect, thoroughly finished unto all good works. (2 Timothy 3:16-17 KJV)

God's words will always prove true and right, no matter who questions them. (Romans 3:4)

Heaven and earth shall pass away but my words shall not pass away. (Mark 13:31 KJV)

Yea rather, blessed are they that hear the word of God and keep it. (Luke 11:28 KJV)

The Scripture cannot be broken. (John 10:35 KJV)

Sanctify them through thy truth, thy word is truth. (John 17:17 KJV)

But my words and my statutes, which I commanded my servants the prophets, did they not take hold of your fathers? And they returned and said, Like as the Lord of hosts thought to do unto us, according to our ways, and according to our doings, so hath he dealt with us. (Zechariah 1:5-6 KJV)

Remember the lesson they learned – God's Word endures! It caught up with them and punished them; then, at last, they repented.

But God's words stand firm like a great rock and nothing can shake it. It is a foundation stone with these words written on it 'The Lord knows those who are really his' and 'a person who calls himself a Christian should not do things that are wrong.' (2 Timothy 2:19)

But his own plans stand firm forever, his intentions are the same for every generation. (Psalm 33:11)

Dearly loved friends, I have been planning to write you with some thoughts about the Salvation God has given us, but now I find I must write of something else instead, urging you to stoutly defend the truth which God gave, once and for all, to his people to keep without change through the years. (Jude 1:3)

Forever oh Lord, your word stands firm in Heaven. (Psalm 119:89)

It is perfectly clear from these scriptures that we can trust God and his Word completely. And, of equal importance, his instructions are the same for every generation, without change through the years.

The note in my Schofield Bible for Ephesians 3:5 says,

> 'The revelation of' the mystery of the church was foretold but not explained by Christ (Matthew 16:18). The details concerning the doctrine, position, walk and destiny of the church were committed to Paul and his fellow apostles and prophets by the Holy Spirit.

Indeed, this is confirmed by Paul himself and by the apostle Peter as well:

> For no prophecy recorded in scripture was ever thought up by the prophet himself. It was the Holy Spirit within these godly men who gave them true messages from God. (2 Peter 1:20-21)

> You who claim to have the gift of prophecy or any other special ability from the Holy Spirit should be the first to realise that what I am saying is a commandment from the Lord himself. (1 Corinthians 14:37)

If you study this passage, it becomes clear that Paul's teaching came as a direct commandment from our Lord himself, and for good reason. But, in reality, all true prophets of God, including the Lord Jesus himself, have encountered opposition and even persecution because of their message. Paul most certainly did. How many of us too have suffered for the truth as he did?

> I call upon this God to witness against me if I'm not telling the absolute truth. (2 Corinthians 1:23)

> But I certify to you, Brethren, that the gospel which was preached of me is not after man. For I neither received it of man, neither was I taught it, but by the revelation of Jesus Christ. (Galatians 1:11-12 KJV)

> From now on please don't argue with me about these things for I carry on my body the scars of the whipping and the wounds from Jesus' enemies that mark me as his slave. (Galatians 6:17)

It is patently obvious from these scriptures that the doctrine that Paul taught and preached to the early church was the truth given to him by God, and even so he met with strong resistance. We are also clearly warned in Scripture that in the day and age in which we live, there would be a real falling away from the truth. Indeed, it is one of the 'signs of the times'.

> There is going to come a time when people won't listen to the truth but will go around looking for teachers who will tell them just what they want to hear. They won't listen to what the Bible says but will blithely follow their own misguided ideas. Stand steady and don't be afraid to suffer for the Lord. (2 Timothy 4:3)

> So we must listen very carefully to the truths we have heard, or we may drift away from them. (Hebrews 2:1)

> See to it that you win your full reward from the Lord, for if you wander beyond the teachings of Christ, you will leave God behind: while you are loyal to Christ's teachings you will have God too. Then you will have both the Father and Son.' (2 John 1:8-9)

> Jesus taught us, 'I will only reveal myself to those who love and obey me. The Father will love them too, and we will come to them and live with them. Anyone who doesn't obey me, doesn't love me.' (John 14:23-24)

Our eternal salvation is not the issue here. The issue is that if we are disobedient then we are not going to receive our full reward from the Lord, neither here on earth nor in eternity. Of vital importance, Gods indwelling presence in our lives is totally conditional on our willingness to obey Jesus.

> You give blessing to the pure but pain to those who leave your paths. (Psalm 18:26)

> But though we, or an angel from Heaven, preach any other gospel to you than that which we have preached unto you, let him be accursed. (Galatians 1:8)

> And remember, it is a message to obey, not just to listen to. (James 1:22)

Today the church needs to take a step backwards – back to the truth. Our Lord Jesus is coming for his Bride soon. Remember the parable of the ten virgins? Five were ready, five were not. Consider the letters to the churches in the book of Revelation.
To the church in Philadelphia:

I know you well, you aren't strong, but you have tried to obey. (Revelation 3:8)

Because you have patiently obeyed me despite the persecution, therefore I will protect you from the time of Great Tribulation and temptation which will come upon the world to test everyone alive. (Revelation 3:10)

Write this letter to the leaders of the church at Laodicea: This message is from the One who stands firm, the Faithful and true witness (of all that is or was or evermore shall be), the primeval source of God's creation. I know you well, you are neither hot nor cold; I wish you were one or the other! But since you are merely luke-warm I shall spit you out of my mouth! You say,' I am rich, with everything I want, I don't need a thing!' And you don't realize that spiritually you are wretched and miserable and poor and blind and naked. My advice to you is to buy pure gold from Me, gold purified by fire, only then will you be truly rich. And to purchase from Me white garments, clean and pure, so you won't be naked and ashamed. And get medicine from Me to heal your eyes and give back your sight.

I continually discipline and punish everyone I love, so I must punish you, unless you turn from your indifference and become enthusiastic about the things of God. Look! I have been standing at the door and I am constantly knocking. If anyone hears me calling him and opens the door, I will come and have fellowship with him and he with me. I will let everyone who conquers sit beside me on my throne, just as I took my place with my Father on his throne when I had conquered. Let those who can hear, listen to what the Spirit is saying to the churches. (Revelation 3:14-22)

The Integrity of the Scriptures: The Way of Truth

I thought we would broaden our understanding by looking at some important facts relating to God's Word. We read:

> In the beginning was the Word, and the Word was with God, and the Word was God. (John 1:1 KJV)

> The Word was made flesh, He lived among us. (John 1:14 KJV)

God and his Word are inseparable. Jesus is the living Word. John further emphasises this:

> For if you wander beyond the teachings of Christ, you will leave God behind; while if you are loyal to Christ's teachings you will have God too. (2 John 1:9)

The Jerusalem Bible puts it this way:

> If anybody does not keep within the teaching of Christ but goes beyond it, he cannot have God with him: Only those who keep to what he [Christ] taught can have the Father and the Son with them.

This is strong stuff. But the simple truth is that God is pure. He is holy. He simply cannot dwell where there is error. Indeed, the Psalms tell us:

> He [God] has magnified His Word above all His name. (Psalm 138:2 KJV)

To a greater or lesser extent, most Christians will at least pay lip service to some of these things, especially the teachings of Jesus in the Gospels. Where people run into trouble is with other parts of Scripture, especially the Epistles of Paul.

We need to come to terms with a most important and profound truth. All Scripture is from God. Not just some of it. Years ago, I was told by a freshly-ordained minister that he had been taught that the Bible was like a river carrying logs of truth. This is absolute rubbish. A lie from the devil. The Bible is the inspired Word of God, and God does not lie. It is impossible for God to lie.

> For no prophecy recorded in scripture was ever thought up by the prophet himself. It was the Holy Spirit within these Godly men who gave them true messages from God. (2 Peter 1:20-21)

> And we will never stop thanking God for this: that when we preached to you, you didn't think of the words we spoke as being just our own, but you accepted what we said as the very Word of God – which of course it was – and it changed your lives when you believed it. (1 Thessalonians. 2:13)

> You who claim to have the gift of the Holy Spirit should be the first to realise that what I am saying is a command from the Lord himself. (1 Corinthians 14:36)

Look! If it is written in the Bible, no matter who the human vessel, then take it as the very Word of God. God uses people to record his messages.

> All scripture is inspired by God and is useful for teaching the truth, rebuking error, correcting faults, and giving instruction for right living. So that the man who serves God may be fully qualified and equipped to do every kind of good work. (2 Timothy 3:16 GNT)

The Bible is God's Word. All of it. Often you will hear that what was relevant 2000 years ago is no longer relevant today. Listen to what God says about it:

> But his own plans stand forever. His intentions are the same for every generation. (Psalm 33:11)

> I have known from earliest days that you will never change. (Psalm 119:152)

> There is utter truth in all your laws; your decrees are eternal. (Psalm 119:160)

> Your truth is as enduring as the Heavens. (Psalm 89:2)

> Urging you to stoutly defend the truth which God gave, once for all, to his people to keep without change through the years, or generations. (Jude 1:3)

> All His commandments are sure, they stand fast forever and ever, and are done in truth and righteousness. (Psalm 111:7-8 KJV)

> God's truth stands firm like a great rock and nothing can shake it. It is a foundation stone with these words written on it: 'The Lord knows those who are truly His.' (2 Timothy 2:19)

I think we have established just how important God's Word is to our lives, our faith and our spiritual growth. Lord, we believe. Help thou our unbelief. The next and very important step is: How do we correctly interpret his Word? Here is some sound advice on this subject from Arnold Fruchtenbaum's excellent book *The Footsteps of the Messiah* (pages 4 and 5):

The Golden Rule of Interpretation

When the plain tense of scripture makes common sense, seek no other sense; therefore, take every word at its primary, ordinary, usual, literal meaning unless the facts of the immediate context, studied in the light of related passages and axiomatic and fundamental truths, indicate clearly otherwise.

Simply put, this law states that all biblical passages are to be taken exactly as they read unless there is something in the text indicating that it should be taken some other way than literally.

The second rule is called the Law of Double Reference.

This law observes the fact that often a passage or block of scripture is speaking of two different persons or two different events that are separated by a long period of time.

A good example can be found where Jesus quotes from Isaiah:

To proclaim the acceptable year of the Lord, and the day of vengeance of our God; to comfort all that mourn; (Isaiah 61:2 KJV)

Jesus stopped in the middle of a sentence. After speaking the words (recorded in Luke 14:19 KJV), 'To proclaim the acceptable year of the Lord', he omitted the second part of the verse, 'and the day of the vengeance of our God'. The comma in the middle of the verse in Isaiah represented a 2000-year time span.

There is one vital requirement we need when it comes to rightly interpreting Scripture. The help and empowering of the blessed Holy Spirit.

> But the comforter which is the Holy Spirit whom the Father will send in my name, will teach you everything and make you remember all that I have told you. (John 14:26 GNT)

> But when the Spirit of Truth comes, he will lead you into all the Truth. He will not speak on his own, but he will speak of what he hears and tell you of things to come.' (John 16:13 GNT)

> But you have received the Holy Spirit and he lives within you, in your hearts, so that you don't need anyone to teach you what is right. For he teaches you all things, and he is the Truth, and no liar, and so just as he has said, you must live in Christ, never to depart from him. (1 John 2:27)

Basically, that means we must live in Christ's teachings, whether they come directly from his mouth, or through his apostles' letters.

> Keep alive in yourselves what you were taught in the beginning: as long as what you were taught in the beginning is alive in you, you will live in the Son and in the Father. (1 John 2:24 Jerusalem Bible)

It is vital we stay grounded in the Bible as it was taught in the beginning. We must pray and ask God to keep us from deception and false teaching.

> Sanctify us in the Truth Lord. Thy word is Truth... (John 17:17 KJV)

The words of the Lord's Prayer:

> Lead us not into temptation but deliver us from evil. (Matthew 6:13 KJV)

The prayer of Jabez:

> May your hand be upon me, to keep me from evil. (1 Chronicles 4:10 KJV)

The Psalmist:

> Let thy loving-kindness and thy truth continually preserve me. (Psalm 40:11 KJV)

> Oh, send your loving-kindness and truth to watch over me. (Psalm 61:7)

We must understand the meaning of the following passage:

> For the word of God is living and powerful, and sharper than any two-edged sword, piercing even to the dividing asunder of soul and spirit. (Hebrews 4:12 KJV)

There are two edges to the Sword of Truth. Jesus demonstrated this beautifully when he countered Satan's testing in the wilderness. Satan used scripture to test Jesus.

He is a master at it –from when he started in the Garden of Eden – and nothing has changed.

Jesus taught us:

> Ye shall know the Truth, and the Truth shall set you free. (John 8:32 KJV)

But to really know the truth one has to have a balanced understanding of the whole of what the Scriptures teach.

> Judge not, that ye be not judged. (Matthew 7:1 KJV)

Nevertheless, Paul says:

> It isn't our job to judge outsiders. But it is certainly our job to judge and deal strongly with those who are members of the church, and who are sinning in these ways. (1 Corinthians 5:12)

Of the men of Crete Paul says:

> These men of Crete are all liars, they are like lazy animals, living only to satisfy their stomachs. They are rotten and disobedient; worthless so far as doing anything good is concerned. (Titus 1:12&16)

> Now here is a command, dear brothers; given in the name of our Lord Jesus Christ by his authority. Stay away from any Christian who spends his days in laziness and does not follow the ideal of hard work we set up for you. (2 Thessalonians 3:6)

We really need discernment, and it is perfectly in order for us to ask God for this:

> If you want to know what God wants you to do, ask him, and he will gladly tell you, for he is always ready to give a bountiful supply of wisdom to all who ask him; he will not resent it. (James 1:5)

> For the Lord is good and glad to teach you the proper path to all who go astray. He will teach the ways that are right and best

to those who humbly turn to him. And when we obey him every path he guides us on is fragrant with his loving-kindness and truth. (Psalm 25:8)

I will instruct you says the Lord and guide you along the best pathway for your life: I will advise you and watch your progress. (Psalm 32:8)

The following is just a suggestion, but it has worked for me. As you read your Bible, record what the scriptures say about certain subjects or issues. This way, you can gain a full understanding of what the Bible teaches about each matter.

*He is a rugged mountain where I can hide;
He is my Saviour,
a rock where none can reach me,
and a tower of safety.
(Psalm 18:2)*

Work Out Your Own Salvation

I would like to start this message with a question. Are you living in the fullness of your salvation – do you fully understand what Paul is saying in the following verses?

> Therefore, my dear friends, as you have always obeyed – not only in my presence, but now much more in my absence – continue to work out your salvation with fear and trembling. (Philippians 2:12-13 NIV)

Why with fear and trembling? Because if we get it wrong, the consequences are serious. Do we really understand what it means to continue to work out our salvation? I do not think I can cover all this means in one brief message, but we can look at some aspects of it. We read:

> For I am not ashamed of the gospel of Christ, for it is the power of God unto salvation to everyone that believeth. (Romans 1:16 KJV)

According to the note in the Schofield Bible (Page 1211), the Hebrew and Greek words for 'salvation' imply the ideas of deliverance, safety, preservation, healing and soundness.

> Salvation is the great inclusive word of the Gospel, gathering into itself all the redemptive acts and processes: such as justification,

redemption, grace, propitiation, imputation, forgiveness, sanctification and glorification. Salvation is in three stages.

1. A Christian has been saved from the guilt and penalty of sin, and is safe (Luke 7:50, 1 Corinthians 1:18, 2 Corinthians 2:15, Ephesians 2:5,8, 2 Timothy 1:9).

2. The Christian is being saved from the habit and dominion of sin (Romans 6:14, 2 Corinthians 3:18, Galatians 2:19-20, Philippians 1:19, Philippians 2:12-13, 2 Thessalonians 2:13). This is a work in progress.

3. A Christian will be saved at the Lord's return, from all the bodily infirmities, that are the result of sin and God's curse upon a sinful world (Romans 8:18-23, 1 Corinthians 15:42-44) and brought into entire conformity to Christ (Romans 13:11, Hebrews 10:36, 1 Peter 1:5, 1 John 3:2).

'Salvation is by grace through faith, is a free gift and wholly without works.' (Ephesians. 2:9-10, Titus 3:5-8)

All this seems to be in conflict with the following passage, which says:

Continue to work out your salvation with fear and trembling. (Philippians 2:12 NIV)

To work out our salvation is firstly to discover what salvation really means and all that it encompasses, and then to work it out by applying it in our own lives through faith. Sounds easy. Let us now look at some aspects of salvation.

Blessed be the Lord, who daily loads us with benefits, even the God of our salvation. He that is our God is the God of our salvation. (Psalm 68:19-20 KJV)

There are simply no areas in our lives where God's great plan of salvation does not apply. The question is, are we living in victory in all these areas of our lives? Hence the admonition to work out our own salvation. As I said before, we cannot cover every aspect of this subject in one message, but I can encourage each one of you to begin working on it for yourselves. To start with, I want to dispel some myths. You cannot work out your own salvation by just attending church on Sunday mornings, nor can you work out your own salvation by just listening to your minister or even great men of God, past and present (though they may well have much to teach us).

To work out our own salvation, we must take the following three steps:

1. We must come to Jesus

He will introduce us to his Father, who will give the Holy Spirit to those who ask him. The blessed Holy Spirit will make the things of God come alive for us. We have to develop our own personal relationship with the Holy Spirit, who will lead us into all truth. We have to come to that place of abiding which Jesus speaks of.

> Abide in me, and I in you. As the branch cannot bear fruit by itself, unless it abides in the vine, neither can you, unless you abide in me. I am the Vine, you are the branches. He who abides in Me, and I in him, he it is who bears much fruit, for apart from me you can do nothing. (John 15:4-5 RSV)

2. We must seek him

> His purpose in all this is that we should seek after God, and perhaps feel our way towards him and find him, though he is not far from any one of us. (Acts 17:27)

God says:

> And ye shall seek me and find me when ye shall search for me with all your heart (Jeremiah 29:13 RSV)

3. We must seek him with all our heart

If we are half-hearted in our faith, we will receive the same fate as those Christians in the Laodicean church.

> 'I know you well – you are neither hot nor cold; I wish you were one or the other! But since you are merely lukewarm, I will spit you out of my mouth!' (Revelation 3:15-16)

> He is a rewarder of them that diligently seek him. (Hebrews 11:6 KJV)

The Greek word for 'seek' is a very strong word, 'ek-zay-teh-o', meaning 'search', 'crave', 'demand'. There is a very good reason for seeking God. He is a rewarder of those who diligently seek him, but it also works the other way around.

> The Lord is with you, while you be with him, and if you seek him, he will be found of you, but if you forsake him, he will forsake you. (2 Chronicles 15:2 KJV)

> And as long as he sought the Lord, God made him prosper.' (2 Chronicles 26:5 KJV)

I want to just touch on a few areas that are practical examples of working out our own salvation. There are times in my life when I feel tired and worn down from many years of hard work and punishing my body. My stomach causes problems, sometimes I have difficulty getting my breath, my back gets sore, my joints seize up. Then, like Jonah, I remember the Lord.

> When I had lost all hope, I turned my thoughts once more to the Lord (Jonah 2:7)

We think we have problems! There was Jonah, three days and three nights in the whale's belly, out in the ocean somewhere as a result of being disobedient to God. He was half-dead from lack of air, water and food. What does he say?

> They that regard lying vanities forsake their own mercy. (Jonah 2:8 KJV)

Praise God for Jonah. It is high time we started to recognise these lies of the devil for what they are – lying vanities. It is high time we started to believe God and his promises instead of our symptoms.
The following is one of my favourite Psalms:

> Bless the Lord, oh my soul, and forget not all his benefits. Who forgives all your sins, who heals all your diseases. (Psalm 103:2 KJV)

Forgives? No problem. Heals? This promise of healing is in that very same verse.

> So that my youth is renewed like the eagle's. (Psalm 103:5)

Then there is that wonderful passage in Isaiah:

> He gives power to the faint; and to those who lack might he increases their strength. Even the youths shall faint and grow

weary, and young men shall utterly fall. But they that wait upon the Lord shall renew their strength; they shall mount up with wings like eagles; they shall run, and not be weary, and they shall walk, and not faint. (Isaiah 40:29-31 RSV)

Do we believe the circumstances, or do we believe God's Word? This is what faith is all about. Without faith it is impossible to please him. It is one thing knowing God's Word; it is another thing to appropriate it and live it out in our own lives.

Look at Job:

How enviable the man whom God corrects! Oh, do not despise the chastening of the Lord when you sin, for though he wounds, he binds and heals again. He will deliver you again and again, so that no evil can touch you. He will keep you from death in famine, and from the power of the sword in time of war. You will be safe from slander; no need to fear the future. You shall laugh at war and famine; wild animals will leave you alone. Dangerous animals will be at peace with you. You need not worry about your home while you are gone; nothing shall be stolen from your barns. Your sons shall become important men; your descendants shall be as numerous as grass. You shall live a long, good life; like standing grain, you'll not be harvested until it's time; I have found from experience that all of this is true. For your own good, listen to my counsel. (Job 5:17-27)

What I want from you is your true thanks; I want your promises fulfilled. I want you to trust me in your times of trouble, so I can rescue you, and you can give me glory. (Psalm 50:14-15)

Now, I do not know in which areas in your life you are having problems, but I do know that if you honestly and humbly seek God's face, search his Word and believe it in spite of the circumstances and (this is a very big and!) if you are prepared to obey him and do things his way, then you will gain the victory; you will work out your own salvation in that area of your life.

Is your problem a rebellious child?

> ...and I will save thy children. (Isaiah 49:2)

> He will tell how you and all your household shall be saved. (Acts 11:14)

Is it an unsaved husband or wife? Jesus said,

> You can ask him for anything, using my name, and I will do it. (John 14:13)

But don't try browbeating your spouse with scriptures. Let them see Christ in you. You will never *nag* them into the Kingdom. You may well love them in with 'chaste and gentle behaviour'. You may have to pray and fast for them and seek God's face in the matter. Remember Jacob, who wrestled with God all night in prayer. He wouldn't let go of God till he got the answer he wanted. You see, he meant business. He was working out his own salvation over a particular issue. In his case, it was his guilty conscience for cheating his brother out of his inheritance.

There are areas in each of our lives that we have to work through in order to gain the victory. There are too many Christians today who still have areas in their lives where they are not living in victory. They have not yet worked out their own salvation in some area or another, and until they do, they cannot continue to grow and go forward in the Lord. Now I must stress that eternal salvation is not the issue here. This passage states clearly:

> For no other foundation can anyone lay than that which is laid, which is Jesus Christ. Now if anyone builds on the foundation with gold, silver, precious stones, wood, hay, straw; each person's work will become manifest; for the day will disclose it because it will be revealed with fire, and the fire will test what sort of work each of us has done. If the work survives, we shall receive a reward. If anyone's work is burned up, they will suffer loss, though they themselves will be saved, but as through fire. (1 Corinthians 3:11 KJV)

Eternal salvation is not the issue. The issue is spiritual growth. Are we going to enter the Kingdom of Heaven at the Rapture as fruit-bearing Christians, ready to receive a crown and rewards, or are we going to be cast into outer darkness (the Tribulation) to have our faith tested by fire? That is the issue. That is why it is so important to work out our salvation in fear and trembling.

Is there some secret sin in your life? Is there unforgiveness in your heart against some person? Are you in bondage to some sin committed by one or more of your ancestors? Has one of your ancestors been a member of the Masonic Lodge or some occult group? Even yoga is dangerous. The Bible says we are all born into sin, every one of us. Are you sick, tired, and not experiencing the joy of the Lord? Is God's peace missing? Is his presence missing in your life? Are you truly walking by the Spirit and not the flesh? Is Jesus truly Lord of every area of your life? Is there a problem or problems in your marriage, your family relations or your work situation? God's will for us – God's great plan of salvation for us – is that we live in victory in every area of our lives.

> How shall we escape if we neglect so great a salvation; which at first began to be spoken by the Lord, and was confirmed to us by those who heard him. (Hebrews 2:3 KJV)

Jesus does not want us just to be converts. He doesn't want us just to be good, regular attenders at church on Sunday. He wants us to be joyful, Spirit-filled, fruit-bearing disciples – really living in victory in every area of our lives. That is why we are exhorted to work out our own salvation.

If the Holy Spirit has quickened something in your heart, do something about it. Jesus paid a very high price for our salvation. Don't let the devil rob you of that which is rightfully yours in Christ. The following verse is often used in the context of Jesus offering the gift of salvation to the unsaved. But the truth is that Jesus is speaking to believers rather than unbelievers; or, more correctly, he is speaking to unbelieving believers.

> Behold I stand at the door and knock: if you hear my voice and open the door, I will come into you, and sup with you, and you with me. (Revelation 3:20, KJV)

Let us pray. Father God, we thank you for your Word. We thank you for the Living Word – our Lord Jesus, our Saviour and Redeemer. And Father God, we thank you for the blessed Holy Spirit, our Comforter and Guide, whom you promised would lead us into all truth.

Father God, I ask you to send the Holy Spirit to minister to each of us. To search into the inner corners of our hearts and bring to light those areas in our lives that are holding us back from spiritual growth. Lord, help us to deal with those areas that are keeping us from growing spiritually and becoming good fruit-bearing disciples.

Lord Jesus, please forgive us for the many times we have kept the door shut on you, when you have desired to come in and sup with us and have us sup with you.

Holy Spirit, help us to be overcomers; to truly work out our salvation in fear and trembling as we have been instructed to. In Jesus' name we ask and pray. Amen.

Salt – Light – Restraining

Ye are the salt of the earth... (Matthew 5:13 KJV).

Or, as the Living Bible puts it, 'You are the world's seasoning, to make it tolerable.'

That's powerful stuff. Ordinary Christians, you and me, young and old – we are the world's seasoning to make it tolerable. We are the salt which preserves the society we live in.

> If you lose your flavour, what will happen to the world? And you yourselves will be thrown out and trampled underfoot as worthless. You are the world's light. A city on a hill, glowing in the night for all to see. Don't hide your light. Let it shine for all, let your good deeds glow for all to see, so that they will praise your Heavenly Father. (Matthew 5:13-14)

So, to recap. We are the world's seasoning in order to make it tolerable. We are the world's light, glowing in the dark for all to see. Let your good deeds glow, so they will praise our Heavenly Father. As I said before, this is powerful teaching from Jesus.

Paul picks up on a similar theme:

> Now I implore you, brethren, by the certainty of the coming of our Lord Jesus Christ and of our meeting him together, to keep your heads and not be thrown off your balance by any prediction, or message or letter purporting to come from us, and saying that

the Day of the Lord has already come. Don't let anyone deceive you by any means whatever.

That day will not come before there arises first a definite rejection of God and the appearance of the lawless man. He is the product of all that leads to death, and he sets himself up in opposition to every religion. He even takes his seat in the Sanctuary of God, to show that he really claims to be God.

You must surely remember how I talked about this when I was with you. You now know about the 'restraining power' which prevents him from being revealed until the proper time.

Evil is already insidiously at work but its activities are secret until what I have called 'the restraining power' is removed. When that happens, the lawless man will be plainly seen. (2 Thessalonians 2:1-6 Phillips)

The phrase I want to pick out from these verses is *restraining power*. Who or what is this restraining power holding back the forces of evil in our society? It is us, the believers, or more correctly the Holy Spirit working through us.

So, we are the salt to preserve. We are the seasoning to make society tolerable.

We are the light shining in the darkness. We are the restraining power keeping the forces of evil in check, until God decrees the time is right and removes this restraining power. That is pretty awesome stuff.

Where do we start? We start by believing it. If Jesus says we are the salt preserving society, he means exactly that. And he asks,

Ye are the salt of the earth: but if the salt have lost his savour, wherewith shall it be salted? (Matthew 5:13 KJV)

If we lose our savour what will happen to the world? He means that too. Our lives, our words, our deeds, our witness and our prayers have an enormous effect on the world around us.

Now some of us may move in wider circles than others. It doesn't matter. If we are faithful in little, God will make us rulers over much. The important thing is to retain our savour, our saltiness.

> I am the Vine, you are the branches. He that abideth in me, and I in him, the same bringeth forth much fruit, for without me you can do nothing. If a man abides not in me, he is cast forth as a branch, and is withered and men gather them, and cast them into the fire, and they are burned. If you abide in me, and my words abide in you, you shall ask what you will, and it shall be done unto you. In this is my Father glorified, that ye bear much fruit, so shall you be my disciples. (John 15:5 KJV)

The point here is, we can't be salt, light and a restraining influence if we are not abiding. Nor can we be asking what we will (and getting our prayers answered) and bearing fruit if we are not abiding.

> But the Godly shall flourish. Even in old age they will still produce fruit and be vital and green. This honours the Lord and exhibits his faithful care. (Psalm 92:12-14)

I had a friend, a Department of Conservation (DOC) Ranger, who once told me that the very old trees in the bush were some of the most fruitful and supported the most life. Yes, even the ones starting to go (or die) in the head. I was most encouraged.

Salt has a number of uses. In spite of the health warnings, it is probably the best and most used seasoning of all. Similarly, we too can have an enormous seasoning effect on the immediate world around us, through kindness, generosity, good deeds and being a loyal and true friend. The right word spoken at the right time can uplift and encourage. Just by being Christians in deeds as well as words. Our work ethic, personal integrity. A simple visit, and our prayers – especially our prayers. Humility, gratitude, patience. Can others see Jesus in us?

And you don't need to travel to China or Africa to find needs. Just start with those around you, those whom God brings across your path each day. He may well end up sending some of us overseas as missionaries, but we must leave that to him, we are simply his servants. Salt can sting, especially if it gets into a raw wound, but at the same time, it cleanses, heals and preserves. If we are to be salt in our society, we may see all of these things happening around us.

We must stand firm against false teaching and compromise, remembering that the Bible is the inspired Word of God, all of it. Homosexuality and gay marriage can never be accepted by the Christian Church. Abortion is wrong; it is wrong to murder innocent babies. Freemasonry can never be accepted. The God of Freemasons is Lucifer. The God of Islam, Jehovah's Witnesses and Mormons is not the God and Father of our Lord Jesus Christ.

The church has become so hell-bent on pleasing people and the feminists, it has compromised truth in so many ways. We might find some of this rather unpalatable, some hard to understand and some controversial. But God says he has refined his Word like silver, seven times so that it is pure. He also says heaven and earth will pass away, but his Word will stand forever. When he says his Word is to be kept without change throughout the generations, we had better believe it and obey.

When Jesus claims he is the Living Word and, even more, when he claims,

> I and the Father are One... (John 10:30 KJV)

> I am the Alpha and the Omega, the beginning and the end... (Revelation 1:8 KJV)

> I am the way, the Truth and the Life, no one comes to the Father, but by me... (John 14:6 KJV)

We had better believe him!

> Neither is there salvation in any other name, for there is no other name under Heaven, given among men, whereby we may be saved other than the name of Jesus. (Acts 4:12 KJV)

We had better believe it, teach it, and speak out against compromise and false teaching, even in the church. I guess you could say that's preserving. Never has there been a time in church history when the Word of God has been more under attack than today. Surely these words of Paul ring out true today:

> For the time will come when they will not endure sound doctrine, but after their own lusts, they shall heap for themselves teachers who will tell them just what they want to hear. And they shall turn away their ears from the truth, and blithely follow their own misguided ideas. Stand steady, and don't be afraid of suffering for the Lord. (2 Timothy 4:3-6 KJV)

Sadly, today, too often ministers, pastors, church leaders and big-name Christian authors have compromised God's word so as not to upset people or 'rock the boat.' The 'in' words are 'inclusiveness' and 'tolerance'. Jeremiah warned this would happen.

> Many pastors have destroyed my vineyard, they have trampled my portion underfoot. (Jeremiah 12:10 KJV)

And as for my flocks, they eat that which you have trampled with your feet, and they drink that which you have fouled with your feet. (Ezekiel 34:19 KJV)

Our whole focus should be to obey and please God in all we say and do, and not be merely man pleasers. In Jesus' message to the Philadelphian church he says:

I know you well; you aren't strong, but you have tried to obey and have not denied my name. Therefore I have opened a door to you that no one can shut. Note this: I will force those supporting the causes of Satan while claiming to be mine (but they aren't – they are lying) to fall at your feet and acknowledge that you are the ones I love.

And what is his promise?

Because you have patiently obeyed me despite the persecution, therefore I will protect you from the time of Great Tribulation and temptation, which will come upon the world to test everyone alive. (Revelation 3:8-10)

It is high time we came to accept the fact that we can't have it both ways. If we desire to serve Jesus, we have to separate ourselves from the world. True, we live in the world, but we are not our own. We have been bought with a price; redeemed from the world by the precious blood of our Saviour. He has a right to call the shots. When he says believe in me and believe *in* my word, we had better do just that. Believe. Not trample, water down, compromise or adulterate it to soothe our itching ears.

The Greek word for 'believe' can be translated 'even'. It refers to something fixed in time and state. Something which cannot be changed. There are some things in God's Word which don't seem too palatable. There are large parts of the Bible which deal with issues of judgment and punishment. And, make no mistake, we are on the very brink of seeing the fulfilment of the Scriptures in this regard, but rarely is this ever preached. There are issues which are hard to come to terms with. 1 Corinthians chapter 11 is a classic example. The first half of this chapter deals with submission of wives to husbands, spiritual covering and protection from evil, and is mainly ignored, But we have made a major doctrine in the second half. We hear scriptures from there being quoted every time we hold a communion service.

This verse is another example:

Who forgiveth all thine iniquities [sins]; who healeth all thy diseases... (Psalm 103:3 KJV)

Yet we go to the doctor! How can this be? Has God made a mistake? I don't think so. He refined his Word seven times, remember.

Salt cleanses and heals. Now we can't do that ourselves, but the blood of Jesus certainly can. And we can lift others up to God in prayer, bringing them before the Throne of Grace and ask for cleansing, healing, deliverance and salvation (or whatever their needs might be).

It is no surprise we are told (Matthew 5:13) that Christians are 'the salt of the earth', and in the next verse (Matthew 5:14) that we are 'the light of the world'. As our saltiness improves, so our light shines brighter. Like some insects, we too are drawn to light. If you are ever caught out in the dark and see a light in the distance, you are drawn to it. I've been out hunting in the bush and been caught out in darkness without a torch. Not a good situation on a dark night.

In such a situation the most welcome sight you could see is a campfire burning or a light shining. So it is for us. If your light is shining brightly people will naturally be drawn to you when they are in trouble. Jesus emphasises the importance of this:

> Don't hide your light. Let it shine for all; let your good deeds glow for all to see, so that they will praise your Heavenly Father. (Matthew 5:15-16)

This does not mean you can blow your own trumpet. Nevertheless, godly people and godly families shine out in today's world. Jesus asked the question:

> When someone lights a lamp, does he put a box over it to shut out the light? Of course not. The light could not be seen or used. A lamp is placed on a stand to shine and be useful. All that is now hidden will someday come to light. (Mark 4:21-22)

Another time Jesus said:

> Who ever heard of someone lighting a lamp and then covering it up to keep it from shining. No, lamps are mounted in the open where they can be seen. (Luke 8:16)

This illustrates the fact that one day everything in our hearts will be brought into the light and made plain to all.

> If you have ears, listen! And be sure to put into practice what you hear. The more you do this, the more you will understand what I tell you. (Mark 4:23-24)

> So be careful how you listen; for whoever has, to him shall be given more; and whoever does not have, even what he thinks he has, shall be taken away from him. (Luke 8:18)

I think we can see the importance Jesus places on allowing our light to shine. People have got to see Jesus in us. I remember Winkie Pratney telling us a story at a camp at Orama on Great Barrier Island.

He was at high school when he became a Christian. One day another student came up to him. 'Are you a Christian?' he asked timidly. 'Yes,' replied Winkie loudly. 'I am too', the other student replied quietly. 'Well, where have you been all those years when I was headed to hell?' Winkie asked.

Do you receive or have read the *Intercessors for NZ* magazine? You don't need to read many copies to realise just how much influence the prayers of faithful Christians have on the affairs of a nation.

> ...the reason you don't have what you want is that you don't ask God for it. (James 4:2b)

But if we are in that position of abiding; if we are in a right relationship with God, then Jesus says to us:

> If ye abide in me, and my words abide in you, ye shall ask what ye will, and it shall be done unto you. (John 15:7 KJV)

There was a time (please Lord, forgive me) when I used to get concerned about the influence of the 'one-world government movement' in New Zealand and what they are seeking to do here. Until I read this scripture:

> As for the work this man of rebellion and hell will do when he comes, it is already going on, but he himself will not come until the one who is holding him back steps out of the way. (2 Thessalonians 2:7)

The important thing is that we can all pray. It doesn't matter what age we are, even if we are in a wheelchair or are bed-ridden. Much time, or little time, we can pray. Whether we are reading the paper, listening to the news on TV or radio, at a meeting or anywhere else; if you feel burdened or prompted by the Holy Spirit, then simply pray. No wonder Jesus instructed us to pray without ceasing. Our prayers have the potential to have a big influence on the world around us, especially when we are able to discern God's will in the situation.

It is the restraining influence of the Holy Spirit, working through Christians, that is holding in check the forces of evil in the world, until the 'Bride' has made herself ready.

I well remember Peter Morrow, when he was in Orama many years ago, saying that the most important people in his church were little old ladies who prayed regularly.

Now I am sure God does not mind if we are little or big, male or female, young or old, adult or child. If we are praying regularly in his will, we have a big impact on our nation and the world-at-large.

The Word for Today, July 27 2002.

Father, your word says: 'Woe to those who call evil good'; but that is exactly what we have done and are continually doing in today's society. We have lost our spiritual equilibrium and revised our values. We've ridiculed the absolute truth of your Word and called it pluralism, suggesting alternative meanings that you never intended.

We reward laziness and call it welfare. Exploit the poor and call it the lottery. Kill our unborn babies and call it choice. Neglect to discipline our children and call it building self-esteem. Abuse power and call it politics. Pollute the airways, via radio and TV with profanity and pornography and call it freedom of expression. Ridicule the time-honoured values of our forefathers and call it enlightenment. Search us Oh God and know our hearts. Cleanse us and set us free.

John Knox was one of the well-known Christian reformers of history. There were others too, such as Martin Luther, John Wesley and C.T. Studd. John Knox spoke out against the evils of his era. 'The monstrous tyranny of women in places of influence'. This really upset Queen Elizabeth I. He would be in big trouble today.

We too must speak out against the incredible nonsense permeating our society and (sadly, much worse) the very church itself. Political correctness, gender neutrality – remember God created us, male and female – and so-called cultural sensitivity. When we are born again, the past is meant to be crucified. Most of this New Age teaching has nothing to do with the Kingdom of God. We will let Paul have the final say:

> For we speak as messengers from God, trusted by him to tell the truth, we change his message not one bit to suit the taste of those who hear it; for we serve God alone, who examines our heart's deepest thoughts. (1 Thessalonians 2:4).

> You can see that I am not trying to please you with sweet talk and flattery; no, I am trying to please God. If I were still trying to please men I could not be Christ's servant. (Galatians 1:10)

Listen and Obey

Today we will look at what Scripture says about hearing God's voice and being obedient to what he says. It is no coincidence that the first word of the first commandment is:

> Hear, O Israel: The Lord our God is one Lord. (Deuteronomy 6:4 KJV)

That word 'hear' (or 'listen'), repeated so many times in the New Testament, is the key word in this message.
Jesus said,

> Yea, rather; blessed are they that hear the word of God and keep it. (Luke 11:28 KJV)

The Living Bible puts that verse like this:

> Yes, but even more blessed are all who hear the word of God and put it into practice.

In John's epistle it says:

> Loving God means doing what he tells us to do, and really, that isn't hard at all. For every child of God can obey him, defeating sin and evil pleasure by trusting Christ to help him. (1 John 5:3-4)

Do you hear what the Spirit is saying? We can trust Christ to help us defeat sin and evil pleasure. But it is conditional. What is the condition? Obedience. Why do you think obedience so important? Jesus gives us the answer:

> Because I will only reveal myself to those who love me and obey me. The Father will love them too, and we will come to them and live with them. Anyone who doesn't obey me, doesn't love me (John 14:23)

This is further reinforced:

> See to it that you win your full reward from the Lord. For if you wander beyond the teachings of Christ, you will leave God behind; while if you are loyal to Christ's teaching you will have both the Father and the Son. (2 John 8-9)

Peter warns us:

> He is the stone that some will stumble over because they will not listen to God's Word, nor obey it, and so this punishment must follow – that they will fall. (1 Peter 2:8)

If we are not willing to obey, we are going to stumble and fall – it's just that simple. Why are we going to fall? The answer is simple – when we are disobedient, we leave God behind; when we are obedient, we are with God. It is God who keeps us from stumbling and sinning.

> So if we stay close to him, obedient to him, we won't be sinning either; but as for those who keep on sinning, they should realize this. They sin because they have never really known him or become his. (1 John 3:6)

Listen and Obey

It is quite possible to be a regular church-going Christian and not really know Jesus and his ways. And, worse still, to have Jesus say when we meet him, 'Depart from me, I don't know you'. Remember Philip, who had been with him for all of his ministry. Jesus said to him:

> Have I been such a long time with you, and yet thou hast not known me, Philip? (John 14:9 KJV)

Now I know that the issue with Philip was Christ's deity (who Christ really was), but the simple truth is we can all be blind at times, even when we have been with him a long time. Sadly, in the church today there is an increasing amount of spiritual blindness and deafness. The point is, seeing and knowing are closely linked. If we can't see him, we won't get to know him. Jesus said:

> I will only reveal myself to those who love me and obey me. (John 14:23)

We will not be able to see him if he does not reveal himself to us. Let us go back to where we started. 'Blessed are they that hear the word of God and keep it.' The following Old Testament passage spells it out so clearly:

> Obedience is far better than sacrifice. He is much more interested in you listening to him, than in you offering the fat of rams to him. For rebellion is as bad as the sin of witchcraft. (1 Samuel 15:22)

James reassures us:

> But if anyone keeps looking steadily into God's law for free men,

he will not only remember it but he will do what it says, and God will greatly bless him in everything he does. (James 1:25)

Isn't that wonderful, and isn't that incentive enough to want to live in obedience? God will greatly bless you in everything that you do if you are obedient. In the book of Revelation, we find our Lord's final instructions to the Christian church and, as we study the letters to the churches, there is one message that rings out loud and clear – those who listen and do what it says will be blessed. Obedience and blessing – they go together. In the letters to the seven churches, we find that this message is emphasised over and over again. To every single church without exception. To the church at Ephesus:

> Let this message sink into the ears of anyone who listens to what the Spirit is saying to the churches. (Revelation 2:7)

Let it sink in – it is not to be ignored. To church at Smyrna:

> Let everyone who can hear, listen to what the Spirit is saying to the churches. (Revelation 2:11)

The inference is that there are some who can't hear. Their ears are closed. To the church at Pergamos:

> Let everyone who can hear, listen to what Spirit is saying. (Revelation 2:12)

To church at Thyatira:

> Pay attention to what I am saying. (Revelation 2:22)

and

> Let all who can hear, listen to what the Spirit is saying to the churches. (Revelation 2:29)

To the church at Sardis:

> Let all who can hear, listen to what the Spirit is saying to the churches. (Revelation 3:1)

To the church at Philadelphia:

> You aren't strong, but you have tried to obey. (Revelation 3:8)

and

> Let all who can hear, listen to what the Spirit is saying to the churches. (Revelation 3:13)

And finally, to the church at Laodicea:

> This message is from the one who stands firm; the faithful and true witness. (Revelation 3:14)

He doesn't compromise the truth and he doesn't lie. His Word doesn't change to suit our whims. Now he is trying to gain our attention. And

> Look I have been standing at the door and knocking. If anyone hears me calling him and opens the door, I will come in and fellowship with him and he with me' (Revelation 3:20)

We are missing out on so much. His final words to the church before the Rapture or Translation (when Christ returns for his bride) occurs: 'Let those who can hear, listen to what the Spirit is saying to the churches.' I know of nowhere else in Scripture where the same message is repeated over and over again, so many times in such a short space. What is going on here? And again, his words: 'Look! I have been standing at the door and I am constantly knocking.'

Why is Jesus speaking like this? These are his final instructions to his church. It is very obvious that we have not been listening as we should, and consequently we are missing some important truths. But worse, while we are playing church, he is shut outside trying to gain our attention. This begs the questions: What are the Holy Spirit and Jesus himself saying to us? Where have we got it wrong? Have we missed something? Where do we start? What is the most important thing?

> Now the most important thing about a servant is that he does just what is Master tells him to do. (1 Corinthians 4:2)

The truth is that we are not our own. We have been bought with a price; so he has a perfect right to set the terms. He is our master. We have been bought and paid for with his blood. We need to study and re-study the Scriptures with honest hearts and open ears, and seek to be obedient to every command which Christ has given us, his chosen people. We must always remember that the details concerning the doctrine, position, walk and destiny of the church were committed to Paul and his fellow apostles.

> In olden times God did not share this plan with his people, but now he has revealed it by the Holy Spirit to his apostles and prophets. (Ephesians 3:5)

> For no prophecy recorded in scripture was ever thought up by the prophet himself. It was the Holy Spirit within these godly men who gave them true messages from God. (2 Peter 1:20-21)

> And we will never stop thanking God for this: that when we preached to you, you didn't think of the words we spoke as being just our own, but you accepted what we said as the very word of God – which of course it was – and it changed your lives when you believed it. (1 Thessalonians 2:13)

Do you want your life to change for the better? Then it's simple – start believing the very words of God. They will change your life when you believe them, obey them and put them into practice. In this we need the help and empowering of the Holy Spirit, and we need to cry out to our Heavenly Father: 'Sanctify us in truth. Thy Word is truth.' We need to remember that God's truth stands firm. Jesus' words to the Laodicean Church are 'from the one who stands firm, the faithful and true witness'. Or, as the Apostle Paul says:

> But God's truth stands firm like a great rock, and nothing can shake it. It is a foundation stone with these words written on it: The Lord knows those who are really his and a person who calls himself a Christian should not do things that are wrong. (2 Timothy 2:19)

We also need to remember Jude's admonition:

> I must write... urging us to stoutly defend the truth which God gave once for all, to his people to keep, without change throughout the years. (Jude 1:3)

We are guilty of a huge error of judgment when we assume that

God's Word is no longer relevant today. Or that the culture has changed. Or that man knows better. Nothing could be further from the truth. We need to be very careful to ensure that we are not being influenced by 'big-name' Christian authors and speakers, or by the ways of the world, rather than believing in God and his unchanging Word.

The church today is allowing itself to be influenced by such nonsense as political correctness and the aspirations of the feminist movement, both within and outside the church. We are more concerned about pleasing others than obeying God, all in the guise of loving one another. The 'in' words are 'inclusiveness' and 'tolerance'.

Let us remember Paul's testimony:

> For we speak as messengers from God, trusted by him to tell the truth: We change his message not one bit to suit the taste of those who hear it, for we serve God alone, who examines our heart's deepest thoughts. (1 Thessalonians 2:4)

We do well at this point to go right back to the Adamic covenant:

> From now on you and the woman will be enemies, as will your offspring and hers. You will strike his heel, but he will crush your head. Then God said to the woman, 'You shall bear children in intense pain and suffering; yet even so, you shall welcome your husband's affections and he shall be your master. And to Adam, God said:
>
> Because you listened to your wife and ate the fruit when I told you not to, I have placed a curse upon the soil. All your life you will struggle to extract a living from it. It will grow thorns and thistles for you, and you shall eat its grasses. (Genesis 3:15-19)

I quote from the note in the Schofield Bible (Page 7) Genesis 3:15; the creation covenant:

> The Adamic covenant conditions life of fallen man – conditions which must remain till, in the Kingdom age, *'The creation itself also shall be delivered from the bondage of corruption into the glorious liberty of the children of God'* (Romans 8:21 KJV).
>
> The elements of the covenant are:
>
> 1. The serpent, Satan's tool, is cursed and becomes God's graphic warning in nature of the effects of sin – from the most beautiful and subtle of creatures to a loathsome reptile.
>
> 2. The first promise of a Redeemer (vs 15)
>
> 3. The changed status of the woman, in three particulars:
>   a) Multiplied conception.
>   b) Sorrow (pain) in motherhood.
>   c) The headship of man (compare to Genesis 1:26-27). Sin's disorder makes necessary a headship; it is vested in the man (Ephesians 5:22-25; 1 Corinthians 11:7-9; 1 Corinthians 14:34; 1 Timothy 2:11-14).
>
> 4. The light occupation of Eden (Genesis 2:15) changed to burdensome labour because of the earth being cursed.
>
> 5. The inevitable sorrow of life (vs 17).
>
> 6. The brevity of life and the tragic certainty of death to Adam and his descendants (vs 19). Also see Romans 5:12-21. Nevertheless, the curse upon the ground is for man's sake. It is not good for man to live without toil.

Not one of the conditions of this covenant have changed, nor will they change until Jesus returns to establish his Millennium Kingdom. There is a mistaken belief today that women are no longer subject to the conditions of this covenant. They misinterpret the following verse:

> So there is no difference between Jews and Gentiles, between slaves and free men, between men and women; you are all one in union with Christ Jesus. (Galatians 3:28 GNT)

Certainly, Jesus set us free from the curses and bondages of the Old Testament law by fulfilling the law for us but in no way did he alter any of the conditions of the Adamic covenant. Not one. In too many instances today, we are following the ways of the world and not God's. We are going the way of Cain, who wanted religion on his terms – not God's. He rejected God's way of atonement for sin through shed blood. And what happened? God rejected his offering. That is scary. We too forget God's words.

> This plan of mine is not what you would work out, neither are my thoughts the same as yours. For just as the Heavens are higher than the earth, so are my ways higher than yours and my thoughts than yours. (Isaiah 55:8-9)

Let us get back to the basics in our daily lives, seeking to obey him and live our lives on his terms, not our own.

> Then we will no longer be like children, forever changing our minds about what we believe because someone has told us something different or has cleverly lied to us and made the lie sound like the truth. Instead we lovingly follow the truth at all times – speaking truly, dealing truly, living truly – and so become more and more in every way like Christ who is the head of his body, the church. (Ephesians 4:14-16)

> It is true that the way to live a Godly life is not an easy matter. But the answer lies in Christ. (1 Timothy 3:16)

And remember the Lord's promises:

> Those who are faithful in little, I will make rulers over ten cities. (Luke 19:17 KJV)

> But oh, that my people would listen to me! Oh, that Israel would follow me, walking in my paths. How quickly then I would subdue her enemies! How soon my hands would be upon her foes! Those who hate the Lord would cringe before him; their desolation would last forever. But he would feed you with the choicest foods. He would satisfy you with the honey for the taking. (Psalm 81:13-16)

All of God's wonderful promises are conditional. 'But oh, that my people would listen to me!'

What Measure Ye Measure

Today our topic is 'what measure ye measure', because Jesus spoke out on the subject. He raises the issue of measuring three times in the New Testament. When Jesus raises a subject three times, you know it is important. We will start with a reading from NIV translation:

> Do not judge or you too will be judged. For, in the same way you judge others, you will be judged and with the measure you use, it will be measured to you. (Matthew 7:1-2 NIV)

Today's English Version puts it this way:

> Do not judge others, so that God will not judge you, because God will judge you in the same way you judge others, and he will apply to you the same rules you apply to others.

The commentary on these verses is interesting. It basically says that we must be very careful in what spirit we are judging a person or events. The truth is, we are meant to judge all manner of events pertaining to life and the church, particularly in matters relating to behaviour, moral standards and the doctrines we follow, but always remembering to love one another. Indeed, Jesus said,

> By their fruits, ye shall know them. (Matthew 7:20 KJV)

Nevertheless, our judging is to be in the right spirit – not harsh, critical or condemning. If our words are spoken in love and bring conviction and change, that is fine, but if they bring condemnation and persecution to righteous people, then we too can expect the same measure of judgement.

A wonderful example of God's grace in this respect is the apostle Paul, who started off judging in the wrong spirit, but ended up being mightily used in the Lord's service. Speaking of judgement, unless we repent, he will apply the same rules to us that we apply to others. This applies equally to world events.

> And be sure to put into practice what you hear. The more you do this, the more you will understand what I tell you. To him who has shall be given; from him who has not shall be taken away even what he has. (Mark 4:24-25)

This teaching can be summed up in one word – obedience. Obedience to what we hear in God's Word. And when we are obedient, we receive more. If we want more of God, greater understanding of his Word, and more spiritual power, then we need to start by being obedient in little things. He gives us more as we continue in obedience. He extends our territory and understanding. So it goes on. Jesus said:

> I will only reveal myself to those who love me and obey me. The Father will love them too, and we will come to them and live with them. Anyone who doesn't obey me doesn't love me. (John 14:23)

We need to spend time meditating on the importance of these words of Jesus. We simply cannot have it both ways. If we love the world more than Jesus, we will never really come to know him.

And how then can we come to know him unless he reveals himself to us? As always, the choice is ours.

> Whatever measure you use to give, large or small – will be used to measure what is given back to you. (Luke 6:38)

Here we have really basic, core teaching for life itself, especially the Christian life. This same rule applies to Christians and non-Christians alike – we reap what we sow. This is just so profoundly true. We should allow this Scripture to sink deep into our hearts. Let's read it again:

> Whatever measure we use to give, large or small, will be used to measure what is given back to us.

This is the secret of God's abundance, and it pertains to every aspect of life and encompasses both our dealings with God as well as with our fellow man. What measure do you use? Perhaps we need to go back to Luke, as this will give us a better understanding of where Jesus is coming from.

> But I tell you who hear me: Love your enemies, Do good to those who hate you. Bless those who curse you, and pray for those who mistreat you. If someone strikes you on one cheek, turn to him the other one also. If someone takes your cloak, do not stop him from taking your tunic. Give to everyone who asks you, and if anyone takes what belongs to you, do not demand it back. Do to others as you would have them do to you.
>
> If you love those who love you, what credit is that to you? Even sinners love those who love them. And if you do good to those who are good to you, what credit is that to you? Even sinners do that.

> And if you lend to those from whom you expect repayment, what credit is that to you? Even 'sinners' lend to 'sinners' expecting to be repaid in full. But love your enemies, do good to them, and lend to them without expecting to get anything back. Then your reward will be great, and you will be sons of the Most High, because he is kind to the ungrateful and the wicked.
> Be merciful just as your Father is merciful. Do not judge, and you will not be judged.
> Do not condemn, and you will not be condemned. Forgive, and you will be forgiven.
> Give, and it will be given to you. A good measure, pressed down, shaken together and running over, will be poured into your lap. For with the measure you use, it will be measured to you. (Luke 6:27-38 KJV)

That says it all, doesn't it? This reaping and sowing principle applies in so many areas of our lives. In fact, it covers every area of our lives. We cannot possibly cover all of Jesus' teaching here, but will concentrate on a few main points.

This message is for those whose ears are spiritually open

> Consider carefully what you hear. (Mark 4:24 NIV)

> Those who listen to it being read and do what it says will also be blessed. (Revelation 1:3)

These passages promise a special blessing to those who hear and take to heart what they hear. Look! Our understanding of scripture and our growth in Christ are in direct proportion to how we listen, take note of what we hear, and then put into practise these truths in our daily living. Jesus said,

The more you do this the more you will understand what I tell you. (Mark 4:24)

Our measuring applies to every area of life. Hence the scale of Jesus' teaching on this subject.

Do not judge and you will not be judged
We have already had a brief look at judging in the right spirit. We need much wisdom in this area.

> It isn't our job to judge outsiders, but it is certainly our job to judge and deal strongly with those who are members of the church. (1 Corinthians 5:12)

It is especially important that we are not sitting under false teaching. We need the help and empowering of the Holy Spirit in this matter. In every area of our life, our judgement needs to be under the guidance of the Holy Spirit. Probably never more so than now as God is beginning to stir the nations; even New Zealand is being stirred. Listen to Amos:

> Those who are wise will not try to interfere with the Lord in the dread day of punishment. (Amos 5:13)

Or Isaiah:

> The Lord, the God of Battle has spoken, who can change his plans? When his hand moves, who can stop him? (Isaiah 14:27)

Let us never forget our God is the God of Battle. Probably no issue causes more division than the Israeli – Palestinian conflict, yet it is not our role to be judgemental of Israel or Palestine. Scripture makes it clear what our role is:

> Take no rest all you who pray, and give God no rest until he establishes Jerusalem and makes her respected and admired throughout the earth. (Isaiah 62:7)

What is our role? It is to pray and keep praying. As God begins to stir our own nation (which he is), we need to be careful how we judge events as they unfold. So often we blame individuals or nations when it is just the hand of God moving against his enemies.

The following is a quote from *Intercessors for New Zealand*, November 2003:

> The issue is not 'whose side God is on' (as though God was partisan and took sides with certain people) but 'whose side am I on? Am I on God's side?'

You see, God is not on anybody's side. He stands for truth, righteousness, holiness and justice; for godliness and the fulfilment of his Word. Remember, God does move in battle from time to time against his enemies.

Forgive and you will be forgiven. According to our measure of forgiveness, so we are forgiven. We could spend this whole message just on this issue alone. Our own spiritual freedom is dependent on our willingness to forgive others. If we want to stay spiritually bound, then we simply need to carry right on harbouring unforgiveness. Because the measure we use in this respect is the measure used against us by God. Jesus picked this up in the prayer he gave us, known as the Lord's Prayer:

> Forgive us our trespasses as we forgive those who trespass against us. (Matthew 6:6 KJV)

This is perhaps more clearly understood if we say: 'Forgive us to the level we are willing to forgive others', because that is the way it is. According to our measure, so God measures also. We set the scales. This is a pretty good incentive to get rid of some old grievances, I would suggest, unforgiveness keeps us bound, whereas Jesus longs for us to be free. This measuring applies to literally every area of our lives and our dealings with others. God and mankind. Our time, finances, family and work. When we show generosity from a grateful heart, God is generous to us. He is limited only by our choices and decisions. He loves to give and longs to bless. It is his very nature to do these things. But as with all his promises, they are conditional. The condition here is simple: the measure we use for others, he will use for us. It applies equally to our Christian life, our willingness to obey Jesus and his Word, and our willingness to lay down our lives for him.

If we want more of Jesus, all we need do is lay down more of ourselves in obedience and service to him. We must never forget we are not our own. We have been bought with a price. He has the right of ownership. The more we hold back, the more we hold him back. The more we die to self and the pleasures of this world, the more he lives in us.

Let us pray. Father God, in this time of growing clamour in our nation and throughout the world, may we learn how to walk in the fear of the Lord and in the comfort of the Holy Spirit. Father God, speak to our hearts, I ask. Open our ears to hear what the Spirit is saying at this time. Help us to rightly discern the truth from your Word, not to judge according to the flesh, and not to be sidetracked by the clamour of the media.

May we, with humble and loving hearts, continue in service to you and each other in your church and your Kingdom.

Father, grant us kind and generous hearts, that we might give freely and receive freely from you. Father, we love you, we respect you and your Word, and we fear you. For you alone are worthy of our fear, our love and our gratitude.

Grant that we might live our lives doing loving deeds, in truth, giving full measure of ourselves that we might receive of your abundance. Lead us not into temptation but deliver us from evil. Cleanse our hearts of all unforgiveness and bitterness. I ask that you might freely forgive us of our own trespasses. Fill us afresh with your Spirit, Lord the blessed Holy Spirit, that we might bear much fruit. Fruit which remains.

In the precious name of Jesus we pray. Amen.

Repent, for the Kingdom of Heaven is at Hand

Not everyone who sayeth unto me, Lord, Lord shall enter the Kingdom of Heaven, but he that doeth the will of my Father who is in Heaven. ['For the decisive question is whether they obey my Father in Heaven' – Living Bible.] Many will say to me in that day, 'Lord, Lord, have we not prophesised in thy name? And in thy name have cast out demons? And in thy name have done many wonderful works?' And then I will profess unto them, 'I never knew you, depart from me, you who work iniquity.' (Matthew 7:21-23 KJV)

The issue here is not salvation. It is about our reigning with Christ in his Millennium Kingdom (the Kingdom of Heaven) here on earth. Back to our text. How can this be? Here we have a group who have been ministering in Jesus' name, and it is a large group. He says 'many' have been prophesying in his name, casting out demons, and doing many wonderful works, and he says to them, 'I never knew you, depart from Me, ye that work iniquity.'

The reason for this is simple. They were not doing the will of his Father. They were not obeying God. They were using Jesus' name to support their own doctrine, or more correctly the devil's doctrine. Jesus and his Father had long departed from the scene.

> For if you wander beyond the teachings of Christ, you will leave God behind, while if you are loyal to Christ's teachings you will

have God too. Then you will have both the Father and the Son. (2 John 1:9)

These people had fallen for the oldest trick in the devil's armoury, the first weapon in his arsenal – 'Did God really say...?' Nothing has changed. Our whole Christian walk is conditional on this one thing – are we being obedient to God and his unchanging Word, or are we being deceived by Satan and our own fleshly desires, wanting to conform to the ways of the world? Paul states it plainly:

> But God's truth stands firm like a great rock and nothing can shake it. It is a foundation stone with these words written on it. 'The Lord knows those who are really His.' (2 Timothy 2:19)

We are known by our obedience to God and his unchanging Word. That is why Jude exhorts us:

> To stoutly defend the truth, which God gave, once for all, to his people to keep without change, through the years. (Jude 1:3)

Or, as some translations say, 'throughout the generations'.
This is why Jesus says to people who were even doing miracles using his name:

> I never knew you. (Matthew 7:23 KJV)

He says the same to the five virgins lacking oil in their lamps:

> Go away! It is too late! (Matthew 25:12)

The oil spoken of here is the blessed Holy Spirit, the presence of God in our lives. It is not rocket science. If we walk in obedience to Jesus and his commandments, then we will have God's Holy Spirit with us and in us. That means we will have plenty of oil in our lamps. However, if we wander away from Christ's teachings, we leave God behind. No God, no oil and – much worse – he does not know us. He is not able to know us in that state.

Our whole purpose in our Christian walk is to bring pleasure to our Creator.

> For thy pleasure they are and were created. (Revelation 4:11 KJV)

We were created to be tested in our faithfulness and our obedience to him. The blessings and rewards for those who are faithful and obedient are simply beyond our comprehension, both in this life and the life to come.

> For since the beginning of the world men have not heard, nor perceived by the ear, neither hath the eye seen, O God, beside thee, what he hath prepared for him that waiteth for him. (Isaiah 64:4 KJV)

> But as it is written, Eye hath not seen, nor ear heard, neither have entered into the heart of man, the things which God hath prepared for them that love him. (1 Corinthians 2:9 KJV)

But the converse also applies. Just as there are rewards and blessings for obedience, so also are there consequences for disobedience. Always there are consequences. For those unbelievers whose sins are not washed clean by the blood of Jesus, there lies ahead eternal damnation.

> And all who trust him – God's Son – to save them have eternal life;

those who don't believe and obey him shall never see heaven, but the wrath of God remains upon them. (John 3:36)

So also, there will be intense suffering and frustration for those believers who find themselves cast into outer darkness as a consequence of following their own misguided form of religion. Jesus warns us clearly:

> There shall be weeping, and wailing, and gnashing of teeth. (Matthew 8:12 KJV)

He warns five more times in Matthew: Matthew 13:42; 13:50; 22:13; 24:51 and 25:30.

In every case he is talking to churchgoers, to Jew and Gentile alike. I emphasise again that these Christians have not necessarily lost their salvation. But by being cast out into outer darkness, it does mean they will have to endure the absolute horror and trauma of the Tribulation, to have their faith tested by fire.

> It is a day of darkness and gloom, of black clouds and thick darkness. (Joel 2:2)

> I counsel thee to buy of me gold tried in the fire, that thou mayest be rich; and white raiment, that thou mayest be clothed, and that the shame of thy nakedness do not appear; and anoint thine eyes with eye salve, that thou mayest see. (Revelation 3:18 KJV)

The basic reason for this is their pursuing a form of religion that is based on man's terms, not God's. Jesus said:

> Not all who sound religious are really godly people. They may

refer to me as 'Lord,' but still won't enter the Kingdom of Heaven. For the decisive question is whether they obey my Father in heaven. At the Judgment many will tell me, 'Lord, Lord, we told others about you and used your name to cast out demons and to do many other great miracles.' But I will reply, 'You have never been mine. Go away, for your deeds are evil.' (Matthew 7:21-23)

This is the second oldest weapon in the devil's arsenal – the sin of Cain – religion on man's terms, not God's. God rejected Cain's offering, just as Jesus still does today. Our offering of service, in whatever field, has to be on his terms. This is totally non-negotiable. God does not change. His Word does not change. He speaks no idle words. His standards and commands for today are exactly the same as when Jesus walked this earth. Whether you agree or disagree makes no difference whatsoever. God's Word stands firm, like a great rock, and nothing can change it. What he says will happen and nothing we say or do will alter that fact.

The late Derek Prince once said:

> The Bible is faultless in its reliability. God has only one standard for His word. Absolute perfection.

We need to understand that the Word of God is totally and absolutely authoritative. We do well to heed it and obey it. No amount of 'grace' teaching can exonerate the church from simple obedience. It is by grace we are saved and enter into the Kingdom of God, but it is only through obedience that we can enter into the Kingdom of Heaven. Study the Scriptures.

> Blessed are they who are part of the first resurrection... (Revelation 20:6 KJV)

No wonder there will be weeping, wailing and gnashing of teeth on the part of those who 'miss the boat' in the Rapture of the believers. But oh, the arrogance of man that he considers he knows better than his Creator and the author of the Scriptures. We need to come to terms with the fact that God's ways are not the ways of the world.

Both the church and the world need to come to terms with the fact that life is on his terms, not ours. He made the rules, and they are not negotiable. Certainly, he gives us free choice, but we must live with the consequences of the choices we make. Listen to the words of Jesus:

> All who listen to My instructions and follow them are wise, like a man who builds his house on solid rock. (Matthew 7:26 ESV)

It is not rocket science. As God himself says:

> My words are plain and clear to anyone with half a mind, if it is only open. (Proverbs 8:9)

Even a person with limited intellectual capacity can understand if his or her mind is not closed to the truth. The Scriptures do not need to be re-interpreted for today. God is not incompetent.

> The words of the Lord are pure words; as silver tried in a furnace of earth, purified seven times. (Psalm 12:6 NKJV)

> All his commandments are sure. They stand fast forever and ever, and are done in truth and righteousness. (Psalm 111:7 KJV)

> God's words will always prove true and right, no matter who questions them. (Romans 3:4)

As Arnold Fruchtenbaum teaches in his excellent book *The Footsteps of the Messiah*:

> When the plain sense of scripture makes good sense, seek no other sense.

We need to heed our Lord's words:

> Man shall not live by bread alone, but by every word that proceedeth out of the mouth of God. (Matthew 4:4 KJV)

The Living Bible puts it this way:

> Obedience to every word of God is what we need.

One of the fastest growing mission fields in the world today is the Christian Church. We have latched on to the first part of the Great Commission, 'Go into all the world.' But in far too many cases have ignored the second and vitally important part, 'Teaching them to obey all I have commanded you.'

As a consequence, we now have the situation spelled out by our Lord in his letter to the Laodicean church:

> Since you are merely lukewarm I will spit [correct translation is vomit] you out of my mouth. You say:' I am rich with everything I want; I don't need a thing!' And you don't realize that spiritually you are wretched, and miserable, and poor, and blind, and naked. My advice to you is to buy pure gold from me, gold purified by fire, only then will you be truly rich. (Revelation 3:16-18)

Lukewarm Christians are headed straight into the fire of the Tribulation. Listen to any number of God's prophets worldwide, and you will quickly come to realise just how imminent the Tribulation is. It may well happen any day now, and sadly, a great number of Christians are not ready for the Kingdom of Heaven in their present state.

One of the biggest issues facing the church today is that of women in positions of leadership. Particularly where women are exercising authority over men, as in the role of elders, pastors and teachers. This is straight-out rebellion and disobedience to God's clearly stated instructions (or, more correctly, commandments).

From Genesis to Revelation, the Scriptures are clear on this issue. In what is referred to as the Adamic Covenant (Genesis 3:15), God sets out a number of conditions; conditions which must remain till, in the Kingdom age,

> the creation itself shall be delivered from the bondage of corruption into the glorious liberty of the children of God. (Romans 8:21 KJV)

According to the note in the Schofield Bible (Page 7) Genesis 3:15, on the Adamic Covenant, the conditions are as follows:

1. The serpent, Satan's tool, is cursed.
2. The promise of a Redeemer.
3. The changed state or status of women in three particulars or ways.
    a. Multiplied conception.
    b. Sorrow and pain in motherhood.
    c. The headship of the man.
4. The easy life in Eden changed to one of toil because of the earth being cursed.
5. The inevitable sorrow of life.
6. The brevity of life and the certainty of death.

Not one of these conditions has changed, nor will they change, until Jesus returns and begins his Millennium Reign on earth. Jesus' First Coming did not change any of the conditions of this covenant, nor did his death on the cross. Even though he did heal the sick and raise the dead, they still all died again in due course.

The position of women is clearly reaffirmed in the New Testament:

> Women should be silent during the church meetings. They are not to take part in the discussion, for they are subordinate to men as the Scriptures also declare. If they have any questions to ask, let them ask their husbands at home, for it is improper for women to express their opinions in church meetings. You disagree? And do you think that the knowledge of God's will begins and ends with you Corinthians? Well, you are mistaken! You who claim to have the gift of prophecy or any other special ability from the Holy Spirit should be the first to realize that what I am saying is a commandment from the Lord himself. (1 Corinthians 14:34-37)

> I never let women teach men or lord it over them. Let them be silent in your church meetings. Why? Because God made Adam first, and afterwards he made Eve. And it was not Adam who was fooled by Satan, but Eve, and sin was the result. So God sent pain and suffering to women when their children are born, but he will save their souls if they trust in him, living quiet, good, and loving lives. (1 Timothy 2:12-15)

These instructions are actual commandments of our Lord, and are totally consistent with the Adamic Covenant. All this in spite of both men and women's efforts to pervert the Scriptures, just as we have been clearly warned:

> For there is going to come a time when people won't listen to the truth, but will go around looking for teachers who will tell them just what they want to hear. They won't listen to what the Bible says but will blithely follow their own misguided ideas. Stand steady, and don't be afraid of suffering for the Lord. Bring others to Christ. Leave nothing undone that you ought to do. (2 Timothy 4:3-5)

In his letter to the church in Thyatira which, on the face of it, is a good church, Jesus spells out the awful consequences of disobedience to this command of his:

> I am aware of all your good deeds-your kindness to the poor, your gifts and service to them, also I know your love, and faith and patience, and I can see your constant improvement in all these things. Yet I have this against you. You are permitting that woman Jezebel, who calls herself a prophetess, to teach and seduce my servants to commit fornication and to eat meat sacrificed to idols. (Revelation 2:19-20 KJV)

The fornication referred to here by our Lord is spiritual not physical. It could well be that during Christ's Millennium reign women will be co-rulers with men, as indeed Eve was with Adam before the fall. But Paul states clearly,

> I never let women teach men or lord it over them. Let them be silent in your church meetings. (1 Timothy 2:12 TLB, also see Jeremiah 3:2; Ezekiel 16:15-17; Ezekiel 16 & 29)

As for meat sacrificed to idols, this is best understood from Jesus' own words:

My meat is to do the will of him who sent me. (John 4:3 KJV)

Labour not for the meat which perishes [false doctrine] but for that meat which endures to everlasting life. (John 6:27 KJV)

For my flesh is meat indeed, and my blood is drink indeed. (John 6:55 KJV)

Back to the letter to the church at Thyatira:

I gave her time to change her mind and attitude, but she refused. Pay attention now to what I am saying; I will lay her upon a sickbed of intense affliction, along with her immoral followers, unless they turn again to me, repenting of their sin with her. And I will strike her children dead. And all the churches shall know that I am he who searches deep within men's (and women's) hearts and minds; I will give to each of you whatever you deserve. (Revelation 2:21-23)

This is a serious warning from Jesus, not to be ignored. It is very obvious that those who follow this false teaching are going to be subject to the horrors and trauma of the Tribulation. Now contrast this message to the one given to the church at Philadelphia:

I know you well; you aren't strong, but you have tried to obey, and have not denied my Name. Therefore, I have opened a door for you that no one can shut. Because you have patiently obeyed me, despite the persecution. Therefore, I will keep you from the time of Great Tribulation which will come upon the world to test everyone alive. (Revelation 3:8 & 10)

The truth is that the church is faced with a real challenge today.

Either it continues on down the track of rebellion and disobedience, following the path of political correctness and bowing down to the false god of humanism (man knows best) in all its evil forms, or it humbles itself, truly repents and turns back to God and his unchanging word and commandments.

> If My people who are called by my name, shall humble themselves, and pray, and seek my face, and turn from their wicked ways, then I will hear from Heaven, and will forgive their sins, and will heal their land. (2 Chronicles 7:14 KJV)

We read the following about John the Baptist:

> For this is he that was spoken of by the prophet Esaias, saying, The voice of one crying in the wilderness, Prepare ye the way of the Lord, make his paths straight. (Matthew 3:3 KJV)

> Repent ye: for the kingdom of heaven is at hand. (Matthew 3:2 KJV)

Jesus himself came with the same message:

> Repent, for the Kingdom of Heaven is at hand. (Matthew 4:17 KJV)

Truly, the church must repent, for the Kingdom of Heaven *is* at hand. We have three final scriptures:

> Keep alive in yourselves what you were taught in the beginning; as long as what you were taught in the beginning is alive in you, you will live in the Son and in the Father. (1 John 2:24 Jerusalem Bible)

See to it that you win your full reward from the Lord. For if you wander beyond the teaching of Christ, you will leave God behind; while if you are loyal to Christ's teachings, you will have God too. Then you will have both the Father and the Son. (2 John 8-9)

Watch yourselves, or all our work will be lost and not get the reward it deserves. If anybody does not keep within the teaching of Christ but goes beyond it, he cannot have God with him: only those who keep to what is taught can have the Father and the Son with them. (2 John 1:8-9 Jerusalem Bible)

Five Steps to Growing in Christ

Do you want more and more of God's kindness and peace? Then learn to know him better and better. For as you know him better, he will give you, through his great power, everything you need for living a truly good life: he even shares his own glory and his own goodness with us! And by that same mighty power he has given us all the other rich and wonderful blessings he promised; for instance, the promise to save us from the lust and rottenness all around us, and to give us his own character.

But to obtain these gifts, you need more than faith; you must also work hard to be good, and even that is not enough. For then you must learn to know God better and discover what he wants you to do. Next, learn to put aside your own desires so that you will become patient and godly, gladly letting God have his way with you. This will make possible the next step, which is for you to enjoy other people and to like them, and finally you will grow to love them deeply. The more you go on in this way, the more you will grow strong spiritually and become fruitful and useful to our Lord Jesus Christ. But anyone who fails to go after these additions to faith is blind indeed, or at least very short-sighted and has forgotten that God delivered him from the old life of sin so that now he can live a strong, good life for the Lord.

So, dear brothers, work hard to prove that you really are among those God has called and chosen, and then you will never stumble or fall away. And God will open wide the gates of heaven for you to enter into the eternal kingdom of our Lord and Saviour Jesus Christ. (2 Peter 1:2-11)

Previously we looked at the importance of growing in Christ from the time we are born again of the Spirit. We saw, from the reading in Hebrews 5:12-13, how it is possible for people to be believers for many years and still be living on milk, simply because they have failed to put into practice the things they have been taught. Indeed, they had reached the stage where because they had been on an 'all milk' diet for so long, their stomachs were no longer able to handle solid food.

We looked at the necessity of leaving our past buried in the grave after we have died to our old life of sin and fleshly desires. And finally, we looked at some of God's instructions relating to this new life in the Spirit. We finished with Paul's instructions:

> But I don't want anyone to think more highly of me then he should from what he can actually see in my life and my message. Forget about all the stories you have heard telling how great I am. Forget about my reputation – good or bad – it is what you can see in my life and my message. (2 Corinthians 12:16)

I would like to tell you a story about two men of God. One was a really big-name Christian. By 'big', I mean really big. He knew Jesus personally, and had been with him from the beginning. He had heard his teaching, witnessed his miracles and even walked on water. He was one of the three who had been on the mountain with Jesus when Moses and Elijah had appeared, and God had spoken. This is an event of such importance that it is recorded in three of the Gospels – Matthew, Mark and Luke. Of course, this man was Peter the Apostle.

On one occasion when he preached 3000 were saved. He

healed a man who had been lame from birth, for 40 years. After he challenged two believers who had lied, they both immediately fell down and died. The Bible says, as a result, terror gripped the whole church. In fact, other believers didn't even dare join with the apostles, but all had the highest regard for them. Peter raised Dorcas from death. Once when he got locked in jail, an angel of the Lord came at night, opened the gates and brought him out. Talk about a big-name Christian. But Peter had a problem. It caused him to deny his Lord and then, according to Paul, later compromised the truth.

> But when Peter came to Antioch I had to oppose him publicly, speaking strongly against what he was doing, for it was very wrong... (Galatians 2:11)

Peter was concerned about pleasing men or what other people thought about him, rather than standing firm in the truth. Contrast him with Paul. He started off badly, murdering Christians. He was zealous alright, but at that stage totally blind to the truth. But what happened when Paul's eyes were opened to the truth? His whole focus changed from one of persecuting believers to being totally focused on serving Christ.

> For me to live is Christ and to die is gain. (Philippians 1:21 KJV)

> For I am the least worthy of all the apostles, and I shouldn't even be called an apostle after the way I treated the church of God. (1 Corinthians 15:9)

Nevertheless, Paul walked in the truth, and it was Paul who corrected Peter when he strayed from the truth. Peter's reaction to Paul's admonition is not recorded, but he refers to Paul as our wise and beloved brother Paul... (2 Peter 3:16)

Peter, to his credit, was able to accept correction, even though he was regarded as a spiritual giant and was held in awe by so many. Humbling, isn't it?

Now we will continue to study more of God's instructions regarding this new life in Christ. The first thing we have to come to terms with is that this new life has a completely new set of instructions and values to live by. The ways of the world do not apply to our new life in Christ.

Certainly we are in the world, but we are no longer part of the world's system of values. When we are born again, we are born as sons and daughters of the living God. We are now members of a big new family.

> To all who received him [Jesus], he gave the right to become children of God. (John 1:12)

> You have received the spirit of adoption whereby we cry Abba Father. (Romans 8:15 KJV)

Actually, we have an interesting situation here – a real enigma if you like – for whilst it is true that we are indeed God's children, yet at the same time we are servants of our master Jesus, who purchased us by his blood in order that we might become children of the Father.

Peter sets out clear instructions regarding our new life:

> From: Simon Peter, a servant and missionary of Jesus Christ.
> To: All of you who have our kind of faith. The faith I speak of is the kind that Jesus Christ our God and Saviour gives to us. How precious it is, and how just and good he is to give this same faith

to each of us. Do you want more and more of God's kindness and peace? Then learn to know him better and better. For as you know him better, he will give you, through his great power, everything you need for living a truly good life: he even shares his own glory and his own goodness with us! And by that same mighty power he has given us all the other rich and wonderful blessings he promised; for instance, the promise to save us from the lust and rottenness all around us, and to give us his own character.

But to obtain these gifts, you need more than faith; you must also work hard to be good, and even that is not enough. For then you must learn to know God better and discover what he wants you to do.

Next, learn to put aside your own desires so that you will become patient and godly, gladly letting God have his way with you. This will make possible the next step, which is for you to enjoy other people and to like them, and finally you will grow to love them deeply.

The more you go on in this way, the more you will grow strong spiritually and become fruitful and useful to our Lord Jesus Christ. But anyone who fails to go after these additions to faith is blind indeed, or at least very short-sighted and has forgotten that God delivered him from the old life of sin so that now he can live a strong, good life for the Lord. So, dear brothers, work hard to prove that you really are among those God has called and chosen, and then you will never stumble or fall away. And God will open wide the gates of heaven for you to enter into the eternal kingdom of our Lord and Saviour Jesus Christ. (2 Peter 1:1-11)

Let us now consider some of the issues raised in the above passage, and what we need to do to obtain these gifts.

Step 1: Work hard to be good

The Jerusalem Bible says:

> But to obtain this you will have to do your upmost yourselves.

The Phillips Modern English Translation puts it this way:

> You must do your utmost from your side and see that your faith carries with it real goodness of life.

People need to see Jesus in us. We have to live our faith and put it into practice. What is it that we have to put into practice? We can start with the discipline of work.

> Work hard and cheerfully at all you do, just as though you were working for the Lord and not merely for your masters [bosses, if you like] remembering that it is the Lord Christ who is going to pay you, giving you your full portion of all he owns. He is the one you are really working for. (Colossians 3:23)

> Never let it be said that Christ's people are poor workers. (1 Timothy 6:1)

> If you don't do your best for him, he will pay you in a way you won't like – for he has no special favourites who can get away with shirking. (Colossians 3:25)

> Now here is a command, dear brothers, given in the name of our Lord Jesus Christ and by his authority. Stay away from any Christian who spends his days in laziness and doesn't follow the ideal of hard work we set up for you. For you all know that

you ought to follow our example; you never saw us loafing. (2 Thessalonians 3:6-7)

There are many reasons why hard work is good. Here are some of them:

Hard work brings prosperity, playing around brings poverty. (Proverbs 28:19)

Telling the truth gives a man great satisfaction, and hard work returns many blessings to him. (Proverbs 12:14)

Notice the emphasis on hard work. There is work, and then there is hard work. Plenty of people have the ability to fill in the day – giving the appearance of working, without actually accomplishing very much at all. Real hard work accomplishes a great deal. Much can be accomplished in a day when we work with integrity, as to the Lord.

So, work hard both at your physical jobs and as a result, grow spiritually. We covered this aspect of spiritual growth in a previous message – 'What measure ye measure'.

And be sure to put into practice what you hear [or what you learn from the Scriptures]. The more you do this, the more you will understand what I tell you. To him who has shall be given; from him who has not shall be taken away even what he has. (Mark 4:24-25)

If we want more of God, more of his presence in our lives, and better understanding of his Word and his ways, then we need to be obedient in little things – and he will give us more.

> So keep on believing what you have been taught from the beginning. If you do, you will always be in close fellowship with both God the Father and his Son. (1 John 2:24)

If we are not willing to listen to him and obey him, we simply will not grow, but remain sickly malnourished spiritual babies. And even worse, when we are not willing to listen and obey, we leave God behind.

> For if you wander beyond the teaching of Christ you will leave God behind. (2 John 1:9)

But as we continue to seek more of him and to walk in obedience, so he reveals more, with extra besides. God always gives back far more than we deserve. That is his way. So, no matter in which area of our lives, the more we give, the more we get back, with extra. This applies in both the physical and spiritual realms. The measure we give determines what measure is given back to us. So, be sure to put into practice what you hear. The more you do this, the more you will understand about what I have been telling you. To him who has will be given more.

Look, salvation is a free gift from God. Forgiveness is free. We cannot earn God's forgiveness, rather it is given by grace and grace alone. But spiritual growth, that is an entirely different story. If we are not willing to listen to what the Spirit is saying (read the letters to the churches in Revelation) and walk in obedience to Jesus' commands, we will not grow – indeed, cannot grow. It is that simple. So, step 1: Work hard to be good and to grow.

Step 2: Learn to know God better and discover what he wants you to do

Here again, this does not just happen. It requires effort, or more correctly, *diligence* on our part. Peter's teaching here is totally consistent with Moses' prayer:

> Now therefore I pray to thee, if I have found Grace [favour] in thy sight, show me now thy Ways, that I might [come to] know thee, that I might find grace in thy sight. (Exodus 33:13 KJV)

Jesus instructs us:

> Yes, I am the Vine; you are the branches. Whoever lives in me and I in him shall produce a large crop of fruit. For apart from me you can't do a thing. (John 15:5)

Show us your ways, oh Lord. We have to get this into our thick skulls: God's ways are not the ways of the world. There is no place in the church for New Age ideology, political correctness or compromising our Lord's clear commandments in order to accommodate the demands of feminists, gay activists, environmentalists and every other disciple of the false god of humanism (or religion on man's terms).

Now back to the story of Peter and Paul. If you remember, Peter stumbled, trying to please men rather than God, whereas Paul's whole focus was on serving and obeying Christ.

> For we speak as messengers from God, trusted by him to tell the truth; we change his message not one bit to suit the taste of those who hear it; for we serve God alone who examines our heart's deepest thoughts. (1 Thessalonians 2:4)

> You can see I'm not trying to please you by sweet talk and flattery; no, I am trying to please God. If I was still trying to please men I could not be Christ's servant. (Galatians 1:10)

Love is not indulgence. First and foremost, Christianity is about relationships. First with our Father God, our Saviour the Lord Jesus Christ and then with each other. But a relationship with the false god of humanism God calls spiritual adultery. (See Jeremiah 3:2 and Ezekiel 16:15-17.) Love desires God's very best for each other, and it is vital that we do love one another, but not by committing spiritual adultery in the process.

A beautiful example of the servant – master relationship can be found in the passage where Abraham instructs his servant to find a wife for his son Isaac:

> So the servant vowed to follow Abraham's instructions. He took with him ten of Abraham's camels loaded with samples of the best of everything his master owned and journeyed to Iraq, to Nahor's village. There he made the camels kneel down outside the town, beside a spring. It was evening, and the women of the village were coming to draw water. 'O Jehovah, the God of my master,' he prayed, 'show kindness to my master Abraham and help me to accomplish the purpose of my journey.' (Genesis 24:9-12)

Look at the servant Eliezer. What a beautiful example of a master-servant relationship. His whole focus was on pleasing his master. There is nothing of self-interest in his prayer, 'Please show kindness to my master by helping me to accomplish the purpose of my journey.' Substitute 'Jesus' for 'Abraham'. That then should be our prayer model.

Note Eliezer's gratefulness after God granted his request, his humility and his eagerness not to be separated from his master by worldly pleasures. He pleaded:

> Don't hinder my return; the Lord has made my mission successful, and I want to report back to my master. (Genesis 24:56)

Compare that with the messages Jesus gives to the Ephesian and Laodicean Churches respectively:

> You have left your first love (Revelation 2:4 NKJV)

> Look! I have been standing at the door, and I am constantly knocking. (Revelation 3:20)

Can you imagine it? Jesus – standing outside his own church, the church that he died for, knocking and wanting to be invited in? There are just so many instances today where the Church is busily doing its own thing and Jesus is left outside the door, knocking. That applies equally in our own lives as well!

Paul got it right when he said:

> Yes, everything else is worthless when compared to the priceless gain of knowing Jesus Christ my Lord, and the power of his resurrection, and the fellowship of his sufferings. I have put aside all else, counting it worth less than nothing, in order that I can have Christ, and become one with him. So, whatever it takes, I will be one who lives in the fresh newness of life of those who are alive from the dead. I don't mean to say I am perfect, I haven't learned all I should even yet, but I keep working toward that day when I will finally be all that Christ saved me for and wants me to be. (Philippians 3:8)

Paul's one desire is to please his Master and Saviour:

> I'm trying to please God. If I were to still trying to please men [or people], I could not be Christ's servant. (Galatians 1:10)

What happens when the church turns away from God, or we as

individuals become more concerned with worldly attractions rather than serving our master, Jesus? You will find Jesus answer in Matthew:

> But I will reply, 'You have never been mine. Go away, for your deeds are evil.' (Matthew 7:23)

We could also read Matthew 25:1-12 or Revelation 3:14-22.

Whilst effort has nothing to do with your salvation, it has everything to do with your spiritual growth. Eight times in the New Testament we are told to make every effort towards becoming like Christ. God, through Christ, has done his part, and we too have to do our part. Jesus said:

> If you love me, obey me. (John 14:15)

Camels

Read Genesis 24:1-27. This is a beautiful story of events which happened around 4000 years ago, which is still as relevant today as when it was written. It is about Abraham sending his servant Eliezer to find a wife for his son Isaac.

In this story, Abraham represents God the Father. His servant, probably the same Eliezer of Damascus mentioned in Genesis 15, is a type of the Holy Spirit, sent by the Father to bring back a bride for his Son. We can all learn from his beautiful prayer:

> 'Oh Jehovah, the God of my master,' he prayed, 'show kindness to my master Abraham and help me to accomplish the purpose of my journey.' (Genesis 24:12)

Our master is Jesus. We too need God's help to accomplish the purpose of our journey in our Master's service. Isaac is a type of Christ, our Master. Rebekah is a sweetie; in her we see the qualities the Holy Spirit is still seeking in the Bride today. The well speaks of the well of salvation. The water Rebekah drew speaks of the Living Water (the Holy Spirit?). Even the camels are important in this story. Camels are very thirsty creatures, especially when they have been without water for a while. They are mean-mannered. They bite, kick and spit cud at you, and, by all accounts, they are very uncomfortable to ride. But the camels had a very important role to play, for they were to carry Rebekah, the bride, to Isaac.

While we cannot do full justice to this story, we will look a bit further at a few more points. Abraham represents God the Father, much loved and respected by his servant.

> You shall not take a wife for my son from the daughters of the Canaanites among whom I live, but you shall go to my country and my people, to take a wife for my son. (Genesis 24:3-4 KJV)

There is a mistaken belief today that it doesn't matter which religion we belong to, that we all worship the same God. Not so! Jesus made it very clear:

> I am the way, the truth and the life. No-one comes to the Father except through me. (John 14:6 KJV)

We are not all God's children. Only those who have had their sins washed clean by the blood of Jesus and have been born again by the Holy Spirit are acceptable in God's sight. If there was any other way, the Father would never have allowed Jesus to suffer and die for us as he did. So, first point. Only someone born again in Jesus can become part of the Bride. No one who denies the deity of Christ can be a Christian – whether they are church-goers, Jehovah's Witnesses, Mormons, Muslims, Hindus or Buddhists. Anyone that denies the Deity of Christ.

Eliezer is a type of the Holy Spirit. Note, he set out with a variety of good things of his master in his hand. Precious gifts he was bearing with him; gifts to prepare the bride for the bridegroom. We read:

> Come in, blessed of the Lord! Why do you stand outside since I have prepared the house and a place for the camels? (Genesis 24:31 KJV)

Today the blessed Holy Spirit is still standing by the well of salvation, waiting to be invited into the house, our bodies, prepared for him by our Saviour, made ready to receive him and the many gifts he comes bearing. To each he gives different gifts, including wisdom, faith, teaching, healing, miracles, prophesy, tongues, discernment – the list goes on. There are those who shy away from these things – but God is good, and his gifts are good also.

> If ye then being evil know how to give good gifts to your children, how much more will your Heavenly Father give good gifts to those who ask him. (Matthew 7:11 KJV)

The gifts are given to empower the Bride in service. And so it is today, just as it was back then. The blessed Holy Spirit still stands, waiting by the well.

We haven't talked about Rebekah yet. But we will talk about the camels first. These camels have a very important role in this story, for they carried Rebekah, the bride, to Isaac. And the Holy Spirit is still using 'camels' today.

> The servant took ten camels from the camels of his master. (Genesis 24:10 KJV)

As we saw before, camels can be very thirsty creatures. And this often necessitates a great number of trips to the well in order to quench their thirst. These camels have got names. Here are some of the names Edward Millar, a missionary in South America, gave to them and some I have added. You can choose names of your own, if you wish.

1. Conflict (physical or spiritual battles). We all have battles in our lives. Try as much as you like, we can't avoid them. Somewhere along our Christian journey, we are going to have to 'ride that camel', and he's a thirsty camel too! We may well have to take a number of trips to the well whilst we are riding that one.

2. Chores (tasks, the daily grind of life). Wherever you are is the perfect environment in which to grow spiritually. Homework. Housework. Jesus himself spent three years in ministry. The first 30 years being prepared. That camel can take much time and energy to get going. Yes, it gets a bit sluggish at times, and thirsty too. It can even be boring to ride. And you need to keep going to the well regularly, just to keep him going.

3. Reproach. That camel's got a nasty nature, it's likely to spit in your face. The truth is, we are supposed to please God rather than men, and we are going to have to put up with reproach from time to time if we really mean business with God. Jesus did, Paul did, John the disciple did.

4. Needs. He's a really thirsty camel. A scrawny old beast, who could have mange. The majority of Christians in Western society haven't had to ride that camel. Those of you who have will know it can require some urgent trips to the well to keep him going, but give him enough water, and he will travel over much dry country.

5. Frustration. He's another thirsty camel. More trips are needed to the well. He's a dangerous one too. Frustration can lead to self-pity. Sympathy can be of the devil. Never sympathise with someone God is just wanting to grow in faith. Love, yes, compassion – yes. Sympathy – no.

6. Troubles. Sneaky camel this one! Boots you when you least expect it, again and again. Bet you don't feel like going to the well for that one. Better do so, though, for he's going to be one of the ones you have to take a turn at riding in order to meet your Isaac.

7. Infirmity (weakness, sickness, whether it be physical, mental, or spiritual). Somewhere along the journey, most of us have to ride this one too. It can be very uncomfortable and painful to ride this camel. We may even need help to draw enough water to keep going. He's got a tendency to want to lie down and rest up. Resting is OK for a bit, but sooner or later, no matter how painful, we are going to have to get him mobile again in order to reach the end of our journey.

8. Persecution. Most Christians in the West have not had to face persecution, but there are many nations where persecution of true believers is endemic.

9. Responsibility. This camel has to carry heavy loads.

10. Pain and sorrow (oppression in its many forms).

All of the above are camels we may have to ride. Yes, the Holy Spirit is still using camels today, as in the story. So often we blame the devil, when it is God sending one of his camels to get watered and ridden for a stretch.

Anyway, we will move on from the camels and come to our heroine, Rebekah. She truly is a sweetie. Let's look at some of her qualities.

Nothing has changed – the blessed Holy Spirit is still patiently waiting by the well of salvation, seeking a Bride for his Master's Son. And he is looking for Christians with special qualities, the ones we see in Rebekah. What are those qualities?

1. She visited the well regularly. Daily in fact. Not just for herself, rather she drew and carried water for her whole household.

2. She showed kindness and hospitality to strangers. Imagine one of your family turning up at home: 'Hi Dad. Hi Mum. I met this old guy and his servants down by the well, and I've invited them to stay. Oh, and they have ten camels too!' The following is one of the overlooked commands in the Bible:

> Be ye hospitable to one another without grumbling. (1 Peter 4:9 KJV) [J.B. Phillips' translation adds 'without secretly wishing you didn't have to']

3. She was obviously fond of animals and concerned for their welfare. The spiritual significance is great. She was prepared to water the camels of a stranger. This can be likened to going to Jesus at the well of salvation to draw water for other people's needs and problems.

4. Eliezer's request was no ordinary request. He was asking for much more than a drink for himself. It was an extraordinary person who would offer to water ten camels voluntarily. That was a huge offer. That was why he waited to see if she would finish the job. She was not only happy to go the extra mile, she persisted till the job was finished. She truly had a serving heart, even though she was of noble birth. Her deeds matched her words. Her 'yes' meant 'yes'. She was super-motivated. She hastened, emptied her pitcher, and ran again and again to the well. Eliezer watched her carefully to see if she would finish the job, so that he would know if she was the one.

Then at last, when the camels had finished drinking, he produced a pair of quarter-ounce gold earrings and two five-ounce gold bracelets for her.

> And the damsel was very fair to look upon, a virgin, neither had any man known her... (Genesis 24:16 KJV)

This verse has very much relevance for the church today. She was keeping herself for her true husband. In far too many instances today, the church has forsaken her true bridegroom, Christ, and prostituted herself with the world.

Rebecca is a type of the 'ecclesia', the called out virgin Bride of Christ (2 Corinthians 11:2 and Ephesians 5:27, as compared with the adulterous church, Revelation 3:20-23).

5. She was prepared to leave her family, indeed everything in her life up to that point and go with the servant, even at very short notice. And note, there was no compulsion here:

> 'Well,' they said, 'we'll call the girl and ask her what she thinks.' So they called Rebekah. 'Are you willing to go with this man?' they asked her. And she replied, 'Yes, I will go.' (Genesis 24:57-58)

6. She was trusting and obedient. She was clear in her faith that God was really leading her in this matter. I am sure there are some good lessons on guidance in this passage. The point is, such was her faith and understanding (not surprising, as she visited the well daily), she was able to obey instantly without doubting.

The whole point of this message is that our Bridegroom, Jesus, is waiting for his 'Bride' to make herself ready. Rebekah, who possessed all those fine qualities, is a type of the bride. We would do well to learn from her. But she still had to ride those camels to get to her Isaac. And the camels came loaded with gifts.

It is in riding those camels through life, on our journey to meet our Isaac (Jesus), that we learn love, joy, peace, patience, kindness, goodness, faithfulness, gentleness, and self-control, the Fruits of the Spirit. Yes, the blessed Holy Spirit still uses 'camels' today to carry us to our Bridegroom – who is soon coming to meet us and take us to be with him.

Let us pray. Lord Jesus, you are the Bridegroom. You are the Isaac in this story, and today your 'Bride' is being made ready for you. Lord, in the parable of the ten virgins, when you came for your Bride, five were ready, five were not. They lacked oil for their lamps.

Lord, as we see those special qualities in Rebekah, we ask that you will help us to seek those qualities in our own lives. Grant us a real thirst for the 'Living Water' and a willingness to carry water for other members of our household, your church.

Lord Jesus, grant us a willingness to water camels, even other people's camels, and the discernment to recognise one of your camels when you bring it to us. To see that it is simply a thirsty, uncomfortable-to-ride camel, not the devil attacking us.

And, Lord Jesus, open our hearts and minds to the presence of the blessed Holy Spirit waiting patiently by the well; waiting with good gifts from the Father. Open our hearts and our minds to his blessed presence.

In your precious name we ask, Lord Jesus. Amen.

Knowing the Faithfulness of God

But all these things that I once thought very worthwhile – now I've thrown them all away so that I can put my trust and hope in Christ alone. Yes, everything else is worthless when compared with the priceless gain of knowing Christ Jesus my Lord. I have put aside all else, counting it worth less than nothing, in order that I can have Christ, and become one with him, no longer counting on being saved by being good enough or by obeying God's laws, but by trusting Christ to save me; for God's way of making us right with himself depends on faith – counting on Christ alone. Now I have given up everything else – I have found it to be the only way to really know Christ and to experience the mighty power that brought him back to life again, and to find out what it means to suffer and to die with him. So whatever it takes, I will be one who lives in the fresh newness of life of those who are alive from the dead. (Philippians 3:7-11)

Paul counted everything in life as being of no consequence compared to this one thing:

That I may know him, and the power of his resurrection. (Philippians 3:10 KJV)

In the midst of all his terrible suffering, Job was still able to say:

For I know my Redeemer liveth.' (Job 19:25 KJV)

And he also said:

And I know that after this body has decayed, this body shall see God. Yes, I shall see him, not as a stranger but as a friend. What a glorious hope. (Job 19:26-27)

So, the first question is: do I know Jesus? Do I know my Redeemer? Do I know the power of his resurrection in my own life? Can I say with total certainty, as Job did – I know my Redeemer lives? I know I shall meet him – not as a stranger, but as a friend?

If we were to leave it there, that would probably be more than enough to discuss now. But there are a couple of other questions we should ask at the same time.

The next question is: does Jesus know me?

Many will say to me in that day, Lord, Lord, have we not prophesied in thy name; and in thy name we have cast out demons. And in thy name done many wonderful works. And then I will profess unto them, I never knew you; depart from me, ye that work iniquity. (Matthew 7:22 KJV)

Jesus said:

'I know My sheep, and they know Me'. (John 10:14)

I know you well – you are neither hot nor cold. (Revelation 3:15)

And this 'knowing' and 'being known' doesn't stop there. It is important to realise that the devil knew who Jesus was, and he knows who are followers of Jesus and who are not.

Why are you bothering us, Jesus of Nazareth – have you come to destroy us demons? I know who you are – the holy Son of God! (Mark 1:24)

Jesus I know, and Paul I know, but who are ye? (Acts 19:15 KJV)

So, you can see it is extremely important not just to know *about* Jesus. We can learn much about him and know much about him, but do we *know him personally*? The question we must ask is – have I experienced the power of his resurrection in my own life? If so, we can be sure of these things:

1. He will know us.
2. The devil will know us.
3. We will have plenty to share about him.
4. Others will be able to see Christ in us.

Recently Charles Stanley was talking about sharing our faith from our own experiences – sharing how we have experienced and proved God's faithfulness in our own lives with others. He told how his own life and ministry had been greatly influenced by a week he spent with his grandfather as a young boy. His grandfather shared with him how God had been utterly faithful to him throughout his life, in the good times and the bad, in his successes and his failures. How God had been faithful at all times and in all things.

What a wonderful lesson and example this is for us to follow. We must not try to paint ourselves as saints. This is about God's faithfulness, not ours. That even when I have 'blown it' and made mistakes, God has been totally faithful and true to his Word. I can bear witness to his unfailing love and protection countless times in my own life. No one will ever be able to convince me otherwise.

I know him! I know his faithfulness! I know his integrity and the integrity of his Word, the Bible. God does not lie. It is impossible for him to lie.

I know that when I stumble and make a mistake, he is faithful and just to forgive my sin and to cleanse me from all unrighteousness. I know from experience that when the Son sets you free you are free indeed.

> If we confess our sins, he is faithful and just to forgive us our sins, and to cleanse us from all unrighteousness. (1 John 1:9 KJV)

> Who forgiveth all thine iniquities; who healeth all thy diseases... (Psalm 103:3 KJV)

> They that wait upon the Lord shall renew their strength. They shall mount up with wings like eagles; they shall run and not be weary; they shall walk and not faint. (Isaiah 40:31)

Praise him, he does just that. I know these things because for over 85 years he has sustained me, blessed me, forgiven me, answered thousands of my prayers and forgiven countless numbers of mistakes I have made.

He has granted me life more abundantly, and spared my life from a great many dangers and accidents. I have been close to drowning three times, run over by a tractor, pounded into the ground by a crazy cow, survived a crash in a helicopter, been rolled on by a four-wheeler motorbike (the bike was wrecked), been in a Land Rover that went over a bank and careered down a steep slope, had numerous close shaves on wheel tractors on steep hills, and many other potentially fatal accidents.

Taped in front of my Bible is the following verse:

Knowing the Faithfulness of God

> You need fear nothing but the Lord of the Armies of Heaven, if you fear him you need fear nothing else, he will be your safety. (Isaiah 8:13)

When it comes to talking about God's kindness and faithfulness, I don't know where to stop. When I was a young man trapping opossums in the Ureweras, I went through a period of intense loneliness and cried out to God to bring the right girl into my life and to bless me with a family. The very next day, I met this beautiful young nurse. We have now been married for 58 years, blessed with seven children, 24 grandchildren and a growing number of great-grandees.

There is a story in the Bible where Jesus changed water into wine. The wedding guests said:

> You have kept the best for the last... (John 2:10)

That is the story of my marriage and my life. He has truly kept the best wine till last. God is totally faithful.

Oh that we would learn to grasp hold of the fullness of our salvation. It covers every area of our lives. And I haven't even mentioned the blessed Holy Spirit, our helper, comforter and teacher, who leads us into all truth and reveals God's secrets to us. For our part, we need to crown him Lord over every part of our lives. That means dying to self and our fleshly desires, and learning to live by the Spirit. Never forgetting that the ways of the Kingdom are totally different to the ways of the world, and that from time to time our faith will be tested.

Jesus was tested. Job was tested. Paul was tested. Joseph was tested. And we can expect to be tested as well. The apostle James wrote:

Count it all joy, my brethren, when you meet various trials. For you know that the testing of your faith produces steadfastness. And let steadfastness have its full effect, that you may be perfect and complete, lacking in nothing. (James 1:2-4 RSV)

Let us pray. Father God, I remember well the words of your servant Edward Miller:

There is a place near to your heart
There is a place where no evil has a part
There is a place where thy will is all supreme
Bring us there, Lord. Bring us there.

In the precious name of Jesus, we ask and pray. Amen.

Conquering Sin

Previously we looked at how important it is to have the right attitude with God, particularly one of faith or belief, rather than unbelief. Also, the utter importance of obedience to all of Jesus' commandments. Even though our salvation may not be in question, we miss out on so many of God's blessings in so many areas of our lives and cannot enter into the Promised Land, which is the place of rest, if we are not obedient, or simply lack of knowledge of his ways, or have unbelief in our hearts.

Today I want to encourage us further in the Lord and show from Scripture what is really the only way we can stand firm in Christ.

In the reading from *The Word for Today*, Saturday 18 November 2000, it says:

> We all think it can only happen to others and not to us, but as sure as fish swim and birds fly, our sinful nature will always mislead us unless we deal with it every day.

In John's gospel it tells us what we must do:

> But those who keep on sinning are against God, for every sin is done against the will of God. And you know that he became a man so that he could take away our sins, and that there is no sin in him, no missing of God's will at any time in any way. So if we stay close to him, obedient to him, we won't be sinning either:

but as for those who keep on sinning, they should realize this: They sin because they have never really known him or become his. (1 John 3:4-6)

John is not speaking here of a state of perfection in which it is impossible for a Christian ever to sin, but is stressing the fact that a Christian cannot keep on practising sin, because he or she is born of God. There are three key points in these verses.

1. Whoever is sinning is sinning against God.
2. Whoever abides in him doesn't keep on sinning.
3. Whoever keeps sinning has not seen him or known him.

Here we will look at three things which are really the keys to a victorious spiritual life.

Abiding
The word 'abiding' appears many times in Scripture, but we will just look at the words of Jesus in John:

> I am the true Vine, and my Father is the Vinedresser. He lops off every branch that does not produce. And He prunes those branches that bear fruit for even larger crops. He has already tended you by pruning you back for greater strength and usefulness by means of the commands I give you. Take care to live in me, and let me live in you. For a branch can't produce fruit when severed from the Vine. Nor can you be fruitful apart from me. (John 15:1-4)

To 'abide in Christ' means:

1. To have no known, unconfessed, unjudged sin. This is a wonderful promise:

If we confess our sins, he is faithful and just to forgive us our sins and to cleanse us from all unrighteousness. (1 John 1:9 KJV)

Remember, if we have unconfessed sin in our lives, the devil has an open door through which he can attack us. In fact, unconfessed sin is a bit like rabbits. First you have one or two, the next thing a plague.

2. To have no interest, nor any part of our life which he cannot share or be part of. In simple words, he has to be Lord of every part of our life. Whatever we are doing, we do it as to the Lord.

3. To know that we can take all our burdens to him and draw all wisdom, life and strength from him. We can be more than conquerors in every situation we may face in life.

I love to be in that place of abiding. Life there is such a joy. But to be in that place and more importantly, to remain in that place means that we must allow nothing into our lives which can separate us from God. But if we do sin, we must deal with it smartly. Christ is the 'vine' and, as branches, we must remain attached to the vine. If we become separated, we quickly become vulnerable and unfruitful, and can end up getting badly burnt.

> If anyone separates from me, he is thrown away like a useless branch, withers and is gathered into a pile with all the others and burned. (John 15:6)

> If you stay in me and obey my commandments you may ask any request you like and it will be granted. (John 15:7)

But how different and truly awesome this next verse is. Any request you like and it will be granted. How can God make such a promise? It is conditional. All of God's promises are conditional. The conditions are simple yet profound. We must stay in him – we must be in that state of abiding and must obey his commandments, all of them.

Abiding means putting Jesus first in all things. We must truly crown him as Lord of our lives. This means allowing no sin to remain unconfessed and thus separate us from him. It means spending time apart from the world and the business of life – waiting on him, listening to him. Abiding does mean taking time out. It does mean studying his Word. And it does mean being fruitful too.

You know sometimes, maybe too many times, we can be so involved with what we call 'the Lord's Work', that we tend to neglect our relationship with the Lord of the work himself, not to mention our own families and our other responsibilities.

Abiding is just so important, and when we are truly abiding in Jesus it doesn't matter what life, or the devil, throws at us. We are unshakeable in him. The old hymn says it so well: 'On Christ the solid Rock I stand; all other ground is sinking sand.'

We can cast all our burdens upon him because he cares about us. He really, really does care. And one of the greatest things of all – sin can't touch us when we are truly abiding. I will read it again:

> So, if we stay close to him, obedient to him, we won't be sinning, but as for those who keep on sinning, they should realize this, they sin because they have never really known him or become his. (1 John 3:6)

The King James version puts it this way:

> Whoever sins has not seen him or known him.

This leads on to the next thing I want us to look at:

Seeing and Knowing Jesus

These two actions seem to be closely connected in Scripture. Jesus said to Phillip, who had been with him for all of his ministry:

> Have I been such a long time with you, and yet hast thou not known me, Phillip? (John 14:9 KJV)

An awful lot of people like Phillip, who go to church, really do not yet know Jesus intimately.

> Anyone who has seen me has seen the Father. (John 14:9)

We see these key words, 'seeing' and' knowing' interconnected in the following passage where Jesus was talking about the Holy Spirit whom he promised to send:

> And I will pray to the Father, and he will give you another comforter, that he may abide with you forever. Even the Spirit of Truth whom the world cannot receive because it seeth him not, neither knoweth him, but ye know him, for he dwells with you and shall be in you. Yet a little while, and the world seeth me no more, but you see me. Because I live, you shall live also. (John 14:16-19 KJV)

Philip had been with Jesus a long time, yet he still had not 'clicked on' to his deity. He could not understand that Jesus is God. Fortunately, in the Christian Church today this is not a major issue, but it is increasingly creeping in. There are a growing number who would deny his deity and the authority of his teaching. There is an increasing amount of spiritual blindness – an increasing number who can't see too well. Equally so, or more so, regarding the person and work of the Holy Spirit of God. There is still a great deal of spiritual blindness regarding the ministry of the Holy Spirit.

The point is, seeing and knowing are closely linked. If we can't see him, we won't get to know him. But, even more important, does he know us?

> If a man loves me, he will keep my words, and my Father will love him and we will come to him, and make our abode with him. (John 14:23 KJV)

There is that 'abiding' word again. When we abide in him, they (both Jesus and the Father) make their abode in us. The Living Bible puts it this way:

> Because I will only reveal myself to those who love me and obey Me. (John 14:23)

Do you want to see Jesus? He will only reveal himself to certain people. Who are they? Those whom the Father and the Son will come and live with (or in). Yes, obedience to Jesus and his commandments is absolutely central to our Christian walk, and determines our worthiness to enter into the Kingdom of Heaven.

> Keep a constant watch. And pray that if possible you may arrive in my presence without having to experience these horrors. (Luke 21:36)

If we love him and obey him, then the Father will love us too, and come and make his home in us.
Now for a very important passage:

> See to it that you win your full reward from the Lord. For if you wander away from the teaching of Christ, you will leave God behind; while if you are loyal to Christ's teachings, you will have

God too. Then you will have both the Father and the Son. (2 John 1:8-9)

We can only come to know the Father through the Son. We can only see the Father through the Son. We will never be accepted by the Father except we are in Jesus, the Son.

> No man knoweth the Son except the Father, neither knoweth any man the Father, except the Son, and he to whomever the Son will reveal him. (Matthew 11:27 KJV)

You cannot see something until it is revealed. It is impossible for anyone to know God the Father except through Jesus. As I have said before, it is just not possible for anyone who denies the deity of Christ to know the true God, whether they be church-goers, Muslims, Jehovah's Witnesses or Mormons. Christ's deity is absolutely central in all things.

The Cross of Calvary is central in all things. Why is this? Jesus cannot reveal to us the Father until we come to the cross and have our sins washed clean and are made acceptable through his blood shed for us. When we are made acceptable, when we are in that place of abiding (and abiding means obeying as well), the whole of the Godhead makes their abode in us and sin can't touch us.

> Don't you realize that you can choose your own master? You can choose sin [with death] or else obedience [with acquittal]. The one to whom you offer yourself; he will take you and be your master and you will be his slave. Thank God that though you once chose to be slaves of sin, now you have obeyed with all your heart the teaching to which God has committed you. And now you are free from your old master, sin: and you have become slaves to your new master, righteousness.' (Romans 6:16-18)

Praise God! But first we have to see him, know him, abide in him and, above all, obey him. No wonder Paul said:

> Yes, everything else is worthless when compared with the priceless gain of knowing Christ Jesus my Lord. (1 Philippians 3:8)

This message was dated 19 November 2000.

Unravelling Some Mysteries

Now we will look at some apparent contradictions in Scripture, and seek to gain understanding from God through his Word, with the help of the blessed Holy Spirit. Jesus warned:

> Many false prophets will appear and lead many astray. (Matthew 24:11 KJV)

> For false messiahs and false prophets will rise up and perform great signs and wonders so as to deceive, if possible, even God's chosen ones. See, I have warned you about this ahead of time. (Matthew 24:24-25 NLT)

In Timothy we read:

> For there is going to come a time where people won't listen to the truth, but will go around looking for teachers who will tell them just what they want to hear. For they won't listen to what the Bible says, but will blithely follow their own misguided ideas. (2 Timothy 4:3-4)

> Stand steady and don't be afraid of suffering for the Lord. Bring others to Christ. Leave nothing undone that you ought to do. (2 Timothy 4:9)

If we desire to walk in truth, we are going to have to learn to swim against the current of New Age theology – and we will suffer persecution, not just from the world, but also from our 'Christian' brothers and sisters and, dare I say it, especially the feminist 'Christians'.

To the church in Philadelphia, the smallest of the seven churches Jesus addresses in his letters in Revelation, he says:

> Because you have patiently obeyed me despite the persecution, therefore I will protect you from the time of Great Tribulation and temptation, which will come upon the world to test everyone alive. (Revelation 3:10)

> For it is my Father's will that everyone who sees his Son and believes on him should have eternal life – that I should raise him at the Last Day. (John 6:40)

There are a great number of other Scriptures which give an absolute assurance of our salvation: Luke 7:50; John 3:15-16; John 3:36; John 6:40; John 10:27-30; Acts 16:31; Romans 5:8; Romans 10:9; Romans 8:29-39; 1 Corinthians 3:15; Ephesians 1:13-14; Ephesians 2:5-8; 4:30; Philippians 1:6; 3:9; 2 Timothy. 1:9; Hebrews 7:25; 1 Peter 1:3-5; 1 John 1:5; 4:15. That's about twenty. I am sure you will find more if you keep searching. If anybody doubts the certainty of their salvation, then these Scriptures should thoroughly reassure them.

Our God is a God of integrity, faithfulness and love. And it is impossible for God to lie. He is pure and holy.

> Though everyone else in the world is a liar, God is not. Do you remember what the book of Psalms says about this? That God's words will always prove true and right, no matter who questions them. (Romans 3:4)

> It is impossible for God to lie. (Hebrews 6:18)

Our God doesn't 'do' lies. So, we can be absolutely assured of our salvation. We have his word on it. Then how can it be that Jesus warns us so many times in Scripture of that which appears to be the very opposite of these assurances? We will start in Matthew.

> Enter through the narrow gate. For wide is the gate and broad is the road that leads to destruction, and many enter through it. But small is the gate and narrow the road that leads to life, and only a few find it. (Matthew 7:13-14 NIV)

Both the Phillips New Testament in Modern English Bible and the Jerusalem Bible translate verse 14 as follows:

> The narrow gate and the hard road lead out into life, and only a few are finding it.
> Watch out for false prophets. They come to you in sheep's clothing, but inwardly they are ferocious wolves. By their fruit you will recognize them. Do people pick grapes from thorn bushes, or figs from thistles? Likewise, every good tree bears good fruit, but a bad tree bears bad fruit. A good tree cannot bear bad fruit, and a bad tree cannot bear good fruit. Every tree that does not bear good fruit is cut down and thrown into the fire. Thus, by their fruit you will recognize them. (Matthew 7:15-20 NIV)

We will pause at this stage and focus on the word *Fire*.

> No one can ever lay another real foundation than that one we already have – Jesus Christ. But there are various kinds of materials that can be used to build on that foundation. Some use gold and silver and precious stones and some build with sticks and hay and

straw. And the quality of each man's work will be seen when the Day of Christ exposes it. For that day's fire will reveal every man's work; the fire will test it and show its real quality. If what a man built on the foundation survives the fire, he will receive a reward. But if any man's work is burnt up then he will lose it (his reward) but he himself will be saved, but as by fire. (1 Corinthians 3:11-15)

I like the J.B. Phillips translation of this passage:

> But if his work is burnt down, he loses it all. He personally will be safe, though rather like a man rescued from a fire.

The word *fire* is used many times in Scripture, and I will take another illustration from Jesus' letter to the Laodicean church. The church which is left behind at the Rapture. Jesus says:

> I counsel you to buy of me gold tried in the fire. (Revelation 3:18 KJV)

These Christians need to have their faith tested by the fire of the Tribulation. Now back to Matthew:

> Not everyone who says to me 'Lord, Lord' will enter into the Kingdom of Heaven, but only he who does the will of my Father who is in Heaven.
> Many will say to me on that day, 'Lord, Lord did we not prophecy in your name, and in your name drive out demons and perform many miracles.' Then I will tell them plainly' 'I never knew you. Away from me you evil doers.'
> Therefore everyone who hears these words of mine and puts them into practice is like a wise man who builds his house on the Rock. Though the rain comes in torrents, and the floods rise and

the storm winds beat against his house, it won't collapse, for it is built on rock. (Matthew 7:21-25)

In Timothy we read:

Gods truth stands firm like a great rock and nothing can shake it. It is a foundation stone with these words written on it: 'The Lord knows those who are really his, 'and 'A person who calls himself a Christian should not be doing things that are wrong.' (2 Timothy 2:19)

Now the parable Jesus told of the ten virgins:

Then shall the kingdom of heaven be likened unto ten virgins, which took their lamps, and went forth to meet the bridegroom. And five of them were wise, and five were foolish. They that were foolish took their lamps, and took no oil with them. But the wise took oil in their vessels with their lamps. While the bridegroom tarried, they all slumbered and slept.

And at midnight there was a cry made, Behold, the bridegroom cometh; go ye out to meet him. Then all those virgins arose, and trimmed their lamps. And the foolish said unto the wise, Give us of your oil; for our lamps are gone out.

But the wise answered, saying, Not so; lest there be not enough for us and you: but go ye rather to them that sell, and buy for yourselves. And while they went to buy, the bridegroom came; and they that were ready went in with him to the marriage: and the door was shut. Afterward came also the other virgins, saying, Lord, Lord, open to us.

But he answered and said, Verily I say unto you, I know you not. Watch therefore, for ye know neither the day nor the hour wherein the Son of man cometh. (Matthew 25:1-13)

Again, those words 'I don't know you.' That is the third time we have read about a group of believers to whom Jesus spoke those fateful words. Seven times in the New Testament Jesus warns: 'there shall be weeping and gnashing of teeth'. See Matthew 8:12; Matthew 13:42; Matthew 13:50; Matthew 22:13; Matthew 24:51; Matthew 25:30. In Luke we read:

> There shall be great weeping and wailing and gnashing of teeth. (Luke 13:28)

In all these cases, Jesus is addressing believers – not unbelievers. In Philippians Paul writes:

> For I have told you often before, and I say it again now with tears in my eyes, there are many who walk along the Christian road who are really enemies of the Cross of Christ. They are heading for destruction for their god is their bellies, they are proud of what they should be ashamed of; and all they think about is life here on earth [worldly things]. (Philippians 3:18-19)

How can we possibly reconcile all these warnings of Jesus and Paul with the 20 or more assurances of salvation we started off with? There are a number of Scriptures which help us understand this mystery. We need to understand that there are two resurrections and two kingdoms. The Kingdom of Heaven, which is only referred to in Matthew and which refers to Christ's thousand-year reign on earth, also called the Millennium, and the Kingdom of God, which is God's eternal Kingdom and which lasts for all of eternity. It never ends.

When Jesus spoke those fateful words, 'Not everyone who says to me "Lord, Lord" will enter into the Kingdom of Heaven' (Matthew 7:21 KJV), he was spelling out very clearly that just because you claim to be a Christian does not mean you will necessarily reign with him in his Millennium Kingdom or be part of his Bride. No wonder he warned seven times: 'There will be weeping and gnashing of teeth.'

The number one requirement is for Jesus needs to 'know' us intimately. The word 'know' here speaks of intimacy. I know about a large number of people, but there are only a few I know intimately. If we desire to be part of the Bride of Christ, he needs to know us intimately. We need to be deeply in love with him, not with the world and its pleasures.

And one of the main prerequisites, in fact it is *the* main prerequisite, is obedience. Jesus said:

> If you love me, obey me... (John 14:15)

And obedience presupposes us loving one another. That is why the scripture teaches us:

> The Lord knows those who are really his. (2 Timothy 2:19)

His Word and his commandments are the foundation stones in their lives, and that is why John taught:

> Make sure you win your full reward from the Lord. For if you wander beyond the teaching of Christ, you will leave God behind, while if you are loyal to Christ's teaching you will have God too. Then you will have both the Father and the Son. (2 John 1:8-9)

Jesus too warns us:

> Watch out! Don't let my sudden coming catch you unawares; don't let me find you living in careless ease; carousing and drink-

ing and occupied with the problems of this life, like all the rest of the world. Keep a constant watch. And pray that if possible, you may arrive in my presence without having to experience these horrors. (Luke 21:34-36)

Are you beginning to get the picture? Not every believer who sits in a church pew on Sunday mornings is going to escape the Tribulation or be taken up in the Rapture (or Translation) of the church before the Tribulation begins. Only those Jesus knows. Only those who have entered through the narrow door and travelled the hard road. Only those who have built their house on the rock of obedience to his Word. Only those who have crucified their flesh on the Cross of Calvary and turned their backs on the pleasures of this world.

I encourage you all to study the letters to the churches in Revelation. There are only two churches out of the seven that are acceptable in their present state, Smyrna – the suffering church – and Philadelphia, the smallest and trying-to-be obedient church. Both these churches were suffering persecution. There will be some saved out of some of the other churches, but a great many are going to have their faith tested by fire during the Tribulation. As we saw before, at least seven times, Jesus warns 'there will be weeping and wailing and gnashing of teeth', by those left behind at the Rapture.

No Christian wants to, or needs to, face the absolute horror and devastation of the seven-year Tribulation; nor do they want to see their family facing it either. That is why he warns us so many times. In Mark chapter 13 alone he warns us six times. He says, 'Stay alert; Be on watch for my return. Keep a sharp lookout. Don't let me find you sleeping. Again I say, watch for my return.' He gives other warnings in Matthew and Luke. The prophet Joel warns us too:

> Let everyone tremble in fear; for the day of the Lord's judgment approaches. (Joel 2:1-2)

There are many terrible events occurring in the world today. But the Tribulation has not started yet. It is imminent. It could start any day. As we saw before, there are two kingdoms – the Kingdom of Heaven and the Kingdom of God – and there are also two resurrections.

> This is the First Resurrection. (The rest of the dead did not come back to life until the thousand years had ended.) Blessed and holy are those who share in the First Resurrection. For them the Second Death holds no terrors, for they will be priests of God and of Christ, and shall reign with him a thousand years. (Revelation 20:5-7)

This includes those taken up in the Rapture (or Translation) before the Tribulation begins, and those who have their faith tested by fire during the Tribulation.

The Second Resurrection is referred to as the Great White Throne judgment:

> And I saw a great white throne and the one who sat upon it, from whose face the earth and sky fled away, but they found no place to hide. I saw the dead, great and small, standing before God; and The Books were opened, including the Book of Life. And the dead were judged according to the things written in The Books, each according to the deeds he had done. The oceans surrendered the bodies buried in them; and the earth and the underworld gave up the dead in them. Each was judged according to his deeds. And Death and Hell were thrown into the Lake of Fire. This is the Second Death – the Lake of Fire. And if anyone's name

was not found recorded in the Book of Life, he was thrown into the Lake of Fire. (Revelation 20:11-15)

This is when the rest of the dead are judged, including those believers who have died through the ages but were not taken up at the time of the Rapture, along with the unbelievers throughout history, plus all those born during the Millennium Reign.

So, to briefly recap. Yes, once saved, we are saved. But only those who truly love Jesus and are 'known' by him will be taken up in the Rapture.

As the late Edward Millar used to teach, 'the Rapture will be for the enraptured'.

I could keep on going, but we will end this section with three scriptures.

> Beg him to save you, all who are humble – all who have tried to obey. Walk humbly and do what is right; perhaps even yet the Lord will protect you from his wrath in that day of doom. (Zephaniah 2:3)

> 'Watch now,' The Lord of Hosts declares, 'the day of judgment is coming, burning like a furnace. The proud and the wicked will be burned up like straw; like a tree they will be consumed – roots and all. But for you who fear my name, the Sun of Righteousness will rise with healing in his wings. And you will go free, leaping with joy like calves let out to pasture.' (Malachi 4:1-2).

My edition of the Living Bible presents 'WATCH NOW' in capitals!

> Watch ye, therefore, and pray always, that you may be accounted worthy to escape all the things that shall come to pass, and to stand before the Son of man. (Luke 21:36 KJV)

Faith for Today

> It was by faith that Abel obeyed God and brought an offering that pleased God more than Cain's offering did. God accepted Abel and proved it by accepting his gift; and though Abel is long dead, we can still learn lessons from him about trusting God. (Hebrews 11:4-6)

This is a classic example of the timelessness and endurance of Scripture and is one of the oldest stories in the Bible. Two brothers each brought an offering to God. They both knew God. Abel brought his offering on God's terms, and both he and his offering were accepted by God. Cain brought an offering on his own terms, not God's. Both he and his offering were rejected. Sadly, 6000 years later, nothing has changed. The Bible backs this up:

> Not all who sound religious are really Godly people. They may refer to me as Lord, but still won't get into the Kingdom of Heaven. For the decisive question is whether they obey my Father in Heaven. At the judgment many will tell me, 'Lord, Lord, we told others about you and used your name to cast out demons and do many other great miracles.' But I will reply, 'You have never been mine. Go away, your deeds are evil.' (Matthew 7:21-23)

We need to consider this passage very carefully. There are a number of points to consider in these verses.

1. *Many will tell me in that day.* Many – not just a few.

2. *We told others about you* (King James Version says 'prophesied in your name'). These are evangelists and prophets that Jesus is referring to.

3. *Cast out demons and did many other great miracles.* Many great miracles. We get all excited about one miracle. But even miracles are not necessarily of God.

> For false Christs shall arise, and false prophets, and will do wonderful miracles so that if it were possible, even God's chosen ones would be deceived. (Matthew 24:24)

4. *I never knew you. Depart from me, ye that work iniquity.*

Today the church needs to take a massive reality-check. Here are these people (they could well be from one of the great megachurches or traditional denominations of today) evangelising, prophesying, casting out demons, doing many miracles all in Jesus' name, and he says, 'You have never been mine. Go away, your deeds are evil.' Wherein lies the problem? These so-called believers were using the authority of Jesus' name to support their own false doctrine.

Jesus goes on to provide us with the answer:

> All who listen to my instructions and follow them are wise, like a man who builds his house on solid rock. (Matthew 7:24)

Consider Paul's instruction to the church.

> But God's truth stands firm like a great rock, and nothing can

shake it. It is a foundation stone with these words written on it. The Lord knows those who are really his, and a person who calls himself a Christian should not be doing things that are wrong. (2 Timothy 2:19)

Do you want to be known by Jesus? Then it's simple. Start believing his Word and obeying it. That is the only foundation on which to build our faith and ministry. It is the only foundation stone that will stand the test of time. We deviate from Truth at our peril. Jesus and truth are inseparable. Jesus said:

I am the Way – yes, and the Truth and the Life. (John 14:6)

When we depart from the Truth, we leave Jesus behind. The apostle John explains this:

Keep alive in yourselves what you were taught in the beginning; as long as what you were taught in the beginning is alive in you, you will live in the Son and in the Father. (1 John 2:24 Jerusalem Bible)

See that you win your full reward from the Lord. For if you wander away from the teaching of Christ, you will leave God behind; while if you are loyal to Christ's teachings, you will have God too. Then you will have both the Father and the Son. (2 John 1:8-9)

We need to meditate on, understand fully, and really take notice of these two verses. If you want to keep something alive, it needs to be nurtured and tended to. What is it that needs to be nurtured, tended and kept alive? That which we were taught in the beginning. Unchanged, original Truth!

We deviate from Jesus' commandments and Truth at our peril.

Jesus and his Word are inseparable. He is the Word of God become flesh. When we depart from Truth we depart from both the Father and the Son.

> Work hard so God can say to you, 'Well done.' Be a good workman, one who does not need to be ashamed when God examines your work. Know what his Word says and means. (2 Timothy 2:15)

The apostles were well aware that there would come a time when the original doctrine which they taught would increasingly come into question, and that it would be twisted to suit the taste of those who heard it. To the extent that a great many believers would become deceived.

> Our wise and beloved brother Paul, has talked about these same things in many of his letters. Some of his comments are not easy to understand and there are people who are deliberately stupid, and always demand some unusual interpretation. They have twisted his letters around to mean something quite different from what he meant, just as they do the other parts of the Scripture – and the result is disaster for them. (2 Peter 3:16)

No wonder Jesus warned:

> Blessed are all who hear the Word of God and put it into practice. (Luke 11:28)

> Go back to what you heard and believed at first; hold to it firmly, and turn to me again. (Revelation 3:32)

> We never try to get anyone to believe that the Bible teaches what it doesn't. All such shameful methods we forego. We stand in the

presence of God as we speak, and so we tell the Truth, as all who know us will agree. (2 Corinthians 4:2)

We are not talking about lost salvation. But to enter into the Kingdom of Heaven and reign with Christ here on earth for a thousand years should be the heart's desire of every born-again Christian.

Remember the parable of the ten virgins? To qualify as one of the five virgins who were ready with sufficient oil in their lamps when the bridegroom appeared unexpectedly. To stand before the Son of Man and to be accounted worthy to escape all the horrors of the Tribulation, should be the earnest prayer of every sincere believer.

Not all who are 'born again' will be part of the First Resurrection and reign with Christ in his Kingdom of Heaven. We need to understand this clearly. Scripture could not be more specific about these things.

No wonder, as we have seen, Jesus warned seven times, 'There shall be weeping and wailing and gnashing of teeth' by those left behind. These are those who were told those fateful words, 'I don't know you. Depart from me ye workers of iniquity.' No wonder the apostle John warned:

Make sure you win your full reward from the Lord. (2 John 1:8)

Our obedience must always be based on trust in him and his unchanging Word. We must simply trust that he *does* know best, even when we don't understand fully. His ways are higher than our ways. Nothing gives us the right to change the Scriptures to suit our own agenda. Remember Cain!

Treasure-Hunting

And this is the secret: that the Gentiles will have their full share with the Jews in all the riches inherited by God's children; both are invited to belong to his church, and all of God's promises of mighty blessings through Christ apply to them both, when they accept the Good News about Christ and what he has done for them. God has given me the wonderful privilege of telling everyone about this plan of his; and he has given me the power and special ability to do it well. Just think! Though I did nothing to deserve it, and though I am the most useless Christian there is, yet I was the one chosen for this special joy of telling the Gentiles of the endless treasures available to them in Christ. (Ephesians 3:6-8)

I want to encourage you. We have just read how Paul was chosen to preach the Good News of the gospel to the Gentiles. Most of you will have heard the Christmas story of how the angel of the Lord spoke to the shepherds and said:

> Don't be afraid, I bring you the most joyful news ever announced, and it is for everyone. (Luke 2:10)

Paul too was writing about the Good News regarding Christ and what he has done for us, and the glad news of the endless treasures available to us in Christ. This most joyful news ever announced; this Good News; these 'glad tidings' that the endless treasures available in Christ are not just for Jews, not just for church-goers or so called religious people, but for everyone. Rich or poor, highly educated or never been to school, top of the social ladder or bottom of society's heap. This Good News is for everyone.

Healthy or sick, Olympic gold medallist or bedridden paraplegic, social celebrity or social outcast, worst of sinners or the most self-righteous, the glad news of the endless treasures available in Christ is truly for everyone. And it's free, with no strings attached.

It is simply not possible to cover the whole subject regarding the endless treasures available to us in him, but we can at least start digging to see what we can unearth.

When God sent an angel down from heaven to announce 'The most joyful news ever announced,' and when the apostle Paul endured imprisonment, beatings and incredible hardships in order to preach this 'glad news of endless treasures in Christ', I think you will agree that we are dealing with something of considerable importance and great value. We are told to:

> Work out your own salvation with fear and trembling. (Philippians 2:12 KJV)

That simply means we are to discover for ourselves and take hold of, by faith, these endless treasures available to us in Christ.

Some Christians never get past the milk stage in their spiritual growth, and remain spiritual babies, as described in Hebrews:

> You have been Christians a long time now, and you ought to be teaching others, but instead you have dropped back to the place where you need someone to teach you all over again the very first principles in God's Word. You are like babies who can drink only milk, not old enough for solid food. And when a person is still living on milk it shows he isn't very far along in the Christian

life, and doesn't know much about the difference between right and wrong. He is still a baby Christian! Still needing to be fed by others instead of being able to feed themselves. (Hebrews 5:12-13)

The first treasure we need to receive from Christ's jewel box is *forgiveness*.

> In whom we have redemption through His blood, the forgiveness of our sins, according to the riches of His grace. (Ephesians 1:7 KJV)

Our sins are forgiven. All of them. We are forgiven and, if we stay close to him, we are set free from the power of sin. Jesus died for all of us on the Cross of Calvary. He paid the price in full. If you are a believer and are still having ongoing trouble with sinfulness, it is probably because of one or more of the following:

1. You are not abiding, staying close to him (see John 15).

2. You are allowing the devil to cast doubts on your rightful inheritance. Remember, he is a thief and a liar. The Bible says,

> Resist the devil, and he will flee from you.' (James 4:7 KJV)

3. You don't really know him, or you are not obeying him. If you love him, you will obey him. It is such a wonderful thing to be forgiven and set free from the power of sin. If that is not a treasure, then I don't know what is.

Another treasure is *joy*.

> I have told you this so that you will be filled with my joy. Yes, your cup of joy will overflow! (John 15:11)

> For the Kingdom of God is not food and drink, but righteousness, and peace, and joy in the Holy Spirit. (Romans 14:17)

Treasure doesn't come much greater than that here on earth. There are not that many non-Christians out there who are full of joy and peace. If God's joy and peace is not good news, then I don't know what is.

> Do not fear anything except the Lord of the Armies of Heaven. If you fear him, you need fear nothing else. He will be your safety.' (Isaiah 8:13)

> God is our refuge and strength, a tested help in times of trouble. And so we need not fear even if the world blows up, and the mountains crumble into the sea. Let the oceans roar and foam; let the mountains tremble! (Psalm 46:1-3)

There are a great many more Scriptures relating to Gods willingness to protect us from danger. And his protection is a true treasure.

The list of God's treasures is endless. The deeper we dig, the more jewels we discover.

> I came that you might have life and have it more abundantly. (John 10:10 KJV)

There is simply no limit to the abundance of life in Jesus. It covers every area of our life and being, including health, work, finances, family life, spiritual growth, faith, power over evil and protection from danger. Look at these verses from Psalm 103:

> I bless the holy name of God with all my heart. Yes, I will bless the Lord and not forget the glorious things he does for me. He forgives all my sins. He heals me. He ransoms me from hell. He surrounds me with loving-kindness and tender mercies. He fills my life with good things! My youth is renewed like the eagle's! (Psalm 103:1-5)

But it takes knowledge and faith to appropriate these promises of God.

> My people perish through lack of knowledge. (Hosea 4:6 KJV)

And it is so true. If we don't spend time with God, getting to know him and his faithfulness, if we don't spend time unearthing or discovering the wonderful treasures tucked away in the Bible, how can we appropriate or take hold of them? God has done so much for us.

There is no end to the riches of his grace available to us in Christ – but we still have to work out our own salvation, and we still have to abide in him in order to bear fruit. You won't get answers to prayer if you don't pray. Perhaps the greatest treasure he gives us in this life is his Spirit:

> If you, being evil, know how to give good gifts to your children, how much more will your Heavenly father give the Holy Spirit to those who ask him. (Luke 11:13 KJV)

We cannot grow into mature, fruit-bearing, wise believers who bring pleasure to our Lord and become part of the Bride without the help and empowering of the blessed Holy Spirit – our Helper, Comforter and Teacher, who alone is able to lead us into all truth and help prepare the Bride for her Bridegroom. And when the going gets tough, it is the Holy Spirit who gives us boldness in the face of persecution. And, on top of all that, the Spirit comes bearing gifts from our Lord to enable us in our walk with God. We can't 'walk the walk' without the Spirit's help.

When it comes to the riches available to us in Christ, the list is endless. We can go on and on. I haven't even mentioned the promise of eternal life and that wonderful verse in Corinthians:

> Eye has not seen, nor ear heard, nor has entered into the heart of man, the things which God has prepared for them that love him. (1 Corinthians 2:9 KJV)

Can you see why Paul was wanting to encourage us? God has so much he desires for us, but we have to do our part. Like getting to know him and his Word, and learning to obey him. In any genuine love affair, it takes two. We need to spend time with him. Jesus said,

> He that abideth in me, and I in him, the same bringeth forth much fruit: for without me ye can do nothing. (John 15:5 KJV)

It is important to express our gratitude to him for all his good gifts. If you were offered a million dollars but didn't accept it, then it would be of no use at all. And you would end up being full of regret after you realise what you have turned down. There is absolutely no limit to what God can do in our individual lives, in our families, in our church, in our district and in our nation. The only thing that limits him is us, and even then he makes a way.

> Oh Lord, I know it is not within the power of man to map his life and plan his course – so you correct me Lord, but please be gentle. Don't do it in your anger, for I would die. (Jeremiah 10:23)

Let us pray. Father God, with awe and deep gratitude we seek to grasp the very richness of your grace and kindness towards us, revealed in Jesus, our Saviour and Redeemer.

Father, open our ears to hear, our eyes to see, and our hearts to understand and obey. Correct us, Lord, but please be gentle. Don't do it in your anger – for surely we would die.

Grant that we may continue to work out our salvation and enjoy more of the riches of your grace and the endless treasures available to us in Christ.

May this year be one of new beginnings and new direction for all of us.

Fill us afresh with your Spirit, Lord. Not just for our sake, Father, but for the sake of your Holy name. Reveal your Glory, Lord, and please forgive us our apathy and unbelief.

In Jesus' name we ask and pray. Amen.

Practical Christianity

Lord, who may go and find refuge and shelter in your tabernacle up on your holy hill? Anyone who leads a blameless life and is truly sincere. Anyone who refuses to slander others, does not listen to gossip, never harms his neighbour, speaks out against sin, criticizes those committing it, commends the faithful followers of the Lord, keeps a promise even if it ruins him, does not crush his debtors with high interest rates, and refuses to testify against the innocent despite the bribes offered him – such a man shall stand firm forever. (Psalm 15)

Since you became alive again, so to speak, when Christ arose from the dead, now set your sights on the rich treasures and joys of heaven where he sits beside God in the place of honor and power. Let heaven fill your thoughts; don't spend your time worrying about things down here. You should have as little desire for this world as a dead person does. Your real life is in heaven with Christ and God. And when Christ who is our real life comes back again, you will shine with him and share in all his glories.

Away then with sinful, earthly things; deaden the evil desires lurking within you; have nothing to do with sexual sin, impurity, lust, and shameful desires; don't worship the good things of life, for that is idolatry. God's terrible anger is upon those who do such things. You used to do them when your life was still part of this world; but now is the time to cast off and throw away all these rotten garments of anger, hatred, cursing, and dirty language.

Don't tell lies to each other; it was your old life with all its wickedness that did that sort of thing; now it is dead and gone. You are living a brand new kind of life that is continually learning more and more of what is right, and trying constantly to be more and more like Christ who created this new life within you. In this new life one's nationality or race or education or social position is unimportant; such things mean nothing. Whether a person has Christ is what matters, and he is equally available to all.

Since you have been chosen by God who has given you this new kind of life, and because of his deep love and concern for you, you should practice tender hearted mercy and kindness to others. Don't worry about making a good impression on them, but be ready to suffer quietly and patiently. Be gentle and ready to forgive; never hold grudges. Remember, the Lord forgave you, so you must forgive others.

Most of all, let love guide your life, for then the whole church will stay together in perfect harmony. Let the peace of heart that comes from Christ be always present in your hearts and lives, for this is your responsibility and privilege as members of his body. And always be thankful.

Remember what Christ taught, and let his words enrich your lives and make you wise; teach them to each other and sing them out in psalms and hymns and spiritual songs, singing to the Lord with thankful hearts. And whatever you do or say, let it be as a representative of the Lord Jesus, and come with him into the presence of God the Father to give him your thanks.

You wives, submit yourselves to your husbands, for that is what the Lord has planned for you. And you husbands must be loving and kind to your wives and not bitter against them nor harsh.

You children must always obey your fathers and mothers, for that pleases the Lord. Fathers, don't scold your children so much that they become discouraged and quit trying.

You slaves must always obey your earthly masters, not only trying to please them when they are watching you but all the time; obey them willingly because of your love for the Lord and because you want to please him. Work hard and cheerfully at all you do, just as though you were working for the Lord and not merely for your masters, remembering that it is the Lord Christ who is going to pay you, giving you your full portion of all he owns. He is the one you are really working for. And if you don't do your best for him, he will pay you in a way that you won't like – for he has no special favourites who can get away with shirking.

You slave owners must be just and fair to all your slaves. Always remember that you, too, have a Master in heaven who is closely watching you.

Don't be weary in prayer; keep at it; watch for God's answers, and remember to be thankful when they come. Don't forget to pray for us too, that God will give us many chances to preach the Good News of Christ for which I am here in jail. Pray that I will be bold enough to tell it freely and fully and make it plain, as, of course, I should.

Make the most of your chances to tell others the Good News. Be wise in all your contacts with them. Let your conversation be gracious as well as sensible, for then you will have the right answer for everyone. (Colossians 3 and 4:1-6)

There is no way we can cover all the ground in these verses. But I would like to speak about practical Christian living. There seems to be a false view that our spiritual life is somehow separate from our daily life in the world. That is not so. It is our normal daily lives and how we live them that will determine our spiritual progress as much or more than anything else. God uses our families, possessions, workplace, our relationships with others, even our praying to teach us and train us and test us for the work and ministry he has ahead for each of us.

> He who is faithful in a very little thing is faithful also in much, and he who is unrighteous in a very little thing is unrighteous also in much. If therefore you have not been faithful in the use of unrighteous mammon, who will entrust the true riches to you? (Luke 16:10 NASB)

Possessions
We must be faithful with money and possessions in order to be entrusted with the true riches, spiritual riches. There are two dangers here – having plenty and wanting to keep it for our own pleasure, my hard work, I earned it. The trouble is we are not our own; this is idolatry. The second danger coveting. Not having much, and envying those who do have, places us in danger of coveting. We want something for nothing. In many cases this is simply a consequence of wasteful lives in the past. Both of these sins Jesus denounces strongly.

We must have the attitude of Paul, who says:

> For I have learned to be content in whatever circumstances I am in. I know how to get along with humble means, and I also know how to live in prosperity, in any and every circumstance I have learned the secret of being filled and going hungry, both of having abundance and suffering need. The danger is that both these things can take our mind off the centrality of Christ. (Philippians 4:11 NASB)

Work

The guidelines are clear:

> Work hard and cheerfully at all you do, just as though you were working for the Lord, and not merely for your masters, remembering that it is the Lord Christ who is going to pay you, giving you full portion of all he owns. He is the one you are really working for. And if you don't do your best for him, he will pay you in a way you don't like – for he has no special favourites who can get away with shirking. (Colossians 3:23-25)

I refuse to believe Jesus was a rough carpenter, or Paul a rough tentmaker. Whatever your job, farmer or housewife, do your best. Or are you one of the bosses? Be fair and just. You too have a master in heaven who is watching you.

> And some soldiers/police were questioning him, saying, 'And what about us, what shall we do? And he said to them, 'Do not take money from anyone by force, or accuse anyone falsely, and be content with your wages.' (Luke 3:14)

Workers, be content with your wages. Remember, we reap what we sow in life. Give freely of yourself to your work, family, friends and church. But keep a balance.

Speech

> And whatever you do or say, let it be as a representative of the Lord Jesus. (Colossians 3:17)

Don't use bad language.

> Say only what is good and helpful to those you are talking to, and what will give them a blessing. (Ephesians 4:29)

There is so much that can be mentioned on the topic of speech and how we talk to others, especially those near to us. Gossip, slander, lies, half-truths, doing your block – all these things will hinder, check, and even stop your spiritual growth. They can lead to falling away and unfruitfulness.

Unforgiveness

> Be gentle and ready to forgive; never hold grudges. Remember the Lord forgave you, so you must forgive others. (Colossians 3:13)

Unforgiveness and bitterness in a person's heart will destroy them faster than any other sin except maybe immorality. If you hold grudges against anyone at all, get rid of it. Hand it over to Jesus. If you can't do it in your own strength, ask Jesus to give you that strength.

Integrity and Truth

> He who walks with integrity, and works righteousness, and speaks truth in his heart... (Psalm 15:2 KJV)

> Don't tell lies to each other. (Colossians 3:9)

I am sure that doesn't mean just with words, but our lives too. You see it too often. On the outside, men and women of God could be good workers in the church, moving in a ministry, praying beautifully, giving generously, but underneath (on the inside) there are problems that need facing up to and dealing with. We might be fooled. But God never is. It is an awful thing going through life carrying a burden of sin because we are afraid or ashamed to face up to it.

We must be completely honest with God, ourselves and each other. If you have a problem, be honest. Admit it. First to yourself and then to God. Don't be afraid to seek help. We have all sinned, every one of us. That doesn't mean you necessarily have to stand up and admit your personal problems to the whole congregation, hang out your dirty washing for all to see. But, if you have a problem, seek help. James says:

> Confess your faults (sins) to one another and pray for each other so that you may be healed. The earnest prayer of a righteous man has great power and wonderful results. (James 5:16 KJV)

Straining Out Gnats
and Swallowing Camels

Listen! I hear the voice of someone shouting, 'Make a road for the Lord through the wilderness, make him a straight, smooth road through the desert. Fill the valleys; level the hills; straighten out the crooked paths and smooth off the rough spots in the road. The glory of the Lord shall be seen by all mankind together.' The Lord has spoken – it shall be. (Isaiah 40:3-5)

John the Baptist, who was now in prison, heard about all the miracles the Messiah was doing, so he sent his disciples to ask Jesus, 'Are you really the one we are waiting for, or shall we keep on looking?' Jesus told them, 'Go back to John and tell him about the miracles you've seen me do – the blind people I've healed, and the lame people now walking without help, and the cured lepers, and the deaf who hear, and the dead raised to life; and tell him about my preaching the Good News to the poor. Then give him this message, 'Blessed are those who don't doubt me.' When John's disciples had gone, Jesus began talking about him to the crowds. 'When you went out into the barren wilderness to see John, what did you expect him to be like? Grass blowing in the wind? Or were you expecting to see a man dressed as a prince in a palace? Or a prophet of God? Yes, and he is more than just a prophet. For John is the man mentioned in the Scriptures – a messenger to precede me, to announce my coming, and prepare people to receive me.

'Truly, of all men ever born, none shines more brightly than John the Baptist. And yet, even the lesser lights in the Kingdom of Heaven will be greater than he is! And from the time John the Baptist began preaching and baptizing until now, ardent multitudes have been crowding toward the Kingdom of Heaven, for all the laws and prophets looked forward to the Messiah. Then John appeared, and if you are willing to understand what I mean, he is Elijah, the one the prophets said would come at the time the Kingdom begins. If ever you were willing to listen, listen now'. 'What shall I say about this nation? These people are like children playing, who say to their little friends, 'We played wedding and you weren't happy, so we played funeral but you weren't sad.' For John the Baptist doesn't even drink wine and often goes without food, and you say, 'He's crazy.' And I, the Messiah, feast and drink, and you complain that I am 'a glutton and a drinking man, and hang around with the worst sort of sinners!' But brilliant men like you can justify your every inconsistency!' (Matthew 11:2-19)

In a real sense, this passage from Matthew is a fulfilment of the Old Testament passage from Isaiah. John came to prepare the way for Jesus. The reason was simple. The people had strayed a mile off-course in virtually every area of God's commandments, and they were not living in victory. They were locked into all sorts of sins and bondages; even their nation was under the control of the Roman Empire.

Hence the prophetic words in Isaiah. Note God's instructions: 'Make a road for the Lord [Jesus] through the wilderness.' It was a wilderness alright. A wilderness of false teaching and half-truths. A wilderness of unbelief, compromise and bondage. The people were living in a spiritual desert. God had been silent for 400 years. But out of the desert God raised up a man for his time, John the Baptist.

And John pointed the people back to God, back to the truth.

He cut through the hypocrisy and ritual and religion, and he called the Jewish nation to repentance – and he pointed them to Jesus – the true Messiah and Saviour.

John was extremely successful in his ministry. So much so that Jesus was led to say,

> Truly, of all men ever born, none shines more brightly than John the Baptist. And yet, even the lesser lights in the Kingdom of Heaven will be greater than he is! (Matthew 11:11)

What set John apart from other men and especially the religious leaders of his day? Jesus asked the crowds.

> When you went out into the barren wilderness to see John, what did you expect him to be like? Grass blowing in the wind? (Matthew 11:7)

Oh, that God would raise up a John the Baptist in the church today. A modern-day Elijah. For a church which seeks to bow and bend to accommodate the whims of every pressure group in society – women's rights, the New World Order, gay liberation, Maori activists, human rights – what about God's rights? A Church which has jumped on the bandwagon of so-called global warming or climate change. A church which seems to have conveniently forgotten that our Lord is about to return and reign here on earth for a thousand years. A church which seeks to form liaisons with just about every cult and false religion in the world today.

And don't believe it can't be happening, because it is. In virtually every denomination you will find error or compromise to some extent. All under the guise of loving one another. And it is fine to love one another, but it is not fine to commit spiritual adultery in the process.

The second question Jesus asked about the peoples' expectation of John was,

> Did you find him dressed in expensive clothes?

Or, as the Good News Translation puts it,

> A man dressed in fancy clothes? (Matthew 11:8 GNT)

Look! Fancy robes, gowns, cassocks and back-to-front collars do not make a man of God. These things speak of tradition, ritual and religion, but not of the authority and power of God.

John came in the spirit of Elijah, to restore truth to God's people. Remember, Elijah challenged the people and said,

> If the Lord be God, follow him; but if Baal, then follow him... (1 Kings 18:21)

I believe that exactly the same situation exists in the church today. Sooner or later we must choose between the false teachings of Baal which have crept into the church, and the truth which we have adulterated, watered down and compromised; all to our detriment. Look, nothing has changed.

Jesus, speaking to the people said:

> And all who heard John preach, even the most wicked of them, agreed that God's requirements were right, and they were baptised by him. (Luke 7:29-30)

All, that is, except the Pharisees and teachers of Moses' law. They rejected Gods plans for them and rejected John's baptism. As I said, nothing has changed. John preached the baptism of repentance. The religious leaders of his day rejected this baptism. Jesus preached the baptism of the Holy Spirit. There are many in the church today, especially among the leaders, who reject God's plan for them in this area.

Yet we greatly need the help and guidance of the Holy Spirit, to enable and empower us in our spiritual growth, to teach us, to lead and guide us into all truth, to bring alive the Scriptures for us, to comfort us and convict us when we need it, and to prepare the Bride for the coming Bridegroom.

The church needs the gifts the Holy Spirit brings for us. Tongues, for when we don't know how to pray in the natural; healing; prophecy; words of knowledge – these good gifts from the Father are given for a reason. To build up and empower the church.

Listen again to what Jesus said:

> 'What can I say about such men?' Jesus asked. 'With what shall I compare them? They are like a group of children who complain to their friends, "You don't like it if we play 'wedding' and you don't like it if we play 'funeral'!" For John the Baptist used to go without food and never took a drop of liquor all his life, and you said, "He must be crazy!" But I eat my food and drink my wine, and you say, "What a glutton Jesus is! And he drinks! And has the lowest sort of friends!" But I am sure you can always justify your inconsistencies.' (Luke 7:31-34)

Where do we start with that lot? Funnily enough, we have latched on well enough with the teetotaller part, but try to get your average Christian to fast, and see where you get. Yet I tell you, if you want to get serious with God – if you really want to see your prayers answered and people saved – try fasting. I can recall a number of times when people have prayed and fasted with very real results.

Rev. Edward Millar fasted and prayed for days on end during

his ministry in South America. The resulting revival saw hundreds of thousands come to salvation.

Let us get back to Jesus. He must have had a good appetite if they called him a glutton – and he drank wine and, according to them, had the lowest sort of friends. Jesus didn't come to save the so-called righteous, he came to save sinners like you and me.

Look, we are straining out gnats and swallowing camels. Frankly, I don't believe God is concerned whether we drink or not, provided what we do is done in faith and does not become a stumbling block to others. The same can be said of the Sabbath. These are not the real issues. The real issues are walking and living by the Spirit; dying to self and the flesh; abiding in Christ; obedience; a grateful heart; walking and living in the fear of the Lord and the comfort of the Holy Spirit; believing Jesus and his commandments; walking in faith; forgiving and being forgiven, and loving one another with the *agape* love of God. This is the type of love which desires God's highest and best for all people – which would see them growing into the very fullness of God's wonderful plan of salvation, set free in Jesus from every sin and bondage and curse. And, make no mistake, we are all born into sin and into bondage, every one of us. Some get set free in Jesus, and a whole lot don't, even regular churchgoers. Far too many are not walking in the freedom, love, peace and joy of the Holy Spirit. And yet Jesus said:

If the Son shall set you free, you shall be free indeed. (John 8:36)

It was Carolyn and my privilege to attend a service in Hastings a while ago.

There was a visiting American speaker who did not impress, but I will tell you what did impress me at that church. The people. They were of all colours and creeds – Samoans, Maori, Indians, Asians and Europeans of many backgrounds. Many were at the bottom end of the social scale. There were ex-drug addicts, alcoholics, prostitutes and homosexuals. Some were way overweight, and some were skinny; some were well off and some were on the dole. And their faces shone with the love of Jesus, for they had been set free and filled with God's Spirit. They were 'going places' in Jesus, and that church was growing so fast.

An interesting thing happened that night. They had an altar call, and a young lady responded and gave her heart to Jesus. What impressed me was that the pastor (it was Mike Connell of Hastings Christian Outreach) prayed over that girl. He took authority in the name of Jesus, and he broke every curse that that girl had inherited from her parents and ancestors and any sins she may have committed herself. He renounced every evil spirit that might have been troubling her up to that point of her life, and she was set free in a wonderful way. I don't remember if he prayed for her to receive the baptism of the Holy Spirit at that stage or not. She certainly hadn't been christened or baptised in water; that would come later. The point I want to make is that there are far too many people, regular churchgoers, still living under a curse of some kind. I will name a few.

The curse of freemasonry. A husband, father or grandfather involved in freemasonry will bring members of the family under this curse. How can this be? In order to join this secret society, one is required to swear an oath of allegiance to their god. The problem is that the god of freemasonry is not our God. Our God is the God of Abraham, Isaac and Jacob, the God and Father of our Lord Jesus Christ, whereas the god of freemasonry is Lucifer. Some of the out-workings of the curse will be marriage breakdowns, suicides, cancer in the left breast of female family members and tragedies of one sort or another.

Any form of dabbling in the occult or witchcraft, or even coming under the influence of hypnotism, can open us up to evil influences.

An evil deed committed by an ancestor can mean we are born under a curse. Incest, sexual perversion, homosexuality, adultery, fornication and pornography are all things which can bring a curse on our lives and those of our families. Merely harbouring unforgiveness in our heart towards another person can open us up to committing the very same sin that we hold against them. Harbouring unforgiveness and grudges can result in our being in bondage to the very same thing ourselves. The list of sin goes on and on. The truth is we are all born into sin – every one of us.

No wonder Jesus and his disciples spent a great deal of time casting out demons and setting people free. The good news is that there is absolutely no need for anyone who believes in the Lord Jesus Christ to remain in bondage to any sin or curse.

But there are many areas in our lives where we may well need to 'work out our own salvation'. We will need the help of the Holy Spirit in this. As the Spirit searches and reveals the hidden things in our hearts, there may well be things we need to renounce, areas where we may need to seek God's (and others') forgiveness, and curses that may need to be broken off us in the name of Jesus.

Remember the angel's message to the shepherds:

> I bring you the most joyful news ever announced, and it is for everyone! The Saviour – yes, the Messiah, the Lord – has been born. (Luke 2:10-11)

The gospel message truly is Good News. Good news to all who will receive it and respond to it. If there is any area in your life where you are not living in total victory? God's great plan of salvation touches every area of our lives, so do something about it. Don't settle for second or third best.

If you have not yet received the baptism of the Holy Spirit (and don't accept the teaching that you received it all when you became a believer, were christened or were baptised in water), God has much more for you. Do something about it. Again, don't settle for second or third best. And if you have received the baptism of the Holy Spirit and you speak in tongues, don't just settle for that. God still has more for you. Much more. Keep seeking God. (More Father, more of your Spirit, please.)

In the book of Acts chapter 2, they were filled with the Spirit and began speaking in other tongues. They went out and began preaching about Jesus, and they started to get persecuted. In Acts chapter 4, the same disciples were praying and seeking God, and guess what? The building shook and they were all filled with the Holy Spirit and were empowered to preach the Word with boldness.

Let us pray. Father God, meet with us today, I ask. Send the blessed Holy Spirit to search our hearts. Into the hidden corners, Lord, to dig up any issues from the past that still need to be dealt with, issues which are holding us back in our spiritual growth, issues which are hindering us from living in the very fullness of your great and wonderful salvation, purchased for us at such great cost by our Lord and Saviour.

Free us, Lord, from every sin, every curse, and every bondage.

Lord, keep us from settling for second or third best, like those Christians described in the book of Hebrews – still spiritual babies, still living on a milk diet. Their stomachs couldn't handle solid food even though they had been believers for a long time.

Fill us afresh with your Spirit, Lord. Set us free and empower us for service, Lord. Service in your Kingdom, service in our community. Grant us boldness, Lord. Boldness to spread the wonderful Good News of your gospel.

Come, Holy Spirit, we need you. Come, sweet Spirit, we pray. Come in your strength and your power. Come in your own gentle way. Father, in Jesus' name we ask. Amen.

Standing Firm, Staying Grounded

This message is based on a number of warnings and instructions in Scripture relating to 'today'.

> There is going to come a time when people won't listen to the truth, but will go around looking for teachers who will tell them just what they want to hear. They won't listen to what the Bible says but will blithely follow their own misguided ideas. (2 Timothy 4:3)

I quote from a number of sources. This first is from a *Prophetic Revival School* email dated 27/5/10. Subject: Brian McLaren and the 'New Liberals.'

> There is a growing movement afoot in the postmodern church that does not abide in God's word; hence they do not know the truth. The movement calls itself, 'Emergent' or 'Emerging church' (E.C.M.) and it is emerging away from orthodox Christianity, spreading its spiritual cancer throughout the globe. E.C.M. 'Change agents' have made inroads into evangelism, big time. What they preach is a counterfeit social gospel. They say they bring 'a message of peace.' Their hope is to make Christianity more palatable to the world. In order to accomplish their lofty goal, the shifters must first repackage the church.

Look, the greatest danger facing Christians today is not so much the world and its attractions, tempting though they may be, but rather believers being led astray by big name theologians, both male and female. They are rife. They are everywhere. In mainline churches, in mega-churches, on TV. They have DVDs and books and online media galore. Scripture clearly warns us this would happen. Jesus himself warns us:

> For false Christs shall arise and false prophets, and will do wonderful miracles, so that if it were possible even God's chosen ones would be deceived. See, I have warned you. (Matthew 24:24)

Quote from Arnold Fruchtenbaum's *The Footsteps of the Messiah*, pp.83-87:

> The Bible itself has given the major admonition by which one must judge all that claims to be of the Lord: the written Word of God.
> Paul states:
>
>> And these things brethren, I have in a figure, transferred to myself and Apollos for your sakes; that in us ye might learn not to go beyond that which is written; that no one of you be puffed up for the one against the other. (1 Corinthians)
>
> Again, it should be emphasized that Paul is writing to a Church which had a strong tendency to move towards the sensational and the experiential. But the focus on the experiential only showed that they were not spiritual, but carnal.
>
>> Dear brothers, I have been talking to you as though you

were still just babies in the Christian life who are not following the Lord but your own desires; I cannot talk to you as I would to healthy Christians who are filled with the Spirit. (1 Corinthians 3:1-3)

Paul must especially admonish a Church of this nature, *not to go beyond the things which are written*. That which is written, of course, is the Holy Scriptures. For any new manifestation or phenomenon, they must go back and test it by the Word of God. If it is something which 'goes beyond that which is written', then it must be rejected out of hand. It is sufficient to know that if it is not in Scripture, they have gone beyond that which is written and, therefore, it is already evident that this thing is not of God. What happens to those who do go beyond that which is written? Paul declares that they become *puffed up for the one against the other*. They develop a spiritual pride that is evident when they go around claiming to be able to judge the Word of God by their experience. There are two further scriptures to consider in this discussion:

> Yea, and all that will live godly in Christ Jesus shall suffer persecution. But evil men and seducers shall wax worse and worse, deceiving, and being deceived. But continue thou in the things which thou hast learned and hast been assured of, knowing of whom thou hast learned them; And that from a child thou hast known the holy scriptures, which are able to make thee wise unto salvation through faith which is in Christ Jesus. All scripture is given by inspiration of God, and is profitable for doctrine, for reproof, for correction, for instruction in righteousness: That the man of God may be perfect, thoroughly furnished unto all good works. (2 Timothy 3:12-17 KJV)

I charge you in the sight of God, and of Christ Jesus, who shall judge the living and the dead, and by his appearing and his Kingdom: preach the word; be urgent in season, out of season; reprove, rebuke, exhort, with all longsuffering and teaching. For the time will come when they will not endure the sound doctrine; but having itching ears, will help to themselves teachers after their own lusts; and will turn away their ears from the truth, and turn aside unto fables. (2 Timothy 4:1-4 KJV)

Paul gives a simple message which is largely ignored by much of the modern movements today: 'Those who seek to live godly lives will suffer persecution'. The truth is that health and wealth are not signs of divine favour or spirituality. Rather, being persecuted for the faith that is a sign of a truly godly person. Paul, then, issues a warning that as time goes on there will be more and more false teachers who are truly imposters and who will go around deceiving others as well and will be deceived themselves.

Quote from *Avoiding Strange Fire* by Jonas Clark, 28 May 2010:

Experiences, even vivid, powerful, and supernatural ones are not measurements for Truth. In my generation some have gold dust, feathers, gems, and people barking and roaring like lions in their meetings. A search through the Scriptures gives no evidence that the Holy Spirit used any of these things to confirm Christ's Word. Others say female angels are healing people. There is no evidence of the existence of female angels in the Word. There are only a few examples of strange fire. Someone may tell you that the things of the Spirit can't be understood by the natural man. That's not true at all because the Holy Spirit can be understood.

He never violates the written Word. The things of the Spirit are understood by the logos, the Bible.

> For whatever God says to us is full of living power: it is sharper than the sharpest dagger, cutting swift and deep into our innermost thoughts and desires with all their parts, exposing us for what we really are. He knows about everyone, everywhere. Everything about us is bare and wide open to the all-seeing eyes of our living God; nothing can be hidden from him to whom we must explain all that we have done. (Hebrews 4:12-13)

The Holy Spirit is not strange, weird or mystical. He is the third part (member) of the Trinity. He is a gentleman, statesman and a loving God that lifts up Christ, the only begotten Son of God. He is not an 'it,' a 'thing,' a 'feeling' or some 'Orphic force.'

In my generation 'Jezebel' and 'Baalim' prophets are prevailing enemies of true prophetic ministry. In the last twenty years these spirits have become sophisticated, have built their own network of churches, followers, training schools, written many books and produced many training videos. These spirits intend to hijack the prophetic ministry and hold themselves out to be experts in their field.

They condemn any criticism by outsiders as irrelevant, unloving, ignorant and judgemental. Both these prophetic groups and others you will encounter have all types of strange signs and wonders at their meetings.

Just remember, not all wonders, no matter how mystical and exciting, are from the Holy Ghost.

> Dearly loved friends, don't always believe everything you

hear just because someone says it is a message from God: test it first to see if it really is. For there are many false teachers around. (1 John 4:1)

Even legitimate miracles in their meetings does not confirm that these ministers are flowing right. Scripture says:

> Many will say to me in that day, 'Lord, Lord, have we not prophesied in thy name? And in thy name cast out devils? And in thy name done many wonderful works?' And then I will profess to them, 'I never knew you; depart from me, ye that work iniquity.' (Matthew 7:22-23)

The passage says, 'Many will say to me in that day', many, not just a few.

Even mega-churches can be built on the sands of materialism and deceiving spirits, all crying 'Lord, Lord' in the process. Throw in a few miracles, slayings in the spirit and gold dust for good measure, and you have mass deception. But listen to what the Bible says:

> But God's truth stands firm like a great Rock, and nothing can shake it. It is a foundational stone with these words written on it. 'The Lord knows those who are really his.' (2 Timothy 2:19)

You want to be known by God? Stay grounded in his unchanging Word. Stay obedient to his commandments. All of them.

J. Lee Grady made this statement, dated 30 April 2010:

> We need the help and empowering of the Holy Spirit. We can truly trust Him because He never does anything to violate the Word of God. As our teacher (1 John 2:27), He knows the dif-

ference between truth and error, and those who depend on him will walk in discernment and avoid deception, pride and carnality.

We need wisdom and discernment. Paul's prayer:

> My prayer for you is that you will overflow more and more with love for others, and at the same time keep on growing in spiritual knowledge and insight, for I want you always to see clearly the difference between right and wrong, and to be inwardly clean, no one being able to criticize you from now until our Lord returns (Philippians 1:9-10).

Some versions say, 'Prepare you for the day of Christ.'

There is a whole message in that text alone. Paul is praying that his converts at Philippi (and we today) will overflow more and more with love for others, but he knows the dangers of love that is not tempered by wisdom, hence his words: 'At the same time keep on growing in spiritual knowledge and discernment'.

The Day of Christ is only for those whom Jesus 'knows'. Those who have been obedient to his commands and are pure and faithful in their doctrine. Not those who have fallen into error. The Day of the Lord awaits these people. Wisdom is so important, for without wisdom and understanding, God's people fall into judgement.

> My people perish through lack of knowledge. (Hosea 4:6 KJV)

Knowledge of God's Word and what it truly says. Some of the most relevant instructions in Scripture regarding this issue can be found in the letters to the churches in Revelation. Not surprisingly. These letters to the churches contain Jesus' final instructions and warnings to his church.

I know how many good things you are doing. I have watched your hard work and your patience; I know you don't tolerate sin among your members, and you have carefully examined the claims of those who say they are apostles but aren't. You have found out how they lie. You have patiently suffered for me without quitting. Yet there is one thing wrong; you don't love me as at first! (Revelation 2:2-4)

Go back to what you heard and believed at first; hold to it firmly and turn to me again. Unless you do, I will come suddenly upon you, unexpected as a thief, and punish you. (Revelation 3:3)

I know you well; you aren't strong, but you have tried to obey and have not denied my Name. Therefore, I have opened a door to you that no one can shut. (Revelation 3:8)

Because you have patiently obeyed me despite the persecution, therefore I will protect you from the time of Great Tribulation and Temptation, which will come upon the world to test everyone alive. (Revelation 3:10)

Then said Jesus to those Jews which believed on him, If ye continue in my word, then are ye my disciples indeed; And ye shall know the truth, and the truth shall make you free. (John 8:31-32 KJV)

Our wise and beloved brother Paul has talked about these same things in many of his letters. Some of his comments are not easy to understand and there are some people who are deliberately stupid, and always demand some unusual interpretation-they have twisted his letters around to mean something quite different from what he meant, just as they do the other parts of the

Scripture – and the result is disaster for them. I am warning you ahead of time, so that you can watch out and not be carried away by the mistakes of these wicked men, lest you yourselves become mixed up too. But grow in Spiritual strength and become better acquainted with our Lord and Saviour Jesus Christ. (2 Peter 3:16-18)

Do you want to be better acquainted with Jesus? You want to be 'known' by him? You want to make it into the Kingdom of Heaven? Then stay grounded in his Word. Here are three final verses, all from the Psalms.

Nothing is perfect, except your words. (Psalm 119:96)

I have known from earliest days that your will never changes. (Psalm 119:152)

There is utter truth in all your laws, your decrees are eternal. (Psalm 119:160)

Tested by the Word of God

During my lifetime I have heard many sermons, messages, daily readings, *Word for Today* and memorised Bible verses, all pertaining to the words Jesus spoke during his ministry. Yet we seldom, if ever, hear any of his final instructions to his church so we will take a brief look at the Letters to the Churches in Revelation. This is important.

We have willingly taken up the command:

> Go ye therefore and teach all nations, baptizing them in the name of the Father, and of the Son, and of the Holy Ghost. (Matthew 28:19)

But, in too many instances, we have ignored the second part of the Great Commission:

> ...teaching them to obey all things whatsoever I have commanded you. (Matthew 28:20)

As a result, a vast gulf has formed between modern-day, western-style Christianity and the true faithful of the church down through the ages. It started with Abel, who was willing to bring his offering to God on God's terms, and it cost him his life. From the very beginning there has been conflict between God's clear instructions on how we are to serve him and man's ideas on how we will serve God.

If we go back to the start of the Christian church, we read,

> They joined with the other believers in regular attendance at the apostles' teaching sessions. (Acts 2:42)

The very first thing the early Christians did was to devote themselves to the 'anointed' word. And it was not easy. God tests our faithfulness in this respect.

I would like to quote from an article by David Wilkinson regarding Joseph. He said,

> Joseph's greatest trial was the Word of God.
> Joseph was tested and tried in many ways but his greatest trial was the word he had received!
>
>> He sent a man before them, even Joseph, who was sold for a servant: Whose feet they hurt with fetters: he was laid in iron: Until the time that his word came: the word of the Lord tried him. (Psalm 105:17-19 KJV)
>
> Consider everything Joseph endured. At only seventeen he was stripped down and cast into a pit to starve to death. His cold-hearted brothers laughed at his pleas for mercy and sold him to Ishmaelite traders who took him by caravan to an Egyptian slave market and sold him as a common slave.
> Yet Joseph's greatest trial wasn't his rejection by his brothers or even the human indignity of being made into a slave or being cast into prison. No, what confused and tried Joseph's spirit was the clear word he had heard from God! God had revealed to Joseph, through dreams, that he would be given great authority, that he would be used for God's glory. His brothers would bow before him and he would be a great deliverer of many people.

I do not believe any of this was an ego trip for Joseph. His heart was so set on God that this word gave him a humble sense of destiny. 'Lord you have put your hand on me to have a part in your great eternal plan.'

Joseph was blessed just by knowing he would play an important role in bringing God's word to pass! But the circumstances in Joseph's life were just the opposite of what God had put in his heart. He was the servant, he had to bow. How could he believe he would one day deliver multitudes when he was a slave himself?

He must have thought:: 'This doesn't make sense. How could God be ordering my steps into prison, into oblivion? God said I was going to be blessed, but he didn't tell me this was going to happen!'

For ten years Joseph faithfully served Potiphar's house but in the end he was misjudged and lied about. His victory over temptation with Potiphar's wife only landed him in jail. During such times he must have pondered the awful questions: Did I hear correctly? Did my pride invent these dreams? Could my brothers have been right? Maybe all these things are happening to me as a discipline for some kind of selfish desire'.

Beloved, there have been times when God has shown me things he has wanted for me; ministry, service, usefulness, yet every circumstance was the very opposite of that word. At such times I thought, 'Oh God, this can't be you speaking, it must be my flesh'. I was tried by God's word to me but God has given us his promises and we can trust them, all of them!'

As God tested Joseph and David Wilkinson, so he will test our faith in obedience to his Word. Far be it that I would ever be guilty of grieving the blessed Holy Spirit by preaching any message that would hinder the work of the Spirit in our lives.

Nevertheless, any form of Christianity that elevates spiritual experiences above the clear teaching of the Word of God is ultimately destined to fail. We are not to be surprised by this.

Jesus explicitly warned us that this is exactly what will occur at this time in the church age. As Jesus said:

> Not all who sound religious are really godly people. They may refer to me as Lord but still won't enter the Kingdom of Heaven. For the decisive question is whether they obey my Father in Heaven. In that day many will say to me: 'Lord, Lord, didn't we preach in your name, cast out demons in your name and do many other great miracles?' But I will reply, 'You have never been mine. Go away for your deeds are evil' (Matthew 7:21).

Most of the translations say, 'I have never known you' or, 'I never knew you.'

Surely this is why John teaches us:

> So keep on believing what you have been taught from the beginning. If you do, you will always be in close fellowship with both God the Father and his Son... (1 John 2:24)

Or, as Today's English Version puts it,

> You will always be in union with the Son and the Father.

Jesus picks this up too:

> Think about those times of your first love (how different now!) and turn back to me again and work as you did before... (Revelation 2:5)

But more on this shortly. This warning is further reinforced:

> Beware of being like them [false teachers and deceivers] and losing the prize that you and I have been working so hard to get. (2 John 1:8)

Comment on working so hard:

> See to it that you win your full reward from the Lord. For if you wander away from the teachings of Christ you will leave God behind; while you are loyal to Christ's teaching you will have God too. Then you will have both the Father and the Son. (2 John 1:8-9)

God is Holy. God is Righteous. God is Truth. God cannot and will not dwell where there is error. God has magnified his Word above his name. There is no teaching in the Bible more relevant to the church today than the letters to the churches in Revelation. The overwhelming message contained in these letters is: 'Listen to what the Spirit is saying' – these are Jesus' final instructions to his church. They have to be relevant, and we ignore them at our own peril even if they are unpalatable to some. The question for us today is quite simply, where do we fit amongst the seven churches and what should be our response?

Ephesus
Are we an Ephesian church, doing a lot of good things?

> I know your deeds, your hard work and your perseverance. I know that you cannot tolerate wicked people, that you have tested those who claim to be apostles but are not, and have found them false. You have persevered and have endured hardships for my name, and have not grown weary. (Revelation 2:2-3 NIV)

Actually, it is very interesting to compare the various translations here:

> I have 'somewhat' against thee, you have left your first love. (KJV)

> You do not love me now as you did at first. (GNT)

> You don't love me as at first. (TLB)

> You have forsaken your first love. (NIV)

> You do not love me as you did at first. (Phillips)

> You have less love now than you used to. (Jerusalem Bible)

> You have abandoned the love you had at first. (RSV)

> You have lost your early love. (NEB)

What happens when a church, or a person, abandons their first love? We get all involved with churchiness and church-related activities. Worse still, we start to listen to man, not God. When we depart from Jesus and his teaching, we lose our way. He is the Way. He alone is Truth. In him alone is Life. Such a church has a form of Godliness but no power. That is why Jesus says,

> Remember how far you have fallen... (Revelation 2:5 NOG).

The Amplified version says it like this:

> Remember then from what heights you have fallen.

The Ephesian church is an apparently good church, doing many good things but nevertheless has obviously fallen from a great height. Jesus' warning:

> Remember therefore from whence thou art fallen, and repent and do the works as at first; or else I will come unto thee quickly and will remove thy candlestick out of his place, unless thou repent. (Revelation 2:5 KJ21)

> If you have ears, then listen to what the Spirit is saying to the churches. (Revelation 2:7 KJV)

Jesus does not mince his words, does he?

Smyrna
Next, we have Smyrna; the persecuted church. Jesus found no fault with this church. He encouraged them to hold on and asked them to be faithful even unto death.

We have not known this kind of persecution, so at this time we cannot claim to be Smyrna Christians.

Pergamos
The church settled in the world. It is interesting that this church is being addressed by,

> He who wields the sharp, double edged sword. (Revelation 2:12)

The Sword of Truth has two edges. So often today we are being fed one-edge theology from a decidedly blunt sword. This church is also doing some good things. They are loyal and have not abandoned their faith, even when one of them was martyred. Nevertheless, this church has compromised God's teaching and

Jesus warns:

> Change your mind and attitude [or simply 'repent' in most versions] or else I will come to you suddenly and fight against them with the sword of my mouth. (Revelation 2:16)

I don't know about you, but I for one do not want to be attacked by Jesus and the sword of his mouth, the Sword of Truth.

Again, the warning:

> Let everyone who can hear, listen to what the Spirit is saying to the churches. (Revelation 2:17)

The inference here is that there are some who will not listen.

Thyatira

The church in idolatry. Again, this sounds a really good church. Jesus says:

> I am aware of all your good deeds – your kindness to the poor, your gifts and service to them; also I know your love and faith and patience, and I can see your constant improvement in all these things. (Revelation 2:19)

This is a 'going places' church, but there is one serious problem:

> You are permitting that woman Jezebel, who calls herself a prophetess, to teach my servants that sex sin is not a serious matter. (Revelation 2:20)

This is not some historical problem Jesus is warning about, because he goes on to say:

As for the rest of you in Thyatira who have not followed this false teaching ['deeper truths,' as they call them – depths of Satan, really], I will ask nothing further of you; only hold tightly to what you have until I come. (Revelation 2:24-25)

This is very obviously a 'today' problem in the Church. Let us not beat about the bush here. I firmly believe this refers to the growing influence of women in today's churches. This has only arisen in the past few years and is in direct conflict with Jesus' instructions to the New Testament Church:

I never let women teach men or lord it over them. Let them be silent in your church... (1 Timothy 2:12)

See also 1 Corinthians 14:34. In fact, from Genesis to Revelation, the Bible is totally consistent on this issue. What is more, for 1800 to 1900 years this was never questioned. The price of disobedience here is serious. Jesus says:

Pay attention now to what I am saying: I will lay her upon a sickbed of intense affliction, along with all her immoral followers unless they turn again to me, repenting of their sin with her and I will strike her children dead. (Revelation 2:22-23)

These people are heading straight into the Tribulation.

Let all who can hear listen to what the Spirit says to the churches. (Revelation 2:29)

Sardis

I know your reputation as an alive and active church, but you are dead. Your deeds are far from right in the sight of God. Go back to what you heard and believed at first. Hold to it firmly and return to me again. Unless you do, I will come suddenly upon you, unexpected as a thief, and punish you. (Revelation 3:1-3)

Can you see and hear Jesus' consistency here? Go back to what you heard and believed at first. Hold to it firmly and turn to me again. The Rapture and Tribulation again.

If you have ears, then, listen to what the Spirit says. (Revelation 3:6)

Philadelphia

I know you well; you aren't strong but you have tried to obey.
Because you have patiently obeyed me despite the persecution, therefore I will protect you from the time of Great Tribulation and temptation which will come upon the world, to test everyone alive. Look, I am coming soon! (Revelation 3:8 & 10-11)

An interesting church but not a strong one. No mention of any social programmes, political involvement, not even any outreach mentioned. Simply obedience, despite the persecution. Again, this letter is addressed to the present day. 'I am coming soon...' If you have ears, then, listen to what the Spirit says.

Laodicea
And lastly, Laodicea. Without exception, these Christians are all headed for the Tribulation in spite of thinking:

I am rich, with everything I want. I don't need a thing. (Revelation 3:17)

Going on, we read some of the saddest words in the Bible.

> Look. I have been standing at the door and I am constantly knocking. (Revelation 3:20)

Why haven't we heard him knocking? Deafness. Spiritual deafness.

Once again, 'Let those who can hear, listen to what the Spirit is saying.'

We have briefly skipped through these letters to the churches. Where do we fit in, either as a church or personally? Only two churches are acceptable in their present state. Smyrna and Philadelphia. Whereas we can't claim to be Smyrna's – we haven't been persecuted to death and I doubt we can claim to be a Philadelphian church. The last church I heard of claiming this label blew up and self-destructed big time. We would not wish to be named as part of Sardis or Laodicea. The other three churches also have major issues to deal with.

Jesus warns:

> Go in by the narrow gate. For the wide gate has a broad road that leads to disaster [RSV and NIV read 'destruction'] and there are many people going that way. The narrow gate and the hard road lead out into life and only a few are finding it. (Matthew 7:13 Phillips)

'Sudden Destruction' means we are suddenly thrust into the Tribulation. We can fool ourselves, delude ourselves but the simple truth is, if we are completely honest before God, we simply do not measure up. You see, God's words will always prove true and right, no matter who questions them.

> When people are saying, 'All is well; everything is quiet and peace-

ful' – then, all of a sudden, disaster will fall upon them as suddenly as a woman's birth pains begin when her child is born. And these people will not be able to get away anywhere – there will be no place to hide. (1 Thessalonians 5:3)

His truth stands firm like a great rock, and nothing can shake it. It is a foundation stone with these words written on it. 'The Lord knows those who are really His.' (2 Timothy 2:19)

We can only be known by God when we walk in obedience to his Word.

At the start of Jesus' ministry it says:

From that time Jesus began to preach and to say, 'Repent, for the Kingdom of Heaven is at hand. (Matthew 4:17 KJ21)

Truly the Kingdom of Heaven is at hand.

Let us pray. Lord Jesus, as we study the letters to the churches it is patently obvious that we do not measure up. Father God, I ask you to send the blessed Holy Spirit; the Spirit of Truth to search our hearts and to remove any hindrances in our lives which cause us to fall short. Open deaf ears to hear and blind eyes to see.

Lord, we remember the words of your prophet Jeremiah when he prayed: 'Oh Lord, I know it is not within the power of man to map his life and plan his course, so you correct me, Lord; but please be gentle. Don't do it in your anger, for I would die.'

In the precious name of Jesus, we ask and pray. Amen.

Role of Women

For we speak as messengers from God, trusted by him to tell the truth; we change his message not one bit to suit the taste of those who hear it; for we serve God alone, who examines our heart's deepest thoughts. (1 Thessalonians 2:4)

Perhaps the biggest question for the church, and indeed individual Christians today is simply this: Is the gospel which Paul preached, and indeed his instructions to the fledgling church, still completely relevant today or are his instructions outdated, particularly regarding issues such as the role of women in the church?

It is important at this point to shift our focus from Paul to the Godhead and listen to what our God has to say about the scriptures.

The words of the Lord are pure words, as silver tried in a furnace of earth, purified seven times. (Psalm 12:6 KJV)

All His commandments are sure. They stand fast forever and ever, and are done in truth and uprighteousness. (Psalm 111:7-8 KJV)

All scripture is given by inspiration of God and is profitable for doctrine, for reproof, for correction, for instruction in righteousness. That the man of God be made perfect, thoroughly furnished unto all good works. (2 Timothy 3:16-17 KJV)

God's words will always prove true and right, no matter who questions them. (Romans 3:4)

Heaven and earth shall pass away, but my words shall not pass away. (Mark 13:31 KJV)

Yea, rather blessed are they that hear the word of God, and keep it. (Luke 11:28 KJV)

The scripture cannot be broken. (John 10:35 KJV)

Sanctify them through thy truth. Thy word is truth. (John 17:17 KJV)

Your fathers and their prophets are now long dead, but remember the lesson they learned, that God's Word endures! It caught up with them and punished them. Then at last they repented. (Zechariah 1:5-6)

But God's word stands firm like a great rock, and nothing can shake it. It is a foundation stone with these words written on it: 'The Lord knows those who are really His' and 'a person who calls himself a Christian should not do things that are wrong'. (2 Timothy 2:19)

But his own plans stand forever. His intentions are the same for every generation. (Psalm 33:11)

Dearly loved friends, I have been planning to write to you with some thoughts about the salvation God has given us, but now I find I must write of something else instead, urging you to stoutly defend the truth which God gave us, once for all, to his people to keep without change through the years. [Or as some translations say, 'Without change through the generations'.] (Jude 1:3)

Forever, Oh Lord, your word stands firm in Heaven. (Psalm 119:89)

It is perfectly clear from these scriptures that we can trust God and his Word completely, and of equal importance, his instructions remain the same for every generation without change. This brings us back to Paul. Did he have it right when he wrote:

Women should be silent during church meetings. They are not to take part in the discussion, for they are subordinate to men as the scriptures declare. (1 Corinthians 14:34)

I do not allow a women to teach or have authority over a man; instead she is to remain quiet. (1 Timothy 2:12 CSB)

Very obviously in this day and age, such teaching is highly provocative and certainly does not fall within the bounds of the current politically correct viewpoint, or of feminists, either within or outside the church.

Where did Paul get his instructions from? This is an interesting study in itself.

The note in the Schofield Bible (Page 1235) on Ephesians 3:5 says,

The revelation of the mystery of the church was foretold but not explained by Christ (Matthew 16:18). The details concerning the doctrine, position, walk and destiny of the Church were committed to Paul and his fellow apostles and prophets by the Holy Spirit. (Ephesians 3:5)

This is confirmed by Paul himself and the apostle Peter as well:

> For no prophecy recorded in scripture was ever thought up by the prophet himself. It was the Holy Spirit within these Godly men who gave them true messages from God. (2 Peter 1:20-21)

Paul says his teaching regarding the role of women in the church came as a direct commandment from our Lord himself.

> You who claim to have the gift of prophecy or any other special ability from the Holy Spirit should be the first to realise that what I am saying is a command from the Lord himself. (1 Corinthians 14:37)

In truth, this should settle the matter once and for all. In reality all true prophets of God, including our Lord Jesus himself, have encountered opposition and even persecution because of their message. Paul most certainly did. How many of us have had to suffer for the truth as he did?

> We stand in the presence of God as we speak and so we tell the truth as all who know us will agree. (2 Corinthians 4:2)

> But I certify to you, brethren, that the gospel which we have preached of me is not after man, neither was I taught it, but by the revelation of Jesus Christ. (Galatians 1:11 KJV)

> From now on please don't argue with me about these things for I carry on my body the scars of the whippings and wounds from Jesus' enemies that mark me as His slave. (Galatians 6:17)

It is patently obvious from these scriptures that the doctrines that Paul taught and preached to the early church were the truth given to him by Jesus, and even then he met with strong resistance. We are also clearly warned in scripture that, in this day and age in which we live, there will be a real falling away from the truth. Indeed, it is one of the 'signs of the times'.

> For there is going to come a time when people won't listen to the truth, but will go around looking for teachers who will tell them what they want to hear. They won't listen to what the Bible says but will blithely follow their own misguided ideas. Stand steady and don't be afraid of suffering for the Lord. (2 Timothy 4:3)

> We must listen very carefully to the truths we have heard, or we may drift away from them. (Hebrews 2:1)

> Our wise and beloved brother Paul has talked about these same things in many of his letters. Some of his comments are not easy to understand and there are some people who are deliberately stupid and always demand some unusual interpretation – they have twisted his letters around to mean something quite different to what he meant, just as they do with other parts of scripture and the result is a disaster for them. (2 Peter 3:15-16)

Perhaps the clearest instructions for women are those from Paul and from Peter:

> You, wives, must submit to your husband's leadership in the same way you submit to the Lord. For a husband is in charge of his wife in the same way Christ is in charge of his body, the church. (He gave his very life to take care of it and be its Saviour!) So, you wives must willingly obey your husbands in everything, just as the church obeys Christ. (Ephesians 5:22-24)

Peter expresses it this way:

> Wives, fit in with your husband's plans; for then if they refuse to listen when you talk to them about the Lord they will be won by your respectful, pure behaviour. Your Godly lives will speak to them better than any words. Don't be concerned about the outward beauty that depends on jewellery, or beautiful clothes, or hair arrangements. Be beautiful inside, in your hearts with lasting charm of a gentle and quiet spirit which is so precious to God. That kind of deep beauty was seen in saintly woman of old, who trusted God and fitted in with their husbands plans. Sarah, for instance, obeyed her husband Abraham, honouring him as head of the house. And if you do the same, you will be following her steps like good daughters and doing what is right; then you will not need to fear offending your husbands. (1 Peter 3:1-6)

These verses are as important for what they don't say as much as for what they do. There is no mention here, or indeed anywhere else in the New Testament of women ministering in the church in a leadership or teaching role. Also, note that the role model God has chosen is Sarah and not Deborah as many would have it today. It is a gentle and quiet spirit which is so precious to God. It is vitally important that both husbands and wives get it right before God, because if either get it wrong, God's blessings and answers to prayer will be hindered.

> You husbands must be careful of your wives, being thoughtful of their needs and honouring them as the weaker sex. Remember that you and your wife are partners in receiving God's blessings, and if you don't treat her as you should, your prayers will not get ready answers. (1 Peter 3:7)

Certainly, women receive the Holy Spirit and also the gifts of the Spirit.

> He [Phillip] had four unmarried daughters who had the gift of prophecy. (Acts 21:9)

But as we see clearly in Peter that it is not so much the gifts which please God as the fruits of the Spirit. Speaking to wives:

> Be beautiful inside, in your hearts, with the lasting charm of a gentle and quiet spirit which is so precious to God. (1 Peter 3:4)

Jesus himself said,

> By their fruits ye shall know them (Matthew 7:20).

Not our gifts, not how we pray or what role we might hold in church. No. It is by our fruits that men and women alike are known by God.

That women are equally important to God is not in question. That they will be equal to men in the Kingdom is also not in question. What is vital for the church to understand is that God in his infinite wisdom has chosen separate roles and separate routes to maturity and blessings for both men and women.

> This plan of mine is not what you would work out, neither are my thoughts the same as your thoughts. For just as the heavens are higher than the earth, so are my ways higher than yours and my thoughts than yours. (Isaiah 55:8-9)

In this life and particularly in the New Testament Church, God never intended that women should be in positions of authority over men or even in teaching positions over men. The scriptures could not be any clearer on this issue. I doubt that many churches and a great number of individual Christians understand the full implications of this passage:

> You wives must submit to your husband's leadership in the same way you submit to the Lord. (Ephesians 5:22)

When woman submit to their husbands they are living in obedience to God. When they rebel against their husband's authority they are rebelling against God. What does God ask of women? That in this life they accept the serving or subservient role.

It is not for us to question God's wisdom. This is the way he has decreed it to be. This does not give husbands the right to treat their wives roughly or in a heavy-handed way. Far from it. Nevertheless, when Christians, from church leaders to new converts, can grasp this truth, I am sure we will see God's blessings flowing freely.

What if we choose to maintain the status-quo and refuse to 'rock the boat'? Listen to John's instructions:

> See to it that you win your full reward from the Lord. For if you wander beyond the teaching of Christ, you will leave God behind; while if you are loyal to Christ's teaching you will have God too. Then you will have both the Father and the Son. (2 John 1:8-9)

Jesus taught:

> I will only reveal myself to those who love me and obey me. The Father will love them too, and we will come to them and live with them. Anyone who doesn't obey me doesn't love me. (John 14:23)

Our eternal salvation is not the issue here. The issue is; we are not going to receive our full reward from the Lord – neither here on earth nor in eternity, and of vital importance – God's indwelling presence in our lives is totally conditional on our willingness to obey Jesus.

> You give blessing to the pure but pain to those who leave your paths. (Psalm 18:26)

> But though we, or an angel from Heaven, preach any other gospel to you than that which we have preached to you, let him be accursed. (Galatians 1:8 KJV)

James makes it clear:

> And remember, it is a message to obey, not just to listen to. (James 1:22)

Today the church needs to take a giant step backwards – back to the truth. Our Lord Jesus is coming for his Bride soon. Remember the parable of the ten virgins. Five were ready. Five were not.

Consider the last two letters to the churches in the Book of Revelation. To the church at Philadelphia he wrote:

> I know you well, you aren't strong, but you have tried to obey and have not denied my name. Because you have patiently obeyed Me despite the persecution, therefore I will protect you ['I will keep you' RSV] 'from the time of Tribulation which is coming upon the world.' (Revelation 3:8-10)

To the church at Laodicea:

> I know you well – you are neither hot nor cold; I wish you were one or the other! You say 'I am rich with everything I want. I

don't need a thing!' and you don't realise that spiritually you are wretched and miserable and poor and blind and naked. My advice to you is to buy pure gold from me, gold purified by fire. And to purchase from me white garments.' (Revelation 3:15; 17-18)

There is going to be a great cost for those left behind when the Bridegroom comes for his Bride. They are headed straight into the fire of the Tribulation to have their faith tested by fire.

Adamic Covenant

So the Lord God said to the serpent, 'This is your punishment: You are singled out from among all the domestic and wild animals of the whole earth – to be cursed. You shall grovel in the dust as long as you live, crawling along on your belly. From now on you and the woman will be enemies, as will your offspring and hers. You will strike his heel, but he will crush your head.' Then God said to the woman, 'You shall bear children in intense pain and suffering; yet even so, you shall welcome your husband's affections, and he shall be your master.' And to Adam, God said, 'Because you listened to your wife and ate the fruit when I told you not to, I have placed a curse upon the soil. All your life you will struggle to extract a living from it. It will grow thorns and thistles for you, and you shall eat its grasses. All your life you will sweat to master it, until your dying day. Then you will return to the ground from which you came. For you were made from the ground, and to the ground you will return.' (Genesis 3:14-19)

A careful study of what is referred to as the Adamic Covenant shines a clear light on this issue.

I quote from the notes in the Schofield Bible (Page 7) Genesis 3:15:

The Adamic Covenant conditions life of fallen man; conditions which must remain in place until during the Kingdom Age. 'The creation itself also shall be delivered from the bondage of corruption into the glorious liberty of the children of God.' (Romans 8:21 KJV) The elements of the covenant are:

1. The serpent, Satan's tool, is cursed (Genesis 3:14, Romans 16:20, 2 Corinthians 11:3,14. Revelation 12:9) and becomes God's graphic warning in nature of the effects of sin; from the most beautiful and subtle of creatures to a loathsome reptile.
2. The first promise of a Redeemer (Genesis 3:15).
3. The changed status of the woman (Genesis 3:16) in three particulars:
   1. Multiplied conception.
   2. Sorrow and pain in motherhood.
   3. The headship of man (compare Genesis 1:26-27). Sin's disorder makes necessary a headship; it is vested in the man (Ephesians 5:22-25; 1 Corinthians 11:7-9; 1 Timothy 2:11-14).
4. The light occupation of Eden (Genesis 2:15) changed to burdensome labour (Genesis 3:18-19) because of the earth being cursed (Genesis 3:17).
5. The inevitable sorrow of life (verse 17).
6. The brevity of life and the tragic certainty of physical death to Adam and all of his descendants (Genesis 3:19, Romans 5:15-21).

Nevertheless, the curse upon the ground is for man's sake. It is not good for man to live without toil.

These conditions, all of them, will remain in force until, in the Kingdom Age, we are delivered from them. Ask yourself...

- Do snakes still slide on their bellies and eat dust?
- Do women still suffer pain in childbirth?
- Do mothers around the world still experience sorrow and pain in motherhood?
- Do men still have to work the land to earn a living from it?

- Do thistles and weeds still grow on the earth?
- Is there still much sorrow and suffering in the world?
- Do men, women and children still die on this earth?

None of these things have changed, nor has the status of women. Not within the family, nor within the church.

Left Behind

I wish to speak about a remarkable man. A man greatly honoured by God, his name is recorded twelve times in the gospels and yet he was not part of the front-line ministry team and in fact, on the face of it, he appeared to have been left behind, or overlooked by Jesus when he chose his disciples. He was an older man, a fisherman who lived by the Sea of Galilee. We are not told the name of the town or place where he actually lived, but it was likely to have been either Bethsaida or Capernaum. Have you worked out to whom we are referring yet? Yes, that is right, Zebedee.

We are first introduced to Zebedee by Matthew.

> A little further up the beach (from where he [Jesus] had called Peter and Andrew) He saw two brothers, James and John, sitting in the boat with their father Zebedee, mending their nets; and called to them to come too. At once they stopped their work, and leaving their father behind, went with Him. (Matthew 4:21-22)

Now on the face of it, Zebedee had just been struck a major blow. His two partners, Peter and Andrew had just been called by Jesus, now his two sons were also called to join the team. It left a major hole in his fishing business, and it was about to get a whole lot worse. His wife, as well, was about join the ministry.

At this point we will stop and look at Zebedee's background. Zebedee was a fisherman on the sea of Galilee. His name was probably the Greek form of 'Zabdi' which means 'giving'. The Hebrew equivalent is 'Zidhdi' (Gift of God). You will see the significance of this as the story unfolds.

Here is a quote from John Bevere's book, *The Bait of Satan*:

> Now the Sea of Galilee is actually a lake. It is located 60 miles from Jerusalem and at one time was 13 miles long and 8 miles wide at its greatest extent. The surface of the lake is about 700ft below sea level and about 150ft deep at its lowest point. The Jordan River flows through it providing much of its water supply but that is augmented by springs in the lake's bed.
>
> The fresh waters of the lake are clean and they have always been well stocked by a variety of fish. Several towns dotted its shores in New Testament times, but almost all of them, Bethsaida, Capernaum and Tiberias stood on its Northern and Western shores because the Eastern slopes rise more precipitously from the water. The sea was the highway for considerable traffic between Damascus and the Mediterranean.
>
> Hot springs along the western shore, especially at Tiberias, brought multitudes to be cured or at least seek relief from various ailments.
>
> The high hills surrounding the below sea-level water, combined with abrupt temperature changes, contributed to sudden violent storms on the lake as various New Testament passages record.
>
> > That evening his disciples went down to the shore to wait for him. But as darkness fell and Jesus still hadn't come back, they got into the boat and headed out across the lake toward Capernaum. But soon a gale swept down upon them as they rowed, and the sea grew very rough. They were three or four miles out when suddenly they saw Jesus walking toward the boat! They were terrified, but he called out to them and told them not to be afraid. Then

they were willing to let him in, and immediately the boat was where they were going! (John 6:16-21 TLB; see Mark 4:35-41 and Mark 6:45-52)

It was on or around this lake that Jesus did many of his wonderful miracles.

Eighteen of the thirty-three recorded miracles of Christ were probably done in the immediate neighbourhood of the sea of Galilee. In the city of Capernaum alone he performed 10 of these. In fact, Jesus, more or less, based his travelling ministry out of Capernaum.

When Jesus heard that John had been arrested, he left Judea and returned home to Nazareth in Galilee; but soon he moved to Capernaum, beside the Lake of Galilee, close to Zebulun and Naphtali. (Matthew 4:13)

Just to diverge here a little, how many of you know there are two seas in Israel? You have the Sea of Galilee, and then there is the Dead Sea. The Sea of Galilee is up north, and it receives waters that originate up in the mountains near Caesarea Philippi. These waters flow down to the top end of the sea of Galilee and so the Sea of Galilee takes in free-flowing water from the northern end. At the same time these same waters, combined with the water from the springs in the lake bed, flow out from the southern end. As a result, the Sea of Galilee is loaded with live marine life. It is full of fish. It is these same living waters that flow down the river Jordan and enter the top end of the Dead Sea. But the Dead Sea only takes in, it doesn't give out.

The result is, every bit of life that comes into the Dead Sea dies. There is a very good lesson there for all of us. If we have the Spirit of God flowing in and not out of our lives, the Spirit dies also.

Remember the chorus,

Freely, freely you have received, freely, freely give. Go in my name and because you believe, others will know that I live.

As the Sea of Galilee was loaded with fish, and the people in Palestine are exceedingly fond of fish and will pay double or triple the price for what they pay for meat, the fishing trade has always been a thriving industry. That gives us some background to the area where Zebedee lived and plied his trade as a fisherman.

Now let us try and discover why he was so greatly honoured by both God and man.

Humility and reverence for the Lord will make you both wise and honoured. (Proverbs 15:33)

Pride ends in destruction; humility ends in honour. (Proverbs 18:12)

That is our first clue. Zebedee was a humble man. Let us go back to where we first found him. In the boat with his sons and hired men mending nets. Zebedee, as we will discover, was a wealthy man of property, had sons and partners and hired servants. He did not need to be in the boats mending nets. He could have been retired and living a life of ease, but Zebedee was a humble, hardworking man.

A lifetime of discipline doesn't change as a man grows older.

By humility and the fear of the Lord are riches, and honour, and life... (Proverbs 22:4 KJV)

The Living Bible translates it, 'long life'.

We are not told how long Zebedee lived, but we are able to

discern from the scriptures that he was a humble, hardworking, successful, hospitable and generous man greatly honoured by God and man. Let us continue in our search to know more of this remarkable man.

> If you won't plough in the cold, you won't eat at the harvest. (Proverbs 20:4)

If you wait for perfect conditions all the time, you won't get a lot done. Obviously conditions on the Sea of Galilee were often far from ideal and, even on a good day, things could change abruptly. Zebedee would have been a very experienced fishermen and sailor. He hadn't reached the position he was in by sitting around waiting for perfect conditions. As we read, the sea was a highway for considerable traffic between Damascus and the Mediterranean and it was quite possible he and his crew were involved in some dangerous rescues over the years.

Jesus refers to James and John as the 'Sons of Thunder'.

> James and John the sons of Zebedee, but Jesus called them 'Sons of Thunder'... (Mark 5:37)

These guys were no wimps. When a certain Samaritan village refused hospitality to Jesus and his team, it was James and John who asked,

> Master, shall we order fire down from Heaven to burn them up? (Luke 9:54)

James was the first of the disciples to be martyred for his faith. He was no wimp, and it is highly unlikely their father was either. Far from it.

Much of the early part of Jesus' ministry was based around Capernaum. As he moved further away, a number of Godly women went with him and provided for his and his disciple's needs. Among these Godly women was Zebedee's wife, Salome. She followed Jesus into his ministry right to the very end. In the light of what unfolds, it is very likely that Jesus had already spent quite some time in Zebedee's home. He knew this family intimately.

Consider Salome's request:

> Then the mother of James and John, the sons of Zebedee, brought them to Jesus and respectfully asked a favour. (Matthew 20:20)

The fact that scripture records them as the sons of Zebedee suggests that it was on this basis that she respectfully asked her favour. The other disciples were indignant. Jesus was not. It is likely that Zebedee was supporting the ministry financially, as were many of the women.

> Joanna, Chuza's wife (Chuza was King Herod's business manager and was in charge of his palace and domestic affairs), Susanna, and many others who were contributing from their private means to the support of Jesus and his disciples. (Luke 8:3)

Zebedee had two sons, two partners and his wife, all involved. We know Peter at least had a family to support. It is almost certain Zebedee was supporting some or all of them. He had probably been supporting Jesus' ministry from the very beginning. Although Jesus was from Nazareth, much of his early ministry was based around the area where Zebedee lived, and so many people close to him were involved. It appears that Zebedee owned property and commanded real respect in Jerusalem, even from the High Priest Annas.

The fact that his son John was sufficiently well known to Annas and was granted access along with Jesus.

> Simon Peter followed along behind, as did another of the disciples who was acquainted with the High Priest. So that other disciple was permitted into the courtyard along with Jesus, while Peter stood outside the gate. Then the other disciple spoke to the girl watching at the gate, and she let Peter in. (John 18:15-16)

John spoke to the servant girl who let Peter enter in. This suggests he enjoyed considerable 'mana' as a son of Zebedee. There is no suggestion that John denied his association with Jesus, which means the fact that he was a son of Zebedee must have carried enormous weight at the time, even with the High Priest. We can only speculate as to why that should be. Zebedee may have been some sort of national hero.

> When Jesus saw his mother standing there beside me, his close friend, he said to her, 'He is your son.' And to me he said, 'She is your mother!' And from then on I took her into my home. (John 19:26-27)

This was Jerusalem, not Capernaum or Bethsaida, and they all remained there, even after the crucifixion and resurrection. It is highly unlikely John owned his own home. He was still young, probably unmarried and without full time income to support Mary. Even though Jesus entrusted his mother to John's care, there seems little doubt the main benefactor would have been Zebedee.

From this we can begin to understand why he, Zebedee, was so greatly honoured by God. He must have been a man of real integrity, a wonderful provider, generous and hospitable, wealthy yet humble and hardworking, a man of high moral standards.

Unselfish in allowing his wife to travel with Jesus and the boys. He must also have been a strong believer. It is highly unlikely Jesus would have placed his mother in the home of an unbeliever, nor would he have been honoured by having his name recorded twelve times. Are you getting the picture?

On the face of it, Jesus seemed to overlook Zebedee at the start of his ministry. You could say he was 'left behind'. But not everyone who is called by Jesus is meant to be on the front line, in the public eye. But even those in the background can also make a huge contribution to his Kingdom. They also can be greatly used and honoured by God.

The key is that wherever we are, whatever we are doing, we must do it, 'As to the Lord.' We are not our own. We are bought with a price, the precious blood of our Saviour. We are born again into his Kingdom, and the rules of the Kingdom are not the rules of this world.

We must understand that God's ways are higher than our ways, we have to learn to walk in obedience to his Word with a humble heart and be content in whatever situation we find ourselves.

No, Zebedee was not called to the frontline – but his two sons were and his full contribution to the Kingdom will never be truly known in this age, but we can all learn greatly from him.

Communes: For Today or Not for Today?

A few weeks ago we watched a video in which the speaker was encouraging us to join together and share our possessions such as occurred in the early church.

> And all the believers met together constantly and shared everything with each other. (Acts 2:44)

> All the believers were of one heart and mind, and no one felt that what he owned was his own; everyone was sharing. (Acts 4:32)

Obviously, 2000 years later, this is very challenging teaching.

It is important for us to study and see what the scriptures say on this matter; to wait upon the Lord for answers.

I went home and prayed about this and asked God for understanding. I will share some of what I believe the scriptures have to say about this and also what others have had to say.

The first thing I discovered: it didn't last!

> And a great wave of persecution of the believers began that day. Sweeping over the church in Jerusalem and everyone, except the apostles, fled into Judea and Samaria. (Acts 8:1)

> The Jerusalem community came into being as a result of Peter's preaching and 3000 were saved at one time. And those who

believed Peter were baptized – about three thousand in all! (Acts 2:41)

Who were these 3000 who were baptised and became part of the church family? In Acts 2:5 we read:

> Many Godly Jews were in Jerusalem that day for the religious celebration, having arrived from many nations.

Here we have a unique situation. 3000 new converts, many visitors to Jerusalem, all needing to be nurtured and established in their faith. This called for a mighty combined effort on the part of the local Christians and, praise God, they responded, big time. But God never intended them to remain in this situation, as when persecution struck, they fled. Read what happened:

> Meanwhile, the believers who fled from Jerusalem, during the persecution after Stephen's death travelled as far as Phoenicia, Cyprus, and Antioch, scattering the Good News. But only to Jews. However, some of the believers who went to Antioch from Cyprus and Cyrene also gave their message about the Lord Jesus to some Greeks. And the Lord honoured this effort so that large numbers of these Gentiles became believers. (Acts 11:19)

I quote now from the book, *God's Generals* by Roberts Liardon:

> Jesus never commanded us to build communes. Jesus commanded us to 'go' not 'huddle.' The book of Acts commune didn't work for long either. Why? So the great commission in Matthew 28:19-20 would be fulfilled. We are to be lights in the world and penetrate Satan's darkness. Huddling together won't accomplish that feat.

Now a note on Acts 4:32, in the Schofield Bible:

> The experience of the Christians of the Jerusalem church, in sharing their possessions is not to be taken as normality for all Christian churches or communities. This voluntary sharing of possessions in the time of persecution is a beautiful evidence of the oneness of believers. However, it should be observed that this communal sharing was; voluntary, in a time of persecution, evidently restricted to the Jerusalem church.

From an edition of a prophetic magazine, *Good News*:

> There is no further mention of Christian communities in the remainder of the New Testament.

> It was not until three years later that I finally went to Jerusalem for a visit with Peter, and stayed with him for fifteen days. And the only other apostle I met was James, our Lords brother. (Galatians 1:18)

Obviously, the commune at Jerusalem had not been reconvened. We now have a number of witnesses all saying the same thing. So, if communities are out, and I firmly believe they are at this stage, what should be our focus?

> But when the Holy Spirit has come upon you, you will receive power to testify about me with great effect, to the people in Jerusalem, throughout Judea, in Samaria, and to the ends of the earth, about my death and resurrection. (Acts 1:8)

Instead of communities, the emphasis is ongoing within the gospel: hospitality and Godly homes.

> After a little thought he [Peter] went to the home of Mary, mother of John Mark, where many were gathered for a prayer meeting. (Acts 12:12)

> To Philemon, our much-loved fellow worker, and to the church that meets in your home, please keep a guest room ready for me. (Philemon 1:22)

Paul speaking to pastors:

> They must enjoy having guests in their home. (Titus 1:8)

> Cheerfully share your home with those who need a meal or a place to stay for the night. (1 Peter 4:9)

I love the J.B. Phillips translation of that verse:

> Be ye hospitable one to the other without secretly wishing you hadn't got to be.

You will note that in all cases we are talking about individual homes made available for the Lord's work. Prayer meetings, church services, hospitality. Hospitality is one of the underrated commands in the Bible.

What about sharing our possessions? No question, the scriptures have a great deal to say about Christian giving and supporting the Lord's work. Where does it start? Where does it end?

> This should be your ambition: to live a quiet life, minding your own business and doing your own work, just as we told you before. As a result, people who are not Christians will trust you,

and respect you and you will not need to depend on others for enough money to pay your bills... (1 Thessalonians 4:11-12)

We gave you this rule: 'He who does not work shall not eat.' Yet we hear that some of you are living in laziness, refusing to work, and wasting your time in gossiping. In the name of the Lord Jesus Christ we appeal to such people – we command them – to quiet down, get to work, and earn their own living. (2 Thessalonians 3:12)

But anyone who won't care for his own relatives when they need help, especially those living in his own family, has no right to say he is a Christian. Such a person is worse than the heathen. (1 Timothy 5:8)

So, first point. God wants us to be independent, not rely on others and support our own families well. Now that we have established what God's will is in these matters, it makes praying easy.

Tom Marshall's advice: God, family, work, church activities (in that order).

Don't worry about anything; instead pray about everything; tell God your needs and don't forget to thank Him for the answers. (Philippians 4:6)

Let Him have all your worries and cares, for He is always thinking about you and watching everything that concerns you. (1 Peter 5:7)

I want you to trust me in your times of trouble so you can give me glory. (Psalm 50:15)

Do you remember the camels story I shared before? One of those camels was named Needs. He was a scrawny old beast. Probably had the mange. Nevertheless, he was one of the camels that carried Rebekah to her Isaac. We each have to ride our different camels at different times. Some of those camels can be incredibly thirsty, can require a number of trips to the well, but it's the camels that carry us to our Isaac, our Jesus. So where does our giving start? It starts with our families. Where does it end? There is no end till Jesus comes.

There is so much more that can be spoken on this subject of communes, but I think we have clearly established that the Acts 2 community was not to be the norm for Christians down through the ages. I firmly believe there is no Biblical mandate to sell all our possessions and move into community at this time. That does not mean that in the future, particularly during the seven-year Tribulation, Christians may well have to move in together to support each other, but this must clearly be a move of God and not man.

All in a Month
(Thessalonians, Message 1)

In considering the first two chapters of 1 Thessalonians, we cannot cover all the points raised so we will look at just a few that shine through. The first thing that stands out is the total love and commitment of the apostles Paul, Silas and Timothy to God and their new converts.

> We always thank God for you and pray for you constantly. (1 Thessalonians 1:2)

The church at Thessalonica was a young church. The apostles had been with them for less than a month. Yet such was the richness of their teaching, that they had taught them many of the great doctrines of the Christian's faith, including the Trinity, the Holy Spirit, Christ's second advent (coming for his Bride), the Day of the Lord (Tribulation), assurance, conversion, election, resurrection, sanctification and Christian behaviour. All in less than a month. Together with the apostles' commitment and the evidence in their own lives, they could say,

> And you know how our very lives were further proof to you of the truth of our message. So you became our followers and the Lord's. (1 Thessalonians 1:5).

There is a powerful message in these words – especially to church leaders, and parents to their children. Remember Paul's words.

> For I don't want anyone to think more highly of me than he should from what he can actually see in my life and my message. (2 Corinthians 12:16)

Back to Thessalonians. Paul says:

> You know how badly we had been treated at Philippi just before we came to you and how much we suffered there. Yet God gave us the courage to boldly repeat the same message to you, even though we were surrounded by enemies. (1 Thessalonians 2:2)

The apostles had been imprisoned at Philippi and been treated roughly. After that, the apostles could have been forgiven if they had backed off. They had been faithful. They already had churches established in other places; Rome, Corinth, Galatia, Ephesus, Philippi and Colossae. They had already suffered greatly and produced much fruit in their ministry, but they were utterly committed to Jesus, the gospel and their fledgling churches. They loved not their own lives, even unto death (Revelation 12:11).

In the parable that Jesus spoke, he said:

> Except a grain of wheat falls to the ground and dies it cannot bring forth fruit. (John 12:24 KJV)

We all must be prepared to die to self and suffer for the gospel. It appears the further the apostles went in their travels, the more they suffered and died to their own well-being, the more and choicer the fruit they produced.

I mean, just think about it. Less than a month at Thessalonica and we have already heard about the depth of teaching the young church had received during that time. Now we read:

> This young church had already become an example to all the other Christians in Greece. And now the word has spread out from you to others everywhere, far beyond their boundaries, for wherever we go we find people telling us about your remarkable faith in God. We don't need to tell them about it. (1 Thessalonians 1:7-8)

Compare this with some of the problems in the earlier churches. Those apostles were totally committed. They said:

> We loved you dearly – so dearly that we gave you not only God's message but our own lives too. (1 Thessalonians 2:8)

It then goes on to paint a beautiful picture not only of the leaders to the young converts in the church, but also as an example for parents to their children.

> You yourselves are our witness, as is God, that we have been pure and honest and faultless toward every one of you. We talked to you as a father to his own children – don't you remember? Pleading with you, encouraging you and even demanding that your daily lives should not embarrass God, but bring joy to Him who invited you into His Kingdom to share His Glory. And we will never stop thanking God for this. (1 Thessalonians 2:10-13)

I read that again because it is so important. Too often we see religion not matched by good fruit, words not matched by deeds.

Another message we can pick up is:

> We speak as messengers from God, trusted by Him to tell the truth. We change His message not one bit to suit the taste of those who hear it, for we serve God alone, who examines our heart's deepest thoughts. (1 Thessalonians 2:4)

They refused to corrupt the gospel to please men or even feminists. The apostles weren't worried about being gender correct, politically correct, culturally sensitive or adulterating the gospel to appease the false god of humanism.

Oh, how the church needs to heed this message today. A church where, in far too many instances, pulpits and the leadership are filled by women usurping the authority of men in teaching roles, in total rebellion to Jesus' clear instruction on this issue.

> Women should be silent during the church meetings. They are not to take part in the discussion, for they are subordinate to men as the Scriptures also declare. (1 Corinthians 14:34)

> I never let women teach men or lord it over them. Let them be silent in your church meetings. (1 Timothy 2:12)

Jesus addresses this issue with the church at Thyatira.

> Yet I have this against you: You are permitting that woman Jezebel, who calls herself a prophetess, to teach my servants that sex sin is not a serious matter; she urges them to practice immorality and to eat meat that has been sacrificed to idols. (Revelation 2:20)

The implications to Jezebel of this rebellion are serious. Jesus spells them out clearly.

> Pay attention now to what I am saying: I will lay her upon a sickbed of intense affliction, along with all her immoral followers, unless they turn again to me, repenting of their sin with her and I will strike her children dead. And all the churches shall know that I am he who searches deep within men's hearts, and minds; I will give to each of you whatever you deserve. (Revelation 2:22-23)

From Genesis to Revelation, the scriptures are clear and unequivocal on this issue.

Women should not be usurping the authority of men, nor be in roles where they are teaching men.

In our passage, Paul also expresses their strong hope of Christ's return.

> Your strong faith and steady looking forward to the return of our Lord Jesus Christ. (1 Thessalonians 1:3)

> And they speak of how you are looking forward to the return of God's Son from Heaven – Jesus whom God brought back to life – and He is our only Saviour from God's terrible anger against sin. (1 Thessalonians 1:10)

Surely, 'God's terrible anger against sin' refers to the Tribulation. This young church, less than a month old, was looking forward to the return of Jesus. How much more so should we be looking forward to the return of our Lord today!

Let us pray. Father please forgive us. We have fallen short in so many ways and we continue to do so. Please forgive us.

Restore us Lord – please bring us to that place of obedience, that place of commitment, that place of truth and fruitfulness which is in you alone, Lord Jesus.

Lord, empower us afresh with your Spirit, who alone is able to rightly interpret the Scriptures for us, and to lead us into all truth.

Empower us to die to our own selfish desires and to the ways of the world, that we might truly be faithful servants who bring you joy and pleasure. We remember the words of your prophet Jeremiah:

> Oh Lord I know it is not within the power of man to map his life and plan his course – so you correct us Lord; but please be gentle. Don't do it in your anger for we would die. (Jeremiah 10:23-24)

Create in us clean hearts, Oh Lord. Put a right spirit within us.

Sanctify us in truth, Lord. Thy Word is truth. Revive us Lord. Revive us we ask.

In Jesus' name we pray. Amen.

When Life Overflows
(Thessalonians, Message 2)

In the first message from Thessalonians, we looked briefly at the first two chapters. To recap briefly; We saw how the apostles Paul, Silas and Timothy were totally committed to God, and saw their love, devotion and commitment to their new converts at Thessalonica.

Nothing, not persecution, weariness or suffering would stop them preaching the whole message of God's wonderful love and the fullness of his plan of salvation available in Christ. The incredible richness of their teaching and how in just a few short weeks they had covered all the major doctrines of the Christian faith.

How their message was imparted as much through deeds as through words and how their own lives were such a shining example of their message.

That nothing would stop them in their endeavour to preach the gospel wherever they went, and how the youngest church of all, at Thessalonica, had become a shining example to all the other older established churches.

How they pleaded, encouraged and even demanded that the daily lives of their new converts should not bring embarrassment to God and to the church, but to bring joy to our Heavenly Father.

In the first chapter, Paul refers to their steadily looking forward to Jesus' return. If they were eagerly awaiting Jesus' return 2000 years ago, how much more should we be awaiting his return today?

Lastly, we read of Paul's uncompromising approach to the gospel.

> For we speak as messengers from God, trusted by him to tell the truth. We change his message not one bit to suit the taste of those who hear it; for we serve God alone, who examines our hearts' deepest thoughts. (1 Thessalonians 2:4)

We now continue from there. To be honest, the first few verses don't seem very relevant to us at present, but we read at the end of this letter Paul writes:

> I command you in the name of the Lord to read this letter to all the Christians and may the rich blessings from our Lord Jesus Christ be with you, every one. Sincerely Paul. (1 Thessalonians 5:27-28)

Yes, I want to be blessed, and I certainly desire for everyone reading this to be blessed. In the next chapters, there are a number of issues raised so we will look briefly at some of them here.

> And then, dear brothers, you suffered what the churches in Judea did, persecution from your own countrymen, just as they suffered from their own people, the Jews. (1 Thessalonians 2:14)

They suffered persecution. Whether we like it or not, if we mean business with Jesus, we are going to cop some flak from our own countrymen – the people we work with, the people we mix and socialise with and even our own flesh and blood. Our own family and the Jews – that's our brothers and sisters in Christ.

If you have any doubts, read the letter to the Philadelphian church in Revelation.

The smallest of the churches, not a mega-church like some of the others, but Jesus said, 'I will keep you from having to go through the Tribulation.' They had tried to obey, despite persecution from the other churches.

Have you ever read the story of Joan of Arc, the Maid of Orleans? The religious leaders had her burnt at the stake. Now they have made her a saint.

It happened to Jesus, Paul and most of the other apostles, and it still happens today, even in the West.

Often when the Spirit of God moves among his people, the ones who oppose it the most are those who have been blessed by God in the past.

> I sent Timothy to visit you to strengthen your faith, and encourage you, and to keep you from becoming faint-hearted in all the troubles you are going through. But, of course you know that such troubles are part of God's plan for us Christians. Even while we were still with you we warned you ahead of time that suffering would soon come – and it did. (1 Thessalonians 3:1-4)

And it will for us too, when we are willing to stand firm in the truth. There is nothing like receiving encouragement when we are going through troubled times.

> For night and day we pray on and for you, asking God to let us see you again, to fill up any little cracks there may yet be in your faith. (1 Thessalonians 3:10)

These verses are not just relevant to church leaders for their congregation but also to us as parents for our children. Indeed for anyone for whom we are seeking salvation or growth in their lives. These verses are relevant to all Christians who are separated from those they want to nurture and grow in Christ. You can just sense the wonderful love and concern of Paul in these words. No parent could love their children more than Paul did his children in the Lord.

Now some very important verses:

> And may the Lord make your love to grow and overflow to each other and to everyone else, just as our love does toward you. This will result in your hearts being made strong, sinless, and holy by God our Father so that you may stand before him guiltless on that day when our Lord Jesus Christ returns with all those who belong to him. (1 Thessalonians 3:12-13)

Can you see how it unfolds? It starts with Paul praying, or our praying, which requires our obedience to Jesus' command to love one another. What happens when these things are all in unison? Our love grows and overflows to each other and to those around us. This will result in our hearts being made strong, sinless and holy by God our Father.

Can you begin to see how incredibly important love is? When we are obedient to the command to love one another, God moves in and makes our hearts strong, sinless and holy. He does all those things for us if we just obey him and love one another. With all those things we try and struggle to obtain in our own strength, we are really misdirecting our energy by trying to be strong, and sinless and holy. All we really need to do is get serious about loving one another and he will do the rest.

Never forget, love is not indulgence. Love seeks God's highest and best for the person we are seeking to love. To truly love, we need to spend time abiding and praying in order to be filled with his Spirit and for his love to flow through us as his vessels. The point is; Love is the key to growth.

Let us pray. Father, we thank you. We thank you for your great love for us. We thank you for building us up and enabling us through your Word and for your wonderful encouragement to us.

We worship you, praise you, thank you Father. We pray and ask that truly you will make our love grow and overflow to each other, and to those we come in contact with, especially in our district. Build your church, Lord. Build your church here in Putere.

One more request, Father. Please surround us with your lovingkindness and truth.

In Jesus' name we ask and pray. Amen.

Being a Christian
(Thessalonians, Message 3)

The main theme flowing through the first three chapters of 1 Thessalonians is the love and commitment of Paul, Silas and Timothy for their new converts.

> And may the Lord make your love to grow and overflow to each other and to everyone else, just as our love does toward you. This will result in your hearts being made strong, sinless, and holy by God our Father so that you may stand before him guiltless on that day when our Lord Jesus Christ returns with all those who belong to him. (1 Thessalonians 3:12-13)

In chapter 4 we will consider a number of issues.

Issue 1: Sexual Morality
We live in a world where immorality is rife and becoming more so every day. It is so important for Christians to remain faithful to God and their wives or husbands in this matter.

> For God has not called us to be dirty minded, but to be holy and clean. If anyone refuses to live by these rules, he (or she) is not disobeying the rules of men, but of God who gives his Holy Spirit to you. (1 Thessalonians 4:7-8)

We cannot have the Spirit of God living in us and be disobedient in this matter.

When lust comes in, the Holy Spirit is grieved. It is that simple. The Spirit of God is holy and cannot abide (live) in the presence of sin. Remember David's cry when he sinned.

> Cast me not away from your presence: and take not your Holy Spirit from me. (Psalm 51:12 KJV)

That's why we need to be careful what we read, listen to, and view as Christians. We certainly live in the world, but in this respect we need to be a world apart. Yet if we do stumble, and sadly we all do at times, we need to be honest and confess our sin. John the apostle puts it like this.

> But if we confess our sins to him, he can be depended on to forgive us and to cleanse us from every wrong. And it is perfectly proper for God to do this for us because Christ died to wash away our sins. (1 John 1:9)

But as King David was aware, we cannot continue to grow spiritually, if we continue to condone or harbour things in our life which are unclean and impure. There is no question, salvation is by grace, but spiritual growth is by choice.

Issue 2: Love

> But concerning the pure brotherly love that there should be among God's people, I don't need to say very much, I'm sure. For God is teaching you to love one another. Indeed, your love is already strong towards all the Christian brothers throughout

the whole nation. Even so dear friends, we beg you to love them more and more. (1 Thessalonians 4:9-10)

You see some Christians finding it easier to 'love' others than their own wives, husbands and children. How often do we see it? Christian couples, each loving the Lord in their own way. Each doing their own thing. Christian parents looking outside their own families (and it is certainly not wrong to look past our own families), but let us look to the well-being of our own children as well. Often it is easier to see the hurts and needs in other people's kids and not see the hurts and needs in our own families.

Husbands, if you want your prayers answered, make sure your wife is not grieving over something you have done or not done, said or not said. Are we as husbands providing well for our family's needs? Are we loving them as Christ loves his church?

And wives, are you serving and submitting to your husbands 'As to the Lord?' This doesn't mean your husband is God. It just means we are obeying the Lord in this matter. Why? Because it is pleasing to God. (Not to mention your husband as well.)

Submission – it doesn't always come easy, especially in this day and age, when the feminists, the world and even the church are all clamouring otherwise. Certainly, the scriptures are clear enough on this issue. Another important thing: obedience to our Lord, and his commandments, brings great blessing.

Issue 3: Ambition

This should be your ambition: to live a quiet life, minding your own business and doing your own work, just as we told you before. As a result, people who are not Christians will trust you and respect you, and you will not need to depend on others for enough money to pay your bills. (1 Thessalonians 4:11-12)

It is wrong to make an absolute out of a principle – even God himself is gracious and forgives mistakes. But I think that healthy Christians who are on the dole should be helped and encouraged to find work and provide for their families. But also, and this is important, to be able to support God's work and be blessed accordingly. Sounds hard! Not really. Just not wanting to settle for second best. Actually, when you study the scriptures, the Bible has a great deal to say about laziness.

Issue 4: The Second Coming
Paul raises this issue because some of his new converts at Thessalonica had lost loved ones and were obviously 'unnecessarily grieving' and he wanted to comfort and encourage them with what has become to the church 'the great Christian hope'.

> Since we believe that since Jesus died and came back to life again, we can also believe that when Jesus returns, God will bring back with Him them also who sleep in Jesus. (1 Thessalonians 4:14)

This is truly remarkable and why is he bringing back with him believers from both the Old Testament and the New and changing the bodies of living believers from mortal to immortal?

> But I am telling you this strange and wonderful secret: we shall not all die, but shall be given new bodies. It will happen in a moment, in the twinkling of an eye. (1 Corinthians 15:51-52)

As quick as you can blink. Why? It is not our Lord's intention that those believers walking in obedience should have to suffer the terrible events of the Tribulation, or the time of God's wrath. At the end of the Tribulation Jesus is coming back as King to rule here for a thousand years, and he is bringing his saints to rule with him.

Speaking of Jesus – the Lamb of God:

> For you were slain, and your blood has bought (or purchased) people from every nation as gifts for God. And you have gathered them into a Kingdom and made them priests of our God: they shall reign upon the earth... (Revelation 5:9-10)

Or as the King James Bible says,

> Redeemed us to God.

Isn't this incredible?

> But as it is written, Eye hath not seen, nor ear heard, neither have entered into the heart of man, the things which God hath prepared for them that love him. (1 Corinthians 2:9 KJV)

Let us pray. Father God, we thank you for your wonderful love. Fill us afresh, Lord – with your Spirit and your love – that we might be vessels of your love to a needy and sin-burdened world.

Let us never forget, Lord, that great and wonderful as your promises are, they are conditional. They are promised for them that love you. Father, we pick up Paul's prayer again:

> And may the Lord make your love grow and overflow to each other and everyone else, just as our love does towards you. (1 Thessalonians 3:12)

Father, I ask you to strengthen our marriages, restore the years which the locust has eaten. May our love be as it was when we were courting, but strengthened by the years. May our love for our children, grandchildren, and now great grandchildren abound even more.

May there be unrestrained love and forgiveness towards all those who have, however long ago, wronged or hurt us. Family members, neighbours, friends, whoever. Cleanse us from all unforgiveness we ask.

Lord, if your Spirit has touched upon anything in our hearts that we need to deal with, help us to do so, honestly and promptly. Build us up, Lord. Pour out your Spirit upon us. Set our districts, our towns, our cities and our nation on fire for Jesus, we pray.

In his precious name, the name of Jesus, we ask. Amen.

Ready for Christ's Return
(Thessalonians, Message 4)

In this message I wish to focus on just one issue – the return of our Lord.

It is important that we focus on this issue because there is still a great deal of misunderstanding and plain error about this subject in the church today.

Every chapter in 1 Thessalonians contains a reference to our Lord's return:

Chapter 1: How you are looking forward to the return of God's Son from Heaven.

Chapter 2: You will bring us much joy as we stand together before our Lord Jesus Christ when He comes back again.

Chapter 3: So that you may stand before Him guiltless on that day when our Lord Jesus Christ returns with all those who belong to Him.

Chapter 4: Then we who are still alive and remain on the earth will be caught up with them in the clouds to meet the Lord in the air and remain with Him forever.

Chapter 5: For God has not chosen to pour out His anger up on us, but to save us through our Lord Jesus Christ. He died for us so that we can live with Him forever, whether we are dead or alive at the time of His return.

This, of course, ties in with Paul's message in Corinthians:

> I tell you this, my brothers: an earthly body made of flesh and blood cannot get into God's Kingdom. These perishable bodies of ours are not the right kind to live forever. But I am telling you this strange and wonderful secret: we shall not all die, but we shall all be given new bodies! It will all happen in a moment, in the twinkling of an eye, when the last trumpet is blown. For there will be a trumpet blast from the sky, and all the Christians who have died will suddenly become alive, with new bodies that will never, never die; and then we who are still alive shall suddenly have new bodies too. For our earthly bodies, the ones we have now that can die, must be transformed into heavenly bodies that cannot perish but will live forever. (1 Corinthians 15:50-53)

It is interesting that Thessalonians, the one book in the Bible which contains so many clear references in every chapter to our Lord's return, is the one book which also contains a commandment in the Lord's name to be read to all the churches. More than just a coincidence I am sure. Take note, pastors!

Why is this so? The reason it is so important to have a clear understanding of this issue is because we need to be ready and waiting for his sudden, and in many cases, unexpected return for his Bride. So many times in the scripture Jesus warns us of the unexpectedness of his sudden return, 'like a thief in the night'.

Or for an opossum hunter, like a trap going off.

In the parable of ten virgins, five were ready and five were not. Jesus warning is clear.

> So stay awake and be prepared, for you do not know the date or moment of my return. (Matthew 25:13)

In Mark chapter 13 alone there are six warnings and, in the letters to the seven churches in Revelation, there are warnings to each church, accompanied by the admonition, 'Listen to what the Spirit is saying.'

It is important to remember that these letters are his final instructions to his church.

> Ephesus: I will come quickly and remove your lamp stand.

> Pergamon: Hold fast till I come.

> Sardis: I will come on thee as a thief, and you will not know what hour I will come.

> Philadelphia: Behold I come quickly.

> Laodicea, the missed-out church: I counsel thee, buy of me gold tried by fire.

The most common question about Jesus' Second Coming is one the disciples asked: 'When is all this going to happen?'

> I really don't need to say anything about that, dear brothers, for you know perfectly well that no one knows. That day of the Lord will come unexpectedly, like a thief in the night. When people are saying, 'All is well; everything is quiet and peaceful' – then, all of a sudden, disaster will fall upon them as suddenly as a woman's birth pains begin when her child is born. And these people will not be able to get away anywhere – there will be no place to hide.

But, dear brothers, you are not in the dark about these things, and you won't be surprised as by a thief when that day of the Lord comes. (1 Thessalonians 5:1-5)

Jesus spoke about this too, in Matthew he said,

So be prepared, for you don't know what day your Lord is coming. (Matthew 24:42)

In Luke:

Watch ye therefore, and pray always, that ye may be accounted worthy to escape all these things that shall come to pass, and to stand before the Son of Man. (Luke 21:36 KJ21)

Now here is an interesting fact. When Jesus returns at the end of the Tribulation to take up his rightful role as King of all the nations and ruler of this world for one thousand years (so much for global warming and the world coming to an end), this will be a totally predictable event.

The Book of Revelation even reveals the number of days of the Tribulation period, the time of the rule of the Antichrist and the number of days that God's two faithful witnesses prophesy during the Tribulation, as 1260 Days.

We are told that the coming world ruler, the Antichrist, will be revealed when he negotiates a peace treaty between Israel and her enemies. We also know that the Antichrist will not be revealed until after the restrainer is removed from the earth. It might appear to some that there are two conflicting sets of Scriptures relating to our Lord's return, but this is not so. When you study the Scriptures carefully, there is no conflict.

The important thing is, Jesus is coming twice. Firstly, before the Tribulation begins, to rescue his Bride from the coming judgment and devastation of God's day of wrath. His Second Coming is at the end of the seven-year Tribulation period to take up his rightful role as King of the nations. It is worth noting Jesus' words:

> In fact, unless those days are shortened, all mankind will perish. But they will be shortened for the sake of God's chosen people. (Matthew 24:22 NLT)

Indeed, such is the grace of God, that even those who are left behind at the Rapture when Jesus comes for his Bride, will not necessarily have lost their salvation. In the letter to the Laodicean Church while it says, 'I will vomit you out of my mouth, his counsel is, buy of me gold purified by Fire... and purchase from me white garments, garments clean and pure' (Revelation 3:18) and concludes the letter with the promise,

> I will let everyone who conquers sit beside me on my throne. (Revelation 3:21)

> After this I saw a vast crowd, too great to count, from all nations and provinces and languages, standing in front of the throne and before the Lamb, clothed in white, with palm branches in their hands. And they were shouting with a mighty shout, 'Salvation comes from our God upon the throne, and from the Lamb. And now all the angels were crowding around the throne and around the Elders and the four Living Beings, and falling face down before the throne and worshiping God. 'Amen!' they said. 'Blessing, and glory, and wisdom, and thanksgiving, and honour, and power, and might, be to our God forever and forever. Amen!' Then one of the twenty-four Elders asked me, Do you know who these are, who are clothed in white, and where they come from?' 'No, sir,'

I replied. 'Please tell me.' 'These are the ones coming out of the Great Tribulation,' he said. (Revelation 7:9-14)

I will tell you something else. It won't be the Gentiles or the Christian church who led them to Christ; they are already up in heaven. These believers, most or all of whom have been 'martyred' for their faith have been led to Christ through the witnessing of the 144,000 faithful Jews, 12,000 from each of the twelve tribes of Israel who were God's servants with his seal on their foreheads. It will be these 144,000 faithful Jews who will fulfil the Great Commission.

Living as a Christian
(Thessalonians, Message 5)

There is so much contained in this chapter, practical suggestions that Paul gives for living as a Christian, firstly warning us to be vigilant.

> So be on your guard, not asleep like the others. Watch for his return and stay sober. (1 Thessalonians 5:6)

He then addresses our attitude to hard working church officers.

> Honour the officers of your church who work hard among you and warn you against all that is wrong. Think highly of them and give them your whole-hearted love because they are straining to help you and remember, no quarrelling among yourselves. (1 Thessalonians 5:12-13)

The trouble is, we don't appreciate being corrected. Next Paul goes on to warn Christians about the disastrous result of laziness.
I have never heard anyone in the church being warned about laziness. But you will be surprised how much the Bible has to say about it. Inclusiveness is the in-word today.

> Dear brothers, warn those who are lazy, comfort those who are frightened, take tender care of those who are weak, and be patient with everyone. See that no one pays back evil for evil,

but always try to do good to each other and to everyone else. Always be joyful. Always keep on praying. No matter what happens, always be thankful, for this is God's will for you who belong to Christ Jesus. (1 Thessalonians 5:4-18)

Away back in the book of Genesis 24, Abraham's trusty servant Eliezer was sent back to Abraham's birthplace to find a bride for his son Isaac. Eliezer asked God to send a girl who would not only offer him a drink, but would offer to water his ten thirsty camels. This was a huge ask. When she offered, he watched to see if she would finish the job. Integrity and a good work ethic are two of the qualities the Holy Spirit is still seeking in the Bride today. Eliezer in the Genesis story was a type of the Holy Spirit; Rebecca a type of the Bride.

> Comfort those who are frightened.

We can relate more easily to that instruction, while Paul says:

> God has not given us the Spirit of fear, but of love, power and a sound mind... (2 Timothy 1:7 KJV)

Still, there are a lot of frightened Christians around.

> Take tender care of those who are weak, be patient with everyone.

Not always easy, is it?

> See that no one pays back evil for evil.

How much damage is caused by our inability to forgive and forget? Not so hard when it is your own family, or even your Christian brothers and sisters, but not so easy when it is a neighbour, or a friend, or a stranger that has done the 'dirty' on you.

Oh, the power and the absolute necessity for a Christian to be able to forgive and to forget. God has washed our sins into the sea of his forgetfulness, and has removed them as far as the east is from the west; and we had better learn to do the same.

Otherwise, our unforgiveness becomes a stumbling block, not just to the person we hold the grudge against, but even more so to ourselves. Jesus said,

> Your heavenly Father will forgive you if you forgive those who sin against you; but if you refuse to forgive them, he will not forgive you... (Matthew 6:14-15)

Another translation:

> Forgive us our trespasses to the level we are willing to forgive those who trespass against us.

Sobering isn't it.

Always try to do good to each other, Always be joyful.

Boy, have I seen some unjoyful Christians in my time. Been guilty of it myself. But this is not the way it is meant to be. If we are walking in obedience, staying close to him, we won't be sinning and we will be full of his joy. Jesus, his peace and his joy, they go together. Remember:

> There is therefore now no condemnation to them which are in Christ Jesus, who walk not after the flesh, but after the Spirit. (Romans 8:1 KJV)

> Always keep on praying. No matter what happens, always be thankful, for this is God's will for you who belong to Christ Jesus. (1 Thessalonians 5:17-18)

No matter what happens, always be thankful. Not so easy is it? Yet there is real spiritual power in praising God and expressing gratitude – even in adversity. It is called the sacrifice of praise. It is powerful. I can recall numerous occasions in lives of believers when God has turned an adverse situation into a time of rejoicing just through praising him and giving thanks when in the natural, things were looking really bad. Praise God, he is sovereign in all situations. And never forget that wonderful promise.

> And we know that all things work together for good to them that love God, to them who are the called according to his purpose. (Romans 8:28 KJV)

Do not smother the Holy Spirit. So often we are guilty, yet we don't even realise we are doing it. We smother the Holy Spirit, who is gentle and not pushy. We are instructed to walk by the Spirit, not by the flesh. So often in life we blame the devil, or God when the real culprit is our flesh. Strong self-will on the throne, me doing 'my thing'. We reap the consequences and we wonder why. Of course, 'it is never our fault', but what is worse it gives the devil access into our lives.

There are a great number of things we can talk about in this chapter, but throughout Thessalonians there is one over-riding theme which Paul keeps emphasising more than any other and that is the return of Jesus. I have deliberately left this till last, even though Paul refers to this event in every chapter.

> Chapter 1:10. And they speak of how you are looking forward to

the return of God's Son from Heaven: Jesus, whom God brought back to life – and He is our only Saviour from God's terrible anger against sin.

Chapter 2:19. Yes, you will bring us much joy as we stand together before our Lord Jesus Christ when He comes back again.

Chapter 3:13. So that we may stand before Him guiltless on that day when our Lord Jesus Christ returns with all those who belong to Him.

Chapter 4:15-19 is much more explicit:

> I can tell you this directly from the Lord: that we who are still living when the Lord returns will not rise to meet him ahead of those who are in their graves.
> For the Lord himself will come down from Heaven with a mighty shout and with the soul-stirring cry of the Archangel and the Great Trumpet Call of God.
> And the believers who are dead will be the first to rise to meet the Lord. Then we who are still alive and remain on the earth will be caught up with them in the clouds to meet the Lord in the air and remain with Him forever. So comfort and encourage each other with this news.

Chapter 5:9-10. For God has not chosen to pour out His anger upon us, but to save us through our Lord Jesus Christ. He died for us so that we can live with Him forever, whether we are dead or alive at the time of His return.

Although these ongoing references to Jesus' return are a common theme running through each chapter, 1 Thessalonians has a four-fold theme:

1. To confirm to the young converts in Thessalonica (and us) the fundamental truths already taught to them.

2. To exhort them (and us) to a life of personal holiness pleasing to the Lord.

3. To comfort them (and us) concerning those who have died.

4. To instruct Christians concerning their hope in the Lord's return.

5. In every chapter of both 1 and 2 Thessalonians the coming or return of the Lord is paramount, yet today we rarely, if ever, hear a message on this subject. This, in spite of Paul's clear instruction.

> I command you in the name of the Lord to read this letter to all the Christians. (1 Thessalonians 5:27)

Thessalonians are not the only books in the Bible that deal with this subject.

> Behold! I show you a mystery: We shall not all sleep [or die], but we shall all be changed. In a moment, in the twinkling of an eye, at the last trump; for the trumpet shall sound, and the dead shall be raised incorruptible, and we shall be changed.
> For this corruptible must put on incorruption, and this mortal must put on immortality'. (1 Corinthians 15.51-53 KJV)

What all this is saying is that there is a generation of Christians who are not going to experience death. They will simply have their bodies changed from mortal to immortal. It seems incredible. Our God is incredible.

Let us pray. Father God, we thank you so much for your word. So rich and full of truth, so encouraging. Sanctify us in the truth, Lord. Thy Word is the truth.

Build us up, Lord. Build us strong, Lord. Strong in Spirit – strong in Jesus – strong in Love.

Lord, if your Word has quickened something in our Spirits today – Help us to respond to you. If we need to forgive someone – show us Lord.

If somebody we know needs encouragement, help us to be your vessel of encouragement. If we need to warn or rebuke someone, may it be in love and in the right spirit.

Grant us wisdom and maturity, Lord, that we might bear fruit, fruit which remains. That we might truly be your disciples, both in word and deed.

Bless us Lord, and Father we ask that you do complete the good work you have started in each of us, not just for our sakes, Father, but in order that we might be more fruitful in service to you, and let us never forget it is for your pleasure that we are created – and not our own – for we are bought with a price: the precious Blood of our Saviour.

In Jesus' name we ask and pray. Amen.

Rapture or Tribulation

Those of you who buy the *Listener* will have noticed on the cover the headline 'Apocalypse Now'. If you have read the article, you would have come across a startling piece of information: a Christian group in America, claiming that the Rapture or Translation of the church is going to take place on the 28 October 1992. In the light of such a startling announcement, I thought it would be good if we had a look at some of the things the Bible has to say about this issue. I doubt if there is any subject in the Bible upon which the teaching today is less clear. Even eminent Bible scholars seem to hold opposing views on the subject, but this certainly did not apply to the apostle Paul. Not only did he teach about the Second Coming even to new converts but said very plainly in the book of 1 Thessalonians,

> I command you in the name of the Lord to read this letter to all the Christians. (1 Thessalonians 5:27)

The richness of Paul's teaching in Thessalonica is evident. During one month the apostle had not only led them to Christ, but had taught them many of the great doctrines of the faith. This includes alluding to the Trinity, the Holy Spirit, the Second Coming. He clearly distinguishes between the Rapture or Translation and the Day of the Lord. He also refers to assurance, conversion, election, resurrection, sanctification and Christian behaviour. All that in that month.

What happened after that? I assume they were busy living it out and passing it on. I am digressing. The point is, the return of Jesus was an important part of Paul's teaching, and I am sure it should be today. Interestingly, the book of Revelation, which has quite a lot to say on this subject also, is the only book in the Bible in which God provides a special blessing to those who read, and hear what it says, and keep the things which are written.

We have to read it, listen to what it says, keep those things in our hearts. Jesus himself had a great deal to say about his return. Perhaps the first and very important thing to note is that scripture differentiates between 'The Day of our Lord Jesus Christ' ('The Day of the Christ') and 'The Day of the Lord.'

There are six scriptures in the New Testament relating to the 'Day of our Lord Jesus Christ' (1 Corinthians 1:8, 1 Corinthians 5:5, 2 Corinthians 1-14, Philippians 1:6, Philippians 1:10, Philippians 2:16). In all six references, the Day of Christ is connected to the reward or blessing of the church. This is in clear contrast to the Day of the Lord which is related to judgment upon sin and unbelief.

> Alas, for the Day the Lord is at hand, and as destruction from the Almighty shall it come. (Joel 1:15 KJV)

> ...a day of darkness and of gloom, a day of clouds and of thick darkness. (Joel 2:2 KJV)

I should explain what the words 'Rapture' or 'Translation' refer to because you won't find them in the Bible. In Corinthians we read:

> But I am telling you this strange and wonderful secret: we shall not all die, but we shall all be given new bodies! It will all happen in a moment, in the twinkling of an eye, when the last trumpet is blown. For there will be a trumpet blast from the sky, and all the

Christians who have died will suddenly become alive, with new bodies that will never, never die; and then we who are still alive shall suddenly have new bodies too. For our earthly bodies, the ones we have now that can die, must be transformed into heavenly bodies that cannot perish but will live forever. (1 Corinthians 15:51-53)

In 1 Thessalonians we read:

For this we say to you by the word of the Lord, that we who are alive and remain until the coming of the Lord shall not precede them which are asleep. For the Lord himself shall descend from Heaven with a shout, with the voice of the Archangel, and with the trump of God: And the dead in Christ shall rise first. Then we who are alive and remain shall be caught up together with them in the clouds, to meet the Lord in the air. And we shall ever be with the Lord. Therefore, comfort one another with these words. (1 Thessalonians: 4:15-17 KJV)

It is quite clear from these scriptures that some Christians will not experience death but will be changed from mortal to immortal. Hence the term Rapture or Translation. The big debate throughout church history has been whether this event will take place prior to the seven-year Tribulation, sometime during the Tribulation or right at the end when Jesus returns to rule the world for a thousand years. As I have pointed out, there is a clear distinction in scripture between 'The Day of the Lord Jesus Christ' and 'The Day of the Lord'. I think there is enough scriptural evidence to suggest that the Day of our Lord Jesus Christ refers to the coming for his Bride, the church. Coming for both the dead and the living with plenty of evidence to show that he is coming when we least expect it.

> Therefore be ye also ready, for in such an hour as you think not, the Son of man shall come. (Matthew 24:44 KJV)

There are a number of other scriptures in which Jesus warns of his unexpected return. Those Paul refers to, and in the letters to the churches in Revelation.

Jesus coming for his church is going to catch a lot of people totally by surprise. That is why Paul says:

> But of the times and the seasons, brethren, ye have no need that I write unto you.
> For yourselves know perfectly that the day of the Lord so cometh as a thief in the night. For when they shall say, Peace and safety; then sudden destruction cometh upon them, as travail upon a woman with child; and they shall not escape.
> But ye, brethren, are not in darkness, that that day should overtake you as a thief. Ye are all the children of light, and the children of the day: We are not of the night, nor of darkness. Therefore let us not sleep, as do others; but let us watch and be sober. For they that sleep, sleep in the night; and they that be drunken are drunken in the night. But let us, who are of the day, be sober, putting on the breastplate of faith and love; and for an helmet, the hope of salvation. For God hath not appointed us to wrath, but to obtain salvation by our Lord Jesus Christ, who died for us, that, whether we wake or sleep, we should live together with him. Wherefore comfort yourselves together, and edify one another, even as also ye do. (1 Thessalonians 5:1-11 KJV)

There is a clear distinction drawn in the chapter between 'they' and 'ye' and 'them' and 'us'. Verse three:

For when *they* shall say peace and safety then sudden destruction cometh upon *them*.

Verse nine,

For God has not appointed *us* to wrath, but to obtain salvation by our Lord Jesus Christ.

Now there are many who would argue that this verse simply refers to eternal life with Jesus and does not necessarily mean we are to be spared from the Tribulation, but there are other scriptures which are more explicit:

For like a snare shall it come on all them that dwell on the face of the whole earth. Watch ye, therefore, and pray always that you be accounted worthy to escape all these things that shall come to pass, and to stand before the Son of man. (Luke 21:35-36 KJV)

Ephesus: Or else I will come unto thee quickly and will remove your lampstand out of its place. (Revelation 2:4)

Sardis: If therefore, thou shalt not watch, I will come on thee as a thief, and thou shalt not know what hour I will come upon thee.

In the letter to the church at Philadelphia, Jesus puts it very clearly and says:

Because you have patiently obeyed me despite the persecution, therefore, I will protect you from the time of great Tribulation and temptation, which will come up in the world to test everyone alive. Look I am coming soon. Hold tightly to the little strength you have – so that no one will take away your crown. (Revelation 3:10-11)

That the church is going to be removed before the time of Tribulation is indicated in 2 Thessalonians:

> And now, what about the coming again of our Lord Jesus Christ and our being gathered together to meet him? Please don't be upset and excited, dear brothers, by the rumour that this day of the Lord has already begun. If you hear of people having visions and special messages from God about this, or letters that are supposed to have come from me, don't believe them. Don't be carried away and deceived regardless of what they say.
>
> For that day will not come until two things happen: first, there will be a time of great rebellion against God, and then the man of rebellion will come – the son of hell. He will defy every god there is and tear down every other object of adoration and worship. He will go in and sit as God in the temple of God, claiming that he himself is God. Don't you remember that I told you this when I was with you? And you know what is keeping him from being here already; for he can come only when his time is ready. (2 Thessalonians 2:1-8)

The restrainer is the Holy Spirit, working through the believers. When the church is translated, the restraining influence on lawlessness will be removed. This world is not going to be a nice place to live in, believe the scriptures. Another confirmation that the church is to be removed is found in the book of Revelation. After the letters to the churches in Revelation, the scene moves to heaven. It is interesting that the church is not mentioned again until the end of Revelation.

I, Jesus, have sent my angel to you to tell the churches all these things. I am both David's Root and his Descendant. I am the bright Morning Star. (Revelation 22:16)

Back to Revelation 4:4. There we see 24 elders with gold crowns, clothed in white raiment:

> Twenty-four smaller thrones surrounded his, with twenty-four Elders sitting on them; all were clothed in white, with golden crowns upon their heads. (Revelation 4:4)

Crowns throughout the New Testament are exclusively presented as rewards for the faithful in the church. The appearance of these elders, already glorified, crowned and enthroned, before the opening of the sealed book of judgments and before the end-time judgments are loosed upon the world, indicates that the church will not be subjected to the wrath and judgments of the Tribulation. The next passage too, seems very clearly to be speaking of the translated church.

> They were singing him a new song with these words: 'You are worthy to take the scroll and break its seals and open it; for you were slain, and your blood has bought people from every nation as gifts for God. And you have gathered them into a kingdom and made them priests of our God; they shall reign upon the earth. (Revelation 5:9-10)

So, where is all this leading? It is leading to the parable of the ten virgins.

> The Kingdom of Heaven can be illustrated by the story of ten

bridesmaids who took their lamps and went to meet the bridegroom. But only five of them were wise enough to fill their lamps with oil, while the other five were foolish and forgot. (Matthew 25:1-3)

They were all virgins which suggest they were all Christians. They all had lamps, and they must have been burning while they were all waiting for the bridegroom. Whilst the bridegroom tarried, they all slumbered and slept. But five were foolish and five were wise, five had extra oil for their lamps. The foolish ones had let their lamps go out, and they had no more oil. Five were ready and five were not. What did the wise advise the foolish to do? 'Go to them that sell and buy it for yourselves'.

There is a whole message in this parable alone. But the points are. They were all Christians. Five were ready. Five were not. The five who were not ready were advised to go and buy more oil. Jesus' warning from this parable was:

> Watch therefore; for you know neither the day nor the hour in which the Son of man cometh. (Matthew 5:13 KJV)

The message of this parable is clearly exemplified in the last two letters to the churches in Revelation.

To the Philadelphia church, the church who was ready, Jesus says,

> Because you have kept the word of my patience, I will keep you from the Tribulation.

But to the Laodicean church, the church who was not ready, he says,

> Because you are lukewarm and neither hot nor cold, I will spit you out of my mouth.

And he goes on to say,

> I council thee to buy of me gold tried in the fire.

Faith purified through Tribulation or fire.

The issues for us are perfectly clear. Jesus is going to come for his Bride, the church. He is going to come unexpectedly and will catch many unawares. Those who are ready and waiting will be taken up. Those who are not ready will be left to face the horrors of the Tribulation.

Let me make this perfectly clear. Salvation is not the issue.

> If any man's work shall be burned, He shall suffer loss; but he himself shall be saved, yet as by fire. (1 Corinthians 3:15 KJV)

There is so much more that can be said. I heard on the news that Mikhail Gorbachev was calling for a Global Government, and there has been much talk and negotiating behind the scenes between Israel and her enemies. There are clear indications that we are moving closer to a One World Government and the Antichrist or world ruler. But as we have seen, this world leader will not be revealed until after the restrainer has been removed. Scripture seems to teach that the Holy Spirit working through the believers or the church is that restrainer.

Let us pray. Lord Jesus, only you know the hour and the day when you will come for your church. But you warned us Lord; 'Watch and pray always that ye may be accounted worthy to escape these things which shall come to pass.'

Lord, make us worthy. Help us to be ready when you come, Lord Jesus, those of us who lack oil for our lamps. We are your vessels, Lord. Recharge us with the oil of the Holy Spirit. Holy Spirit, we know that you came to lead us into all truth, to be our comforter and to prepare the bride for the coming Bridegroom. Dear Holy Spirit, I ask you to complete that work of preparation in our lives in order that we will be ready when our Bridegroom comes. Help us to be ready, I pray.

We need your help please, Holy Spirit. Dig deep into our hearts and our lives. I ask that there may be no sin (not past nor present) to hinder us in our walk with Jesus.

Come, Holy Spirit, we need you. Come, sweet Spirit, we pray. Come in your strength and your power. Come in your own gentle way.

In Jesus' name we ask, amen.

Two Kingdoms – Two Days – Two Resurrections

What on earth is going to happen? I want to clear up some myths and misconceptions which are all too prevalent in the church today. This is not surprising. Scripture warns us clearly that in the last days this would happen.

> There is going to come a time when people won't listen to the truth, but will go around looking for teachers who will tell them just what they want to hear. They won't listen to what the Bible says but will blithely follow their own misguided ideas. (2 Timothy 4:3-4)

> They *will go to church*, yes, but they won't really believe anything they hear. Don't be taken in by *people* like that... (2 Timothy 3:5)

Contrast this with Paul's words:

> For we speak as messengers from God, trusted by him to tell the truth; we change his message not one little bit to suit the taste of those who hear it; for we serve God alone, who examines our heart's deepest thoughts. (1 Thessalonians 2:4)

> Gods words will always prove right no matter who questions them. (Romans 3:4)

> God's truth stands firm like a great rock and nothing can shake it. It is a foundation stone with these words written on it, 'The Lord knows those who are really His.' [Those who listen and obey Him.] (2 Timothy 2:19)

> Those who are really his, hear what he is saying and obey him. For thou [God] has magnified thy word above all thy name? (Psalm 138:2 KJV)

And one final scripture:

> My words are plain and clear to anyone with half a mind, if it is only open. (Proverbs 8:9)

Even a child or a person with limited intelligence can hear what God is saying. Hearing just requires an open mind. That we should have a clear understanding of these matters is made clear. Thessalonians, which deals with these issues, is the only book in the Bible which carries with it a special command from the Lord.

> I command you in the name of the Lord to read this book to all the Christians. (1 Thessalonians 5:27)

The book of Revelation also begins and ends with a special promise.

> If you read this prophecy aloud to the church, you will receive a special blessing from the Lord. Those who listen to it being read and do what it says will also be blessed. For the time is near when these things will all come true. (Revelation 1:3)

There are a number of very important instructions to the church in Revelation, especially in the letters to the churches, which are Jesus' final instructions to his church. It concludes saying,

> Blessed are those who believe it and all else written in the scroll. (Revelation 22:7)

Much confusion exists among believers today simply because many have not learned to distinguish between the 'Kingdom of God' and the 'Kingdom of Heaven'. The note in the Schofield Bible (Page 1002) on Matthew 6:33 states:

> The expression 'Kingdom of God', although used in many cases as synonymous with the 'Kingdom of Heaven', is to be distinguished from it in some instances.
>
> The Kingdom of God is at times viewed as ever-lasting and universal, i.e. the rule of the sovereign God over all creatures and all things.
>
> The Lord has made the Heavens his throne, and his Kingdom rules over all'. (Psalm 103:19)
>
> His Kingdom is an everlasting Kingdom and his dominion, from generation to generation. (Daniel 4:3 NKJV)

Right now the world may be regarded as a province of the great Kingdom of God, currently in revolt. Certainly, the world is not in a state of rest, far from it.

For you and me or anyone else to be subjects of the Kingdom, we must be born again. Jesus said:

> Verily, verily I say unto thee, except a man be born of water and the Spirit, he cannot enter the Kingdom of God. (John 3:5 KJV)

Are you with me so far? Now comes the important part of this section of the message. When we are born of water and the Spirit, or born again, we enter the Kingdom of God as newborn babies (or if you like, 'milk sucking Christians'), but – and it is a very big but – not all who are born again will enter the Kingdom of Heaven.

The Kingdom of Heaven refers to Christ's Millennium Reign on earth. In a sense, the Kingdom of Heaven is under the auspices of the Kingdom of God and at the end of the thousand-year Millennium Rule of Christ, it will once again become part of the Kingdom of God. It is going to take our Lord and his Bride 1000 years to achieve this. Not surprisingly, Jesus himself referred to the devil as ruler of this world.

Note from the Schofield Bible (Page 1248) Corinthians 15:24:

> The Kingdom, once established under David's Divine Son, our Lord Jesus Christ, has for its objective the restoration of the Divine authority on the earth which currently may be regarded as a revolted province of the great Kingdom of God. See also Scofield Bible (Page 1002) Matthew 6:33.

Jesus came as the promised Messiah, for the purpose of restoring the Kingdom again on Earth.

> From that time Jesus began to preach and to say, 'Repent for the Kingdom of Heaven is at hand.' (Matthew 4:17 KJV)

This passage is very relevant:

> See to it that you win your full reward from the Lord. For if you wander beyond the teachings of Christ you will leave God behind; while if you are loyal to Christ's teachings you will have God too. Then you will have both the Father and the Son. (2 John 8-9)

Following Israel's rejection of their King and his Kingdom, the whole focus of Jesus' message changed:

> From that time forth Jesus began to show His disciples how He must go into Jerusalem and suffer many things from the Elders and Chief Priests and Scribes and be killed and be raised again on the third day. (Matthew 16:21 KJV)

Who was it that rejected the Messiah and his message of the Kingdom? That is right. The religious leaders. The established church. Nothing has changed.

However, when we grasp the important distinction between the Kingdom of God and the Kingdom of Heaven, this passage is no longer confusing.

> Not everyone that sayeth unto me, 'Lord, Lord,' shall enter the Kingdom of Heaven, but he that doeth the will of my Father, who is in Heaven. (Matthew 7:21 KJV)

Obedience is the key to entering the Kingdom of Heaven.

Also Matthew 25:1-12 and the parable of the ten virgins. All were virgins; all had lamps; all were waiting for the bridegroom. Five were wise; five were foolish; five were taken; five were left.

Did they lose their salvation? No, not necessarily. See 1 Corinthians 10:3-15. Compare with Revelation 3:14-22.

> I know you well, you aren't strong but you have tried to obey. (Revelation 3:8)

> Because you have patiently obeyed me despite the persecution, therefore I will protect you from the time of Great Tribulation

and temptation that will come upon the world to test everyone alive. Look I am coming soon! Hold tightly to the little strength you have so that no one will take away your crown. (Revelation 3:10-11)

Crowns are associated with Christ's Millennial Kingdom – the Kingdom of Heaven.

I saw four and twenty elders sitting clothed in white raiment; and they had on their heads crowns of gold. (Revelation 4:4 KJV)

Note in the Schofield Bible (page 1356). Revelation 4:4:

The very word 'elder' has church significance. (1 Timothy 5:17 and Titus 1:8) Crowns throughout the New Testament are exclusively presented as rewards to the faithful in the church.

The appearance of these elders, already glorified, crowned and enthroned before the opening of the sealed book of judgements (Revelation 5) and before the end time judgements are loosed upon the world (Revelation 6-18) reaffirms that the faithful are not to be subjected to the judicial wrath and judgements of that time. See John 5:24; Romans 5:9; 1 Thessalonians 1:10; 1 Thessalonians 5:1-11; Revelation 3:10.

The letter to the Laodicean church represents the five foolish virgins. Have they lost their salvation? No. But listen to Jesus's words:

But since you are merely lukewarm, I will spit you out of my mouth. [Left behind at the Rapture. Another translation is 'I will vomit you out of my mouth.'] ... My advice to you is to buy pure gold from me, gold purified by fire... Only then will you be truly rich. I will let anyone who overcomes or conquers, sit beside me on my throne, just as I took my place with My Father on His throne when I had conquered. (Revelation 3:16-21)

Faith tested by persecution and Tribulation: the fifth seal.

And when he broke open the fifth seal, I saw an altar, and underneath it, all the souls of those who had been martyred for preaching the Word of God and for being faithful in their witnessing. They called loudly to the Lord and said, 'Oh sovereign Lord, holy and true, how long will it be before you judge the people of the earth for what they have done to us? When will you avenge our blood against those living on the earth?' White robes were given to each of them and they were told to rest a little longer until their other brothers, fellow servants of Jesus, had been martyred on the earth and joined them. (Revelation 6:9-11)

This group of martyred Christians includes members of the Laodicean Church who responded to Jesus and became overcomers during the early part of the Tribulation.

After this I saw a vast crowd, too great to count, from all nations and provinces and languages, standing in front of the throne and before the Lamb, clothed in white, with palm branches in their hands. And they were shouting with a mighty shout, 'Salvation comes from our God upon the throne, and from the Lamb.' And now all the angels were crowding around the throne and around the Elders and the four Living Beings, and falling face down before the throne and worshiping God. 'Amen!' they said. 'Blessing, and glory, and wisdom, and thanksgiving, and honour, and power, and might, be to our God forever and forever. Amen!'
Then one of the twenty-four Elders asked me, 'Do you know

who these are, who are clothed in white, and where they come from?'

'No, sir,' I replied. 'Please tell me.'

'These are the ones coming out of the Great Tribulation,' he said; 'they washed their robes and whitened them by the blood of the Lamb. That is why they are here before the throne of God, serving him day and night in his temple. The one sitting on the throne will shelter them; they will never be hungry again, nor thirsty, and they will be fully protected from the scorching noontime heat. For the Lamb standing in front of the throne will feed them and be their Shepherd and lead them to the springs of the Water of Life. And God will wipe their tears away.' (Revelation 7:9-17)

The very large group of martyrs, too great to count, are those who have turned to God through the preaching of 144,000 faithful Jews.

It is the Jews who will fulfil or complete the Great Commission, not the Gentiles.

We will now move on to the second part of this message, Two Days. The Day of the Lord and the Day of Christ. The first and most important thing that we must understand about Jesus' return is that there are two very different and specific events which have confused as being the same. This also has led to much false teaching and confusion amongst believers. Scripture clearly differentiates between the Day of our Lord Jesus Christ (Day of Christ), and the Day of the Lord.

The scriptures relating to the Day of our Lord Jesus Christ are: 1 Corinthians 1:8, 1 Corinthians 5:5, 2 Corinthians 1:14, Philippians 1:6, Philippians 1:10 and Philippians 2:16.

In all six references, the Day of Christ is connected to the reward or blessing of the church. This is in clear contrast to 'The

Day of the Lord', which is related to judgement upon sin and unbelief.

> A day of darkness and gloom, a day of clouds and thick darkness. (Joel 2:2 KJV)

The Day of the Lord refers to a specific period of seven years as described in Matthew 24:9-22, Revelation 6-18 and many other places in scripture both the Old and New Testaments.

The Day of the Lord begins after the restrainer is removed and the man of sin is revealed.

> For that day shall not come, except there come the falling away first, and that man of sin be revealed, the son of perdition. (2 Thessalonians 2:3 KJV)

In other parts of scripture, he is referred to as the Antichrist.

The Day of Christ, which precedes the Day of the Lord, is going to catch many by surprise, both those in the world and those in the church. He is coming when we least expect it.

> Therefore, be ye also ready, for in such an hour as ye think not the Son of Man cometh. (Matthew 25:13 KJV)

In the letter to the churches in the book of Revelation, there are a number of references to his unexpected return.

> Ephesus: Or else I will come unto thee quickly, and will remove your lamp stand out of its place.

> Sardis: If therefore thou shalt not watch, I will come to thee as a thief and thou shall not know what hour I will come upon thee.

As we have just seen in the parable of the ten virgins, five were ready and waiting. Five were caught out and Jesus' warning,

> So, stay awake and be prepared, for you do not know the date or the moment of My return. (Matthew 25:13)

Now, this is in total contrast to Jesus' return at the end of the seven-year Tribulation, to take up his rightful role as 'King of the Nations'. This is a totally predictable event.

After the appearance of the Antichrist, or false world ruler, who negotiates a 'peace treaty' between Israel and her enemies, it will literally be possible to number the days until the Tribulation ends and our Lord returns. This is the time referred to in scripture as Daniel's 70th week, a period of seven years.

For those believers enduring the Tribulation, it will be a great source of comfort to know that their Redeemer is coming and when. They will literally be able to count the days to his return.

Jesus is coming twice. Firstly, prior to the Tribulation to gather up his Bride before the trouble starts. Secondly, at the end of the Tribulation to take his rightful place as ruler of the nations and ruler in the Kingdom of Heaven on earth. The Bride, those in the church who are ready, are going to be spared from the Tribulation (Zephaniah 2:3; Malachi 4:1-2; Luke 21:35-36).

> For when they shall say 'Peace and safety,' then sudden destruction cometh upon them. (1 Thessalonians 5:3)

> For God has not appointed us to wrath but to obtain salvation by our Lord Jesus Christ. (1 Thessalonians 5:9)

There is a clear distinction in these two passages. In verse 3, it is 'they' and 'them'. Whereas in verse 9 it talks about 'us'.

Paul's careful alternation of the pronouns 'they' and 'us' throughout this passage is sufficient to show that he never conceived of the church or the 'Bride' remaining on earth during the Tribulation or the time of wrath. There are other scriptures to substantiate this.

> For like a snare shall it come on all them that dwell on the face of the whole earth. Watch ye, therefore and pray always that ye be accounted worthy to escape all these things that shall come to pass, and to stand before the Son of Man. (Luke 21:35-36 KJV)

In the letter to the church at Philadelphia, Jesus puts it very clearly:

> Because ye have patiently obeyed me despite the persecution, therefore I will protect you from the time of Great Tribulation and temptation which will come upon all the world to test everyone alive. Look I am coming soon. Hold tightly to the little strength you have so that no one will ever take away your crown. (Revelation 3:10-11)

Contrast that with the words spoken to the Laodicean Church.

> 'But since you are lukewarm, I will spit [or vomit] you out of my mouth. (Revelation 3:16)

So, Two Kingdoms, Two Days. Now to Two Resurrections.

We have already seen those who are part of the First Resurrection. They include all those Christians described here.

> For thou wast slain and hast redeemed us to God by thy blood out of every kindred, and tongue, and people, and nation. And

hast made us unto our God, a Kingdom of Priests, and we shall reign on Earth. (Revelation 5:9-10)

They called loudly to the Lord and said, 'O Sovereign Lord, holy and true, how long will it be before you judge the people of the earth for what they've done to us? When will you avenge our blood against those living on the earth?' White robes were given to each of them, and they were told to rest a little longer until their other brothers, fellow servants of Jesus, had been martyred on the earth and joined them. (Revelation 6:10-11)

After this I saw a vast crowd, too great to count, from all nations and provinces and languages, standing in front of the throne and before the Lamb, clothed in white, with palm branches in their hands. And they were shouting with a mighty shout, 'Salvation comes from our God upon the throne, and from the Lamb.' And now all the angels were crowding around the throne and around the Elders and the four Living Beings, and falling face down before the throne and worshiping God. 'Amen!' they said. 'Blessing, and glory, and wisdom, and thanksgiving, and honour, and power, and might, be to our God forever and forever. Amen!'

Then one of the twenty-four Elders asked me, 'Do you know who these are, who are clothed in white, and where they come from?'

'No, sir,' I replied. 'Please tell me.'

'These are the ones coming out of the Great Tribulation,' he said; 'they washed their robes and whitened them by the blood of the Lamb. That is why they are here before the throne of God, serving him day and night in his temple. The one sitting on the throne will shelter them; they will never be hungry again, nor thirsty, and they will be fully protected from the scorching noontime heat. For the Lamb standing in front of the throne will feed them and be their Shepherd and lead them to the springs of the Water of Life. And God will wipe their tears away.' (Revelation 7:9-17)

Then I saw thrones, and sitting on them were those who had been given the right to judge. And I saw the souls of those who had been beheaded for their testimony about Jesus, for proclaiming the Word of God, and who had not worshiped the Creature or his statue, nor accepted his mark on their foreheads or their hands. They had come to life again and now they reigned with Christ for a thousand years. This is the First Resurrection. (The rest of the dead did not come back to life until the thousand years had ended.) Blessed and holy are those who share in the First Resurrection. For them the Second Death holds no terrors, for they will be priests of God and of Christ, and shall reign with him a thousand years. (Revelation 20:4-6)

And I saw a Great White Throne and the one who sat upon it, from whose face, the earth and sky fled away but they found no place to hide.

I saw the dead, great and small, standing before God, and the books were opened, including the Book of Life. And the dead were judged according to the things written in the books, each according to the deeds he had done. The oceans surrendered the bodies buried in them; and the earth and underworld gave up the dead in them. Each was judged according to his deeds. 'And death and hell were thrown into the lake of fire. This is the second death – the lake of fire. And if anyone's name was not found in the Book of Life, he was thrown into the lake of fire. (Revelation 20:11-15)

'For forty years I watched them in disgust,' the Lord God says, 'They were a nation whose thoughts and hearts were far away from Me. They refused to accept my laws. Therefore, in my wrath I swore they would never enter the promised land, the place of rest I planned for them'. (Psalm 95:10-11)

The Millennium Reign of Christ represents the seventh day in God's time calendar: the day of rest he planned for the earth (Isaiah 11:10 & 14:7).

Time to Get Serious

We have had a brief look at the letters to the churches in Revelation which contain Jesus' final instructions to his church. In this message, we go back to the start of Jesus' ministry.

> While they were living in Nazareth, John the Baptist began preaching out in the Judean wilderness. His constant theme was, 'Turn from your sins ... turn to God ... for the Kingdom of Heaven is coming soon.' Isaiah the prophet had told about John's ministry centuries before! He had written, I hear a shout from the wilderness, 'Prepare a road for the Lord – straighten out the path where he will walk.' (Matthew 3:1-3)

> With water I baptize those who repent of their sins; but someone else is coming, far greater than I am, so great that I am not worthy to carry his shoes! He shall baptize you with the Holy Spirit and with fire. He will separate the chaff from the grain, burning the chaff with never-ending fire and storing away the grain. (Matthew 3:11-12)

> From then on Jesus began to preach. 'Turn from sin, and turn to God, for the Kingdom of Heaven is near.' (Matthew 4:17)

John the Baptist was described as a voice crying in the wilderness. He was a type of Elijah in his day. And God promises to send yet another Elijah during the Tribulation.

> See, I will send you another prophet like Elijah before the coming of the great and dreadful judgment day of God. His preaching will bring fathers and children together again, to be of one mind and heart, for they will know that if they do not repent, I will come and utterly destroy their land. (Malachi 4:5-6)

The 'great and dreadful judgement day of God', refers to the second half of the Tribulation. That verse shows clearly how utterly important Godly fathers are, and indeed, Godly families.

We need to take notice. God sends his prophets when the church has strayed off track. Nehemiah – John the Baptist – Jesus too, they didn't mess around. When the church strays off track through disobedience, God sends his prophets. Nehemiah was a classic example.

> Some Jewish men had married foreign women and the children could not speak in the language of Judah at all. [I presume that was Hebrew.] So I argued with these parents, and cursed them, and punched a few of them, and knocked them around and pulled out their hair; and they vowed before God that they would not let their children intermarry with non-Jews. (Nehemiah 13:23)

John was a voice crying in the wilderness. It was a wilderness alright. A wilderness of unbelief, false teaching, compromise and straight out disobedience. The God they were worshipping was the false God of humanism, Religion based on man's terms. The sin of Cain. Their deeds did not match their religious talk. Hence John's warning.

> Don't try to get by as you are, thinking we are safe, we are Jews [today read, 'Christians']. (Matthew 3:9)

Jesus' warning to the Laodicean church makes this abundantly clear.

> I know you well – you are neither hot nor cold; I wish you were one or the other! But since you are merely lukewarm, I will spit you out of my mouth! You say, 'I am rich, with everything I want; I don't need a thing!' And you don't realize that spiritually you are wretched and miserable and poor and blind and naked. (Revelation 3:15-17)

Lukewarm is not good enough. Although modern versions say, 'I will spit you out of my mouth.' The original text says, 'I will vomit you out.'

In far too many instances, we have reduced the gospel to a gospel of salvation, a gospel of grace, the wonderful love of God and his glorious promises, and these are all true and a very necessary part of our spiritual life. We have latched on to the first part of the Great Commission – 'Go into all the world and preach the gospel' – but ignore the vitally important second part – 'Teaching them to obey all I command you.'

And the consequences are serious, Jesus warns us:

> At the Judgment many will tell me, 'Lord, Lord, we told others about you and used your name to cast out demons and to do many other great miracles.' But I will reply, 'You have never been mine. Go away, for your deeds are evil.' (Matthew 7:22-23)

Our God is an incredible God. There is no other God remotely like him. But he is so much more than a 'Sugar Daddy' God, to which, in too many cases, the church has reduced him today. He is the Lord of the Armies of Heaven. He is the Lord of Justice. He is a God who demands obedience. Jesus said, 'If you love me, obey me'

(John 14:15). He is the God of wrath. He hates sin in any form. His ways are higher than our ways.

He cannot dwell where there is sin and disobedience – hence so many weak and powerless churches. They may call themselves the House of God, but he has long since departed from the scene, if he was ever there to start with. I quote Mark Steyn from an article he wrote in *Investigate* magazine:

> None of the pillars of what we regard as conventional society is quite as sturdy as it was, and most of them have collapsed. Many mainstream Protestant churches are to one degree or another, post-Christian. If they no longer seem disposed to converting the unbelieving to Christ, they can at least convert them to the boggiest of soft-left political clichés. In this world, if Jesus were alive today, he'd most likely be a gay Anglican Vicar in a committed relationship, driving around in an environmentally-friendly car with an 'Arms are for Hugging' sticker, on the way to interfaith dialogue with a Wiccan and a couple of Wahhabi imams.

Obviously, this is an extreme example, but in far too many instances the church is worshipping a 'False Christ' with a worldly life style. The 'in' words are 'inclusiveness' and 'tolerance.' And it is totally unacceptable to our Heavenly Father and our Lord Jesus Christ. And the consequences are extremely serious.

If Jesus, who knew no sin, walked in the Fear of the Lord, how much more so must we? Look! We need to wake up, we need to come to terms with the fact that when we are born again, it is a totally new life with a totally new life-style, with a totally new set of rules to live by.

All of us. Male and female. We are no longer our own selves – we are bought with a price. We should have as much interest in the things of the world as a dead person.

God's word, not mine.

And if we try and do it alone, we will fail. We need the help and empowerment of the Holy Spirit. And the hardest part of all – we must be willing to die to self. And it is not easy.

The answer lies in Christ. We must abide in him. If the branch is not attached to the vine, it withers and dies and ends up getting burnt. Abiding is absolutely crucial to our spiritual walk and growth. Abiding and obedience.

When we allow the so-called pleasures of the world to crowd Jesus out of our lives, when we allow the world's values system to push aside or over-rule the commandments of Jesus, we are headed for trouble and we will not – cannot – grow spiritually. We simply cannot have it both ways. There is no room in the Kingdom for New-Age theology, or political correctness or cultural correctness, or gender correctness.

The way forward for the church is backwards. Back to the truth. Hence Jesus' words regarding the church at Sardis:

> I know your reputation as a live and active church, but you are dead. Now wake up!
> Strengthen what little remains – for even what is left is at the point of death. Your deeds are far from right in the sight of God. Go back to what you heard and believed at first; hold to it firmly and turn to me again. Unless you do, I will come suddenly upon you, unexpected as a thief, and punish you. (Revelation 3:1-3)

We need to study and think deeply about what Jesus is saying in this letter. It goes right to the heart of modern-day Christianity.

Go back to what you heard and believed at first.

This is totally consistent with what the apostle John writes.

> So keep on believing what you have been taught from the beginning. If you do, you will always be in close fellowship with both God the Father and his Son. (1 John 2:24)

> See to it that you win your full reward from the Lord. For if you wander beyond the teaching of Christ you will leave God behind; while if you are loyal to Christ's teachings, you will have God too. Then you will have both the Father and the Son. (2 John 1:8-9)

Obedience to what Jesus taught us in the beginning is so very important. The way forward for the church is back. Back to the truth.

We need to change our lifestyles and priorities. Every one of us – from church leaders to new converts. The time is so short. He is going to come back – suddenly and unexpectedly – and only for those he 'knows,' only those who are ready.

Luke-warmness is not acceptable. From here on it has to be his way.

Each one of us has to re-examine the Scriptures, especially the New Testament Commandments and seek to obey them in every way.

It is time to stop playing church. People need to see Christ in us. Shining out of us, like lights in a dark world. And that can only come from abiding.

We need to turn off the television and computer and spend more time with him, in his presence and in his Word. Far less time pursuing our own pleasures and more time seeking to know him better, and please him. For his pleasure, we are created. Not ours. We need to understand that Agape love is in total contrast to what the world considers to be love.

> If I gave everything I have to the poor people, and if I were burned

alive for preaching the gospel but didn't love others, it would be of no value whatever.

Love is very patient and kind, never jealous or envious, never boastful or proud.

Never haughty or selfish or rude. Love does not demand its own way. It is not irritable or touchy. It does not hold grudges, and will hardly even notice when others do it wrong. It is never glad about injustices, but rejoices when truth wins out.

If you love someone you will be loyal to him/her no matter what the cost. You will always believe in him, always expect the best of him, and always stand your ground in defending him. (1 Corinthians 13:3-7)

When a Christian is abusive, or rude, or touchy or selfish, all our religious pretence is shown for what it is; just that, religious pretence, and we do much damage to the Kingdom of God.

People have to see a difference in us. They have to see Jesus' love in us. Agape love is different. It is love on a whole new level.

It is love in spite of. It is not indulgence. It is not even based on feeling good about someone. Agape desires God's very best for the other person. Agape comes from God. God's love is Agape love.

Never was Agape love better demonstrated than on the Cross of Calvary.

We need to start demonstrating Agape love to a world crying out for it.

The verses in 1 Corinthians 13 are not just nice words to be read at wedding ceremonies.

The scriptures are so much more than printed words. God's words are living and powerful, sharper than a two-edged sword.

The world needs to be able to see Jesus in us. Remember, he is the Word made flesh. And he instructs us:

> If you refuse to take up your cross and follow Me, you are not worthy of being Mine. If you cling to your life, you will lose it, but if you give it up for Me, you will save it. (Matthew 10:38-40)

Dying to self. It is not easy. Dying to the world and its pleasures. It is not easy.

Dying to our religion. It is not easy. God is not religious. Men (people) are.

Let us come aside from the world and its pleasures and ask the Holy Spirit to bring each one of us to that place where Paul said,

> I do not want anyone to think more highly of me than what they can see in my life and my message. (2 Corinthians 12:6)

That is true Christianity.

Make no mistake. Truly the time is short. A special crown awaits all those who long for his return. The Rapture of the church is imminent.

But in the words of the late Edward Miller, 'The Rapture will be for the enraptured.'

Truly the Kingdom of Heaven is at hand. Our Lord is coming for his Bride. In the parable of the ten virgins – five were ready, five were not.

We must repent and change our ways if we don't want to miss out.

Jesus said:

> Watch and pray always that you might be accounted worthy to escape these things which shall come to pass and stand before the Son of man... (Luke 21:36 KJV)

Blessed and holy are those who share in the First Resurrection.

> For them the second death holds no terrors, for they will be priests of God and of Christ, and shall reign with Him for a thousand years. (Revelation 20:6)

How can anything in this life compare with that? I will let Jesus have the last word:

> Look! I have been standing at the door and I am constantly knocking. If anyone hears Me calling and opens the door, I will come in and fellowship with him, and him with Me. I will let everyone who conquers sit beside Me on my throne, just as I took my place with My Father on his throne, when I had conquered.
> Let those who can hear, listen to what the Spirit is saying to the churches. (Revelation 3:20-23)

*There is a river of joy
flowing through the city of our God
the sacred home of the God above all gods.*
(Psalm 46:4)

Staying Calm During Crises

The Apostle Peter discusses many issues that are very relevant to the church today, for there is much happening in the world and in our nation which suggests that our present world system really is coming to an end.

There is no doubt that God's hand of judgment is upon our nation and upon his church.

> Lo, I am with you always, even to the end of the Age. (Matthew 28:20 KJV)

But we are not to be surprised at what is happening. Peter says,

> Beloved, do not be surprised at the fiery ordeal among you, which comes upon you for your testing, as though some strange thing were happening to you; But to the degree that you share the sufferings of Christ, keep on rejoicing. (1 Peter 4:12-13 NASB)

> Since Christ suffered and underwent pain, you must have the same attitude he did; you must be ready to suffer, too. For remember, when your body suffers, sin loses its power, and you won't be spending the rest of your life chasing after evil desires but will be anxious to do the will of God. You have had enough in the past of the evil things the godless enjoy – sex sin, lust, getting drunk, wild parties, drinking bouts, and the worship of idols, and other terrible sins. Of course, your former friends will be

very surprised when you don't eagerly join them anymore in the wicked things they do, and they will laugh at you in contempt and scorn. But just remember that they must face the Judge of all, living and dead; they will be punished for the way they have lived. That is why the Good News was preached even to those who were dead – killed by the flood – so that although their bodies were punished with death, they could still live in their spirits as God lives. The end of the world is coming soon. Therefore be earnest, thoughtful men of prayer. Most important of all, continue to show deep love for each other, for love makes up for many of your faults. Cheerfully share your home with those who need a meal or a place to stay for the night. (1 Peter 4:1-8)

Of course we cannot cover all Peter discusses in one chapter but there are some good things we can talk about.

And because God is their judge too, the dead had to be told the Good News as well. (1 Peter 4:6 Jerusalem Bible)

After his death, Jesus told the Good News to those who had died in the flood. He did this because they, like us, must face the 'judge of all'. There are an enormous number of 'spiritually dead' people around us today who need to hear the Good News of Jesus. And it is Good News. Nothing has changed. The angels brought good tidings of great joy to the shepherds. Jesus came preaching the Good News of the gospel of the Kingdom. Philip, the evangelist, told the Ethiopian eunuch the Good News of Jesus.

That is exactly what it would have been to the eunuch, Good News. Good as in amazing, astonishing, marvellous, wonderful. You see, in Israel eunuchs were not allowed to be part of God's people. They had been physically disfigured, and so they could not belong. But Philip was able to point out that that was no longer the case; that in Jesus all those barriers were broken down. That the Christian community is a community from which no one is excluded, unless they choose so themselves.

Good News indeed, for someone who had always been excluded because of his disfigurement. Philip had explained to him who Jesus was, that in him God had drawn near to man and that through Jesus there is forgiveness of sin, that men and women are set free from past and present bondages, delivered from demons, healed from sickness and that we might have life, and have it more abundantly. Moreover, nobody, regardless of their colour, their race, their sex or their physical state, whether of high birth or low, rich or poor is excluded from this community who wishes to be included. Nothing. Absolutely nothing. That has got to be Good News.

> As they rode along, they came to a small body of water, and the eunuch said, 'Look! Water! Why can't I be baptized?' 'You can,' Philip answered, 'if you believe with all your heart.' And the eunuch replied, 'I believe that Jesus Christ is the Son of God.' (Acts 8:36)

But we need to preach the full gospel of Jesus Christ. I quote from the latest *Intersermon* magazine.

> We need to preach not just the gospel of 'God loves you', but also, 'he hates your sin'. Jesus died for our sins.

We need to repent, confess and turn from sin in order to receive forgiveness, and we need to forgive others. We need to tell about the cross, repentance, the need for a transformed life and, most important, how to come into victory and remain in victory. Not just 'God loves you as you are, receive this blessing!'

Pray that we will not compromise the gospel by preaching partial truths in order to 'win converts' rather than 'make disciples' That is most important. We must preach the whole gospel. We must heed Paul's warning:

> For the time will come when they will not endure sound doctrine but, wanting to have their ears tickled, they will accumulate for themselves teachers in accordance to their own desires. (2 Timothy 4:3 NASB)

But back to our passage. Peter challenges us:

> The end of the world is coming soon. Therefore be earnest, thoughtful men of prayer.

We are told to be calm or clear minded and self-controlled in order that we might pray. Not walking in the flesh, not looking at the problems around us but looking to Jesus. Taking 'his yoke upon us'. Filled with and led by the blessed Holy Spirit. I like that. We need to pray and we will need to respond to many needs around us. We will need discernment. Lord, in the midst of the clamour and all the turmoil, let us hear your voice, let us meet your needs, let us be vessels of your love.

Which brings us to verse 8 of 1 Peter 4:

> And above everything else be sure that you have real deep love for each other, remembering how love can cover a multitude of sins.

Where do we get this love? Jesus. How do we get this love? Abiding.

> Abide in me, and I in you. As the branch cannot bear fruit of itself,

unless it abides in the vine, so neither can you unless you abide in me. I am the vine, you are the branches, he who abides in me and I in him, he bears much fruit, for apart from me you can do nothing. (John 15:4 KJV)

Fruit comes from abiding. Love comes from abiding. Power comes from abiding.

If you abide in me, and my words abide in you, ask whatever you wish, and it will be done for you. (John 15:7 KJV)

God's promise is expressed in a song we sing:

There is no condemnation for them in Christ Jesus, who walk every day with the Lord. (Romans 8:1 KJV)

You may well ask. How do I abide? Just take time off and be alone with Jesus. It might be praying in English or in tongues. It might be singing praise. It might be meditating on his Word. It might be studying the Bible. It might be just enjoying his presence, just resting in his love. Most important, it is coming apart from the busyness of life, just to be alone with him.

Coming, Ready or Not

The main thrust of this message is the parable of the ten virgins that Jesus tells as part of his teaching.

> Then shall the kingdom of heaven be likened unto ten virgins, which took their lamps, and went forth to meet the bridegroom. And five of them were wise, and five were foolish. They that were foolish took their lamps, and took no oil with them. (Matthew 25:1-3 KJV)

It is no coincidence that this parable follows on immediately from the previous chapter which relates to both Jew and Gentile, saved and unsaved. The parable of the ten virgins is aimed directly at Christians. In considering this, it is important that we understand the time in which we are living, and the things which are happening in the world today and how they relate to this parable.

Certainly, a lot of world attention is focussed on the Middle East at present, and well it might be. It is very obvious as we see events unfolding on the world scene, events which were prophesied thousands of years ago by Old Testament prophets, our Lord Jesus himself, and the apostles in the New Testament. It is important that we understand and how it relates to us as a church and as individual Christians.

Many times in scripture we are warned to 'watch, be on alert, know what is happening.' In Mark 13 alone, Jesus warns us six times ending with,

> Keep a sharp lookout! For you do not know when it will come, at evening, at midnight, early dawn or late daybreak. Don't let me find you sleeping. Watch for my return! This is my message to you and to everyone else. (Mark 13:35-37)

At the end of the first letter to the Thessalonian church, a letter that has much to say about Jesus' unexpected and sudden return for those who are ready. Paul writes:

> I command you in the name of the Lord read this letter to all the Christians. (1 Thessalonians 5:27)

In Revelations it says:

> Blessed is he who reads and those who hear the words of the prophecy, and heed the things which are written in it, for the time is near. (Revelation 1:3 KJV)

Jesus instructs us:

> Learn a lesson from the fig-tree. When its tender shoots appear and are breaking into leaf, you know that summer is near. In the same way when you see all these things, you may know that the end is near, at the very door. I tell you this: the present generation [us] will live to see it all. Heaven and earth will pass away; my words will never pass away. (Matthew 24:32-34 NEB)

The fig-tree in this parable is seen as representing the nation of Israel. The nation of Israel was re-born again as a nation on the 14 May 1948. The fig-tree has put forth its leaves.

Most books written on Bible prophecy seem to agree on at least a few things:

1. Sometime in the not too distant future, there will be a war in the Middle East as described in Ezekiel chapter 38. It is hard to believe that events happening in the region at present are not connected with the fulfilment of this prophecy.

2. This war is going to cause much concern to many people. Perhaps it will involve chemical weapons and even a nuclear attack. Whatever; people will be sickened by what happens.

3. Something is going to trigger a world financial crash which will plunge the world into a major financial crisis, and a major recession which will cause serious hardship and probably outright anarchy. Every man for himself.

4. Twice, David Pawson has come to New Zealand from England to warn us of this impending financial crash.

5. The Rev. Ron McKenzie, the Presbyterian minister at Waikaka Valley in Gore, has issued a similar warning. He warns of serious social upheaval.

6. A world leader will arise (probably from out of Europe) who will bring apparent peace and apparent financial and social stability. He will introduce a new One World Government and a new world money system, and he will be successful in negotiating a Peace Treaty between Israel and her enemies. The signing of the peace treaty will mark the beginning of the seven-year Tribulation, or Day of God's wrath mentioned many times in Scripture.

This world leader (or Antichrist as he is referred to in the Bible) will be hailed as a great leader and will indeed claim to be the Messiah returned to take up his role as King of the nations.

He will appear to be assassinated and then come back to life again. He will have supernatural power. As Jesus was God in human form, this false Messiah will be the devil in human form. He will deceive a great many people including the Jews. Many Christians, including church leaders, will believe that he is the Messiah.

Remember, one of Satan's main attributes is his ability to deceive; he can appear as an angel of light, and Jesus warns us, he will deceive many, even the very elect. There are many other things he will do as he consolidates his position, including requiring people to worship him and to have a number tattooed on them in order to buy, sell or trade. God forbids us to receive this mark.

This false Messiah or Antichrist will ultimately be responsible for the slaughter of millions of Jews and Christians. No one in their right sense wants to have to, or see their loved ones, endure the absolute horror and trauma of the Tribulation. Approximately two thirds of the world's population will be killed; everything in the sea will die. Jesus warns:

> In fact, unless those days are shortened, all mankind will perish. But they will be shortened for the sake of God's chosen people. (Matthew 24:22)

Jesus warns us regarding all these things:

> Keep a constant watch. And pray that if possible, you may be accounted worthy, and arrive in my presence without having to experience all these horrors. (Luke 21:36)

Before the appearance of the Antichrist, before the Tribulation – the day of God's wrath, or the Day of the Lord. Suddenly, unexpected by many, Jesus is going to come down and rescue his Bride from the impending disaster. One thing is certain. His coming is imminent, but it is going to catch a lot of believers by surprise. Hence his warning,

> But I will reply, 'You have never been mine. Go away, for your deeds are evil.' (Matthew 7:23)

and the parable of the ten virgins.

In five of the letters to the churches in the book of Revelation, Jesus admonishes and points out areas where there is need for repentance or overcoming:

Ephesus: You have left your first love.

Pergamon: False teaching.

Thyatira: False prophets – Women in leadership over men.

Sardis: You think you are alive. But you are dead.

Laodicea: Neither hot nor cold-lukewarm, wretched-miserable-poor-blind-naked. A real need for repentance and overcoming in the Laodicean church.

Only two of the churches are acceptable as they are, without having to repent and overcome in a number of areas:

Smyrna: the suffering church. We in the West cannot claim to be Smyrna Christians. We have not had to suffer – even to the point of death – for our faith.

Philadelphia: The smallest –

I know you well; you aren't strong, but you have tried to obey and have not denied my Name. Therefore I have opened a door to you that no one can shut. 'Note this: I will force those supporting the causes of Satan while claiming to be mine (but they aren't – they are lying) to fall at your feet and acknowledge that you are the ones I love. 'Because you have patiently obeyed me despite the persecution, therefore I will protect you from the time of Great Tribulation and temptation, which will come upon the world to test everyone alive. (Revelation 3:8-10)

Remember the letters to the churches in Revelation are Jesus' final instructions for his church before he comes for his Bride. For this reason alone, we ignore his messages at our peril. Without exception, to all seven churches he warns, 'Listen to what the Spirit is saying to the churches.' We too must listen to what the Spirit is saying. Note where Jesus is in relation to the Laodicean church. Outside, knocking, trying to gain entrance into his church. Wanting them to open the door and invite him in.

This brings us back to where we started, the parable of the ten virgins. The message is simple.

Five were wise, and five were foolish. Five were ready and prepared when the bridegroom came, five were not and those that were not ready missed out. The door was shut.

I want to make one thing clear; the issue here is not salvation.

Notice the language of this parable. It was midnight. It speaks of ten virgins, lamps, oil and a bridegroom. This is symbolic language. It is a spiritual picture of events that Jesus is trying to implant in the hearts and minds of his people.

First of all, ten virgins. The term virgin in scripture means clean, pure, holy. They were all Christians washed clean by the blood of Jesus. They had all been born again. They most probably all went to church. They were not five believers and five unbelievers. They all had lamps and not only that, all ten lamps were lit and burning. There is no reason to believe that any of the lamps were brighter than the rest. We read:

> Thy word is a lamp to my feet, and a light to my path. (Psalm 119:105 KJV)

The lamp is God's Word. They all had God's Word. His instructions. They knew the scriptures. And they all had oil, a symbol used in scripture to signify the Holy Spirit.

They all knew the bridegroom was coming. They were all waiting.

The Bible refers to Jesus as the Bridegroom, and indeed the church is often referred to as the Bride of Christ. Jesus Christ is coming back for his Bride.

> This same Jesus who is taken up from you to Heaven, shall come again in the same manner as you have seen Him go. (Acts 1:7 KJV)

He is coming back with a physical body. A body which will have nail holes in his hands and feet.

Now comes the difference. Five were wise. Five were foolish. Certainly, we are not saved by works or what we do. Salvation is by grace, and grace alone. But the issue here is the reward we get.

> See to it that you win your full reward from the Lord. (2 John 1:8)

There are degrees of rewards for Christians. There are different levels of spiritual growth. Babies, young men, fathers. Each time Jesus speaks to the seven churches in Revelation he says, 'I know your works.'

Paul says:

> In a great house there are different vessels, some to honour, some to dishonour. (2 Timothy 2:21 KJV)

We have the choice then of changing from a seldom used vessel to one that is greatly valued and often used. A vessel of honour. Who has the prerogative? Is it God's sovereignty? No, 'if a man purges himself from these, he shall be a vessel of honour'. No question the blessed Holy Spirit will help us with the purging, but it is our choice.

> Let us be glad and rejoice and honour him; for the time has come for the wedding banquet of the Lamb, and his bride has prepared herself. (Revelation 19:7)

It says, 'The Bride has prepared herself, made herself ready,' and yet many Christians think they can drift through life, or even busily be following false doctrine, and that when Jesus comes they will be instantly transformed into St Mary, St John, St Agatha, St Rupert, or whoever. No! The 'Bride' has made herself ready.

The late Rev. Edward Millar used to teach,

> The rapture, when it comes, will be for the enraptured. Those who truly love Jesus.

How does God know those who truly love him? Simple.

> If you love me, you will Obey me.

The deciding factor in this parable was the amount of oil, or the presence of God in their lives. Five of them possessed more oil than the other five and at midnight when the cry was made, 'The bridegroom is coming, go out and meet him,' five had sufficient oil, five did not. Notice from the parable there obviously had been a price to pay to obtain the extra supply of oil they carried in their vessels. (Go to them that sell and buy for yourselves.) The foolish ones had not been prepared to pay the price up to that time – were not prepared.

The price of abiding. The price of prayer. The price of consecrating their lives to Jesus. The price of giving up the pleasures of this world in order to gain the blessings of God. The price of submitting to the Lordship of Jesus in every area of our lives. The price of obedience to every word of God. Let us not wait till the midnight hour before we start to do our preparing for his return. Now is the time to get the oil in our vessels, because suddenly and without warning, the trumpet will blow, Jesus will return to gather up his Bride, the restrainer will be removed, the Antichrist will be revealed, and the Tribulation will begin.

Let us repeat. The issue is not salvation. The issue is that five were prepared and ready when the Bridegroom came. The other five were not. Even when they cried, 'Lord! Lord!' He answered, 'Verily I say to you, I know you not.' I find that incredibly sad.

I am sure that it was not Jesus' fault that he didn't know them. Perhaps they had been so busy doing their own thing, they hadn't spent enough time with him, in order for him to get to know them. Not much time seeking his face. Not much time abiding. If you want that extra oil, there is a price to pay. You may have to be willing to spend more time at his shop. Might have to become a regular customer. Then he will get to know you.

When the Bolshevist revolution occurred in Russia in 1917, the Russian Christian Church was in convention in Moscow. Just six blocks away from the fiercest fighting in which hundreds were being slain. The church closed its convention with a two day debate on whether church officials should wear red or yellow robes in church functions. When the convention adjourned, they had neither robes nor churches in which to wear them. Communism had taken over.

As in Noah's day – they knew not what was happening until the flood came and swept them all away. That is how it will be when the Son of Man comes.

Let us pray. Lord Jesus, I am not sure which is the saddest part of that story. It is so sad that you had to say, 'I know you not,' to half of them, simply because they were not willing to pay the price for extra oil.

Lord Jesus, help us to know you more. Lord, we cannot help but love you when we know you. Lord Jesus, we cannot help but want to obey you, serve you, and please you when we know and love you. Father God, I ask for more oil for our lamps. The oil of the Blessed Holy Spirit. Even if we think we have enough, fill us some more, Lord. Help us to become regular customers.

Come, Holy Spirit, we need you,

Come, Holy Spirit, we pray,

Come in your strength and your power,

Come in your own gentle way.

In Jesus' name we ask and pray. Amen.

Two Faces of Evil

This message was given immediately after the '9/11' attack on the twin towers in America.

No question, we have all been shocked, 'stunned' is probably a better word, by events which have occurred over the past ten days, and I have been thinking a great deal and praying about what I should speak about today.

It is easy, in the light of really major events to take our eyes off the Lord and get caught up in all the action and emotion going on around us.

We need to come aside and listen to what the Spirit of God is saying.

Jesus said:

> Fear not them who kill the body, but are not able to kill the soul, but rather fear Him who is able to destroy both soul and body in hell. (Matthew. 10:28 KJV)

The reference is not to Satan but to God, who alone has power to destroy both soul and body.

Many people were killed in America, but many of those who died are now united with their Saviour. None of us know when our time on earth will come to an end. In the tragedy in Manhattan and the Pentagon, thousands of lives came to an abrupt and sudden stop, but for those whose sins were forgiven and washed clean by the blood of Jesus, their eternal life is assured.

Now I want to talk about another form of evil which is attacking both society and the church today. It is also a clear indication that we are indeed living in the last days of this present age.

I had a friend come to visit last weekend. He brought with him a *Dominion* for me to read. In it was a column entitled 'Honest to God' written by a minister. In part he wrote:

> The church and the world now have a name for these devout folk who insist that because the stories are in the Bible they must be literally true. These people are called fundamentalists and fundamentalists are not always flavour of the month, even in church circles. Liberal minded clergy who are in favour of homosexuality and who insist on gender correctness, and political and cultural correctness, don't always take kindly to those who dare to suggest that these New Age teachings cannot be reconciled with a literal interpretation of the Bible. Hence the great push by so called New Age scholars to discredit any literal interpretation of the scriptures.

What does God have to say about this issue? Plenty.

> You may as well know this too, Timothy, that in the last days it is going to be very difficult to be a Christian. (2 Timothy 3:1)

> For there is going to come a time where people won't listen to the truth, but will go around looking for teachers who will tell them just as they want to hear. They won't listen to what the Bible says but will blithely follow their own misguided ideas. (2 Timothy 3:3-4)

The note in the Schofield Bible on apostasy states,

Apostasy is irremediable and awaits judgement (2 Thessalonians 2:10-12; 2 Peter 2:17,21; Jude 11-15; Revelation 3:14-16).

Paul speaking of the Antichrist says:

> He will completely fool those who are on their way to hell because they have said, 'No' to the truth; they have refused to believe it and love it, and let it save them, so God will allow them to believe lies with all their hearts, and all of them will be justly judged for believing falsehood, refusing the Truth, and enjoying their sins. (2 Thessalonians 2:10-14)

Can you not hear what the Spirit of God is saying? Horrendous as the events in America are, evil and shocking to the extreme as the behaviour of Osama Bin Laden and his terrorist followers might seem, they cannot rob us of our eternal life in Jesus.

But imposters, who masquerade as men of God, ministers of the church are leading God's people away from the truth, and worse, much worse, are leading them to destruction, at best having to face the horrors of the Tribulation and martyrdom for their faith, at worst to eternal destruction. Hence Jesus' warning:

> Fear not them who kill the body, but are not able to kill the soul, but rather fear Him who is able to destroy both soul and body in hell. (Matthew 10:28 KJV)

It is absolutely imperative that we hold fast to the truth in the days ahead. We are clearly warned:

> For the time will come when they will not endure sound doctrine, but after their own lusts, shall heap to themselves teachers, having itching ears... (2 Timothy 4:3 KJV)

For there is going to come a time when people won't listen to the truth but will go around looking for teachers who will tell them just what they want to hear. They won't listen to what the Bible says but will blithely follow their own misguided ideas. Stand steady and don't be afraid of suffering for the Lord. Bring others to Christ. Leave nothing undone that you ought to do. (2 Timothy 4:3-5)

Jesus speaking to the Philadelphian church says:

Because you have patiently obeyed me despite the persecution, therefore I will protect or keep you from the time of Great Tribulation and temptation which will come upon the world to test everyone alive. (Revelation 3:10)

Jesus is addressing these words to us. If we desire to hold fast to the truth, we are going to face opposition, yes, and persecution. And note, the Philadelphian church was not a mega-church.

You aren't strong, but you have tried to obey.

It is imperative that we have absolute trust and faith in the Word of God. All of it. Not just the parts we like the sound of.

The words of the Lord are pure words, like silver tested in a furnace of earth, purified seven times. Thou shalt keep them, Oh Lord, thou shalt preserve them from this generation forever. (Psalm 12:6-7 KJV)

All scripture is given by inspiration of God, and is profitable for doctrine, for reproof, for correction, for instruction in righteousness. That the man of God may be perfect, thoroughly furnished unto all good works. (2 Timothy 3:16-17)

Here is what the Schofield Bible says about this verse:

> Every word of the Holy Scripture is inspired by God or God-breathed. Without impairing the intelligence, individuality, literary style, or personal feelings of the human authors, God supernaturally directed the writing of Scripture so that they recorded, in perfect accuracy, His comprehensive and infallible revelation to man. If God himself had done the writing, the written word would be no more accurate and authoritive than it is.

In the last days of this present church-age, truth and the integrity of God's Word will increasingly come under attack. It will be, and indeed already is, difficult to stand against popular opinion and say, 'This is wrong', 'This is not what the scriptures teach, not what Jesus commanded.'

But in considering world events, we recognise that the trap has not yet sprung,

The Tribulation has not yet started, but don't forget Jesus' warning:

> For like a snare shall it come on all them that dwell on the face of the whole earth. Watch ye, therefore, and pray that ye may be accounted worthy to escape all these things that shall come to pass, and to stand before the Son of man. (Luke 21:35-36 KJV)

Let us recapitulate on three points:

1. We must stand strong in the truth. Whatever happens, and no matter how difficult, we must not bow down to false New-Age doctrines. Remember it says,

> And he will completely deceive those who are on their way

to destruction because they have said 'No' to the Truth. (2 Thessalonians 2:10)

2. We need the help of the Holy Spirit.

When He, the Spirit of Truth, is come, He will guide you into all Truth; for He shall not speak of himself; but whatever He shall hear, that shall He speak, and He will show you things to come. He shall glorify Me; for He shall receive of Mine; and shall show it unto you. (John 16:13-14 KJV)

3. We have received the Holy Spirit.

But you have received the Holy Spirit and he lives within you, in your hearts, so that you don't need anyone to teach you what is right. For He teaches you all things, and He is the Truth, and no liar, and so just as He has said, you must live in Christ, never to depart from Him. (1 John 2:27)

It's called abiding. And remember, if we stay close to Jesus we won't be sinning, or getting led astray. We need the help and empowering of the Holy Spirit as we cannot stand alone. We also need the help and guidance of the Holy Spirit to discern what the will of God is and to know how to pray. To know when to pray for peace and when not to.

4. Even as things are starting to turn to custard in the world and the church, remember we are the restraining influence in society.

We are the salt of the earth... We are the light of the world. (Matthew 5:13-14)

After the Rapture of those who are ready, when Jesus comes for his Bride, things will really deteriorate here on earth, because the restraining influence will have been removed. Remember the parable of the ten virgins, only five were ready.

So, until he comes. We must continue to be salty. We must let our lights shine brightly. We must continue restraining the evil influences in society and the church, through prayer, intercession, example, and when necessary through speaking the truth in love.

> I must work the works of him that sent me, while it is day: the night cometh, when no man can work. (John 9:4 KJV)

We must keep working while it is still day. Be encouraged, hear Jesus' words.

> When you see all these things begin to come to pass, look up, for your redemption draws nigh. (Luke 21:28 KJV)

Understanding the Times

It is imperative we understand the time we are living in.

The leaders of Israel and the Christians in the early church did and it was something Jesus sought to make clear in his ministry.

> From the tribe of Issacher there were 200 leaders of the tribe – all men who understood the temper of the times and knew the best course for Israel to take. (1 Chronicles 12:32)

> These men [the Bereans] were more noble, in that they received the word with all readiness of mind, and searched the scriptures daily, whether those things were true. (Acts 17:11)

In Matthew 24:32 and again in Mark 13:28 Jesus said we are to,

> Learn a parable of the fig tree.

The fig tree represents the nation of Israel who after 2000 years, on May 14, 1948, was reborn.

> Who has heard or seen anything as strange as this? For in one day, suddenly a nation, Israel, shall be born, even before the birth pains come. In a moment, just as Israel's anguish starts. The baby is born; the nation begins. Shall I bring to the point of birth and then not deliver? Asks the Lord your God. No! Never! (Isaiah 66:7-9)

Back to the parable of the fig tree:

> Let the fig tree teach you a lesson. When its branches become green and tender, and it starts putting out leaves, you know summer is near. In the same way, when you see these things happening, you will know that the time is near, ready to begin. Remember this! All these things will happen before the people now living have all died. Heaven and earth will pass away; my words will never pass away. (Mark 13:28-31 TEV)

Most translations say 'this generation shall not pass away'. However, Jesus goes on to say:

> No one knows, however, when that day or hour will come – neither the angels in heaven, nor the Son; only the Father knows. Be on watch, be alert, for you do not know when the time will be. (Mark 13:32-32 TEV)

Here is how various versions translate the call to action:

NIV: Be on guard! Be alert.

KJV: Take ye heed, watch and pray.

Phillips: Keep your eyes open, keep on the alert.

TLB: Stay alert. Be on the watch for my return.

Jerusalem Bible: Be on your guard. Stay awake.

RSV: Take heed, watch.

NEB: Be alert, be watchful.

Too many Christians today have taken the words 'No one knows the day or the hour' as an excuse to keep on as they have been. Ignoring Jesus' repeated warnings, six times in Mark 13; but also in Zephaniah 2:1-3 and Malachi 4:1-2.

> Watch out! Don't let my sudden coming catch you unawares; don't let me find you living in careless ease, carousing and drinking and occupied with the problems of this life, like all the rest of the world. Keep a constant watch. And pray that if possible you may arrive in my presence without having to experience these horrors. (Luke 21:34-36)

> For those will be days of such horror as have never been since the beginning of God's creation, nor never will be again. And unless the Lord shortens that time of calamity, not a soul on earth will survive. (Mark 13:19)

Do you hear and understand what Jesus is saying?

I doubt many Christians in the West today, truly understand the seriousness of the current world situation. Too many are of the belief that because we go to church we are all going to be taken out of this world and spared the horrors of the Tribulation, when Jesus comes for his bride. Ignoring the warning Jesus gave,

> And pray that if possible you may arrive in my presence without having to experience these horrors. (Luke 21:36)

If you need further confirmation of the warnings Jesus gave, read and study the letters to the churches in Revelation chapters 2 and 3.

Only two Churches are acceptable as they are without serious changes.

These letters are Jesus' final instruction before the Tribulation begins. Without exception he warns, 'listen to what the Spirit is saying'.

Jesus also warns a great number of Christians are going to be taken totally by surprise at his coming: Matthew 24:43; Luke 12:39; 1 Thessalonians 5:2 and 5:4; 2 Peter 3:10; Revelation 3:3 and 16:15 – seven warnings, and there are more.

He also warns,

> There will be weeping and wailing and gnashing of teeth by those who ignore his warnings and are left to face the Tribulation and have their faith tested by fire. (Matthew 8:12; 22:13; 24:51 and 25:30)

These warnings in Matthew refer to those believers left behind at the rapture because they lacked sufficient oil, as in the parable of the ten virgins. (See the sermon 'Coming, Ready or Not' earlier in this book.)

The next reference is more serious:

> And there will be great weeping and gnashing of teeth as you stand outside and see Abraham, Isaac, Jacob, and all the prophets within the Kingdom of God. (Luke 13:28)

This group has been locked out of the Kingdom of God. They have no further opportunity to overcome and be saved. They may well be Christians who received the mark of the beast.

It is necessary to stress all those left behind at the rapture and are left to face the horrors of the Tribulation have not at this point lost their salvation, but they do need to become overcomers and have their faith tested by fire.

To those who do overcome, Jesus makes a wonderful promise:

> To him that overcomes, I will give him the right to sit with me on my throne. (Revelation 3:21 NIV)

How did these believers become overcomers during such a difficult time?

> And they overcame him (Satan) by the blood of the Lamb, and by the word of their testimony, and they loved not their lives, even unto death. (Revelation 12:11)

It is going to cost them a great deal of suffering and ultimately their lives, in many cases by beheading or the guillotine.

Sadly, many will fall away during this time, accept the mark of the beast and lose their eternal salvation. This is why the devil is trying so hard to drag as many Christians into the Tribulation as he can. He knows his time is short.

This is why the apostle John sounds a warning:

> Watch out for the false leaders – and there are many of them around – who don't believe Jesus Christ came to earth as a human being with a body like ours. Such people are against the truth and against Christ. Beware of being like them and losing the prize you and I have been working so hard to get. See to it you win your full reward from the Lord. (2 John 7-8)

> But no one knows the date and hour when the end will be – not even the angels. No, nor even God's Son. Only the Father knows. (Matthew 24:26)

The devil's mantra. No need to worry, not likely to happen for another 50 years.

We are the generation who have witnessed the birth of Israel. We are the people living at this time referred to in Matthew 24:30 who will see the return of Jesus for his Bride.

There is much false teaching in the church today, exactly as the apostles warned would occur, at this time.

Paul, Peter, John and Jude all warned about this. Many preach we will see a major revival before the Tribulation occurs, but this is not consistent with what Jesus said:

> But will the Son of Man find faith on earth when He comes. (Luke 18:8).

> As in the days of Noah so shall the coming of the Son of Man be. When I return the world will be as indifferent to the things of God as the people were in Noah's day. They ate and drank and married everything just as usual right up to the day when Noah went into the ark and the flood came and destroyed them all. (Luke 17:26-27)

> And the world will be as it was in the days of Lot: People went about their daily business – eating and drinking, buying and selling, farming and building – until the morning Lot left Sodom. Then fire and brimstone rained down from heaven and destroyed them all. Yes, it will be business as usual, right up until the hour of my return. (Luke 17:28-30)

The letters to the churches in the book of Revelation dispel any doubts of that teaching.

Yes, 'many' will come to salvation during the seven years of tribulation. They are the overcomers mentioned in Revelation 6:9

and those who respond to the preaching of the 144,000 faithful Jewish witnesses in Revelation 7.

The vital message for the church today is that Jesus is going to come suddenly.

> I will come suddenly upon you, unexpected as a thief. Keep a sharp lookout. Don't let me find you sleeping. Watch for my return. (Revelation 3:3)

Is it any wonder Jesus warns us?

> Watch out, don't let my sudden coming catch you unawares, don't let me find you living in careless ease, carousing and drinking, occupied with the problems of this life, like all the rest of the world.
> Keep a constant watch. And pray that if possible you may arrive in my presence without having to experience these horrors. (Luke 21:34-36)

More on the Letters to the Churches
(Revelation 2 & 3)

Although I delved briefly into these letters to the churches in a previous message, 'Tested By the Word of God' (page 264), the truth is these letters contain such a treasure trove of rich and relevant teaching for the church today. We do well to dig a little deeper.

From the very beginning of the church these letters have remained, and continue to do so as a benchmark by which individual churches and individual Christians can measure their spiritual progress.

When Jesus repeats the words, 'Listen to what the Spirit is saying,' seven times in succession, we need to take heed.

Although these seven letters have had relevance throughout church history, the main purpose of this message is to show clearly the importance of these messages to both the church corporate and us as individual believers today, as in, 'to him that has an ear', and, 'to him that overcometh'.

These letters which are Jesus's final instructions before His sudden, and in many instances unexpected, return for His bride show the natural progression of evil and deception which have crept into the church during the past 2000 years.

It started with the Ephesian Church which although doing many good things at the start left its first love for Jesus and ended up falling from a great height to the point where He warned them, 'unless you repent and do the works you did at first, I will come suddenly (the Rapture) and remove your lampstand.'

The note in the McArthur Study Bible on 2 John verses 6 and 9 shines an interesting light on the true meaning of love:

> This is love, that we walk according to His commandments.

The apostle John defines love not as an emotion or sentiment, but as obedience to God's commandments. In John 14:21 Jesus spells it out clearly:

> The one who obeys me is the one who loves me, and because he loves me, my Father will love him; and I will too and I will reveal myself to him.

Note 3 in the Scofield Bible on page 1147 shines more light on this verse:

> The Lord correlates love for Him with obedience to Him. To love Christ means to care enough about Him to keep His commandments.

This should not surprise us. Jesus is the 'word become flesh'. Jesus and His words are inseparable as indeed is God the Father and His word.

> Those who remain obedient to Christ's commandments remain in fellowship with both the Father and the Son. (2 John 1:9)

> Stay always within the boundaries where God's love can reach you and bless you. (Jude 1:21)

These boundaries are contained within the commandments of Christ.

Where the Ephesian Church found itself in trouble, then and equally so today, was by being led astray by false teaching and turning back to worldly pleasures.

We will now move on to the next letter to Smyrna the suffering church. I am sure it is no coincidence that Jesus held up Smyrna as an example to Ephesus. Whereas Ephesus had fallen so far that Jesus warned them unless they repented He would remove their lampstand, He found no fault with Smyrna, but encouraged them to hold on and be faithful even unto death. It's worth recalling from Acts 9:31,

> The believers learned how to walk in the fear of the Lord and the comfort of the Holy Spirit.

The fear of the Lord ensures that we hate those things which God hates. The comfort of the Holy Spirit keeps us walking on the path of Truth. This is true Christianity.

Notice Jesus's words of encouragement to the Smyrna Christians:

> Do not fear what you are about to suffer. Behold, the devil is about to throw some of you into prison, that you may be tested. Be faithful unto death and I will give you the crown of life. The one who conquers will not be hurt by the second death.

Next we go to the Church in Pergamum. This church is being addressed by Him who wields the sharp and double bladed sword. This sword signifies judgement on those who attack His people and destroy His church (Revelation 16). Also, the double bladed sword represents the two edges to the sword of Truth encompassed in Jesus's commandments.

So often today the church is being fed single edge theology. Half truths from a blunt sword. Here are some examples:

> 'Go into all the world and preach the gospel...' (Mark 16:15)

The church has willingly taken up this portion of the commandment but the more important part of the message '...teaching them to obey all I have commanded you', is often overlooked.

> For God so loved the world that He gave His only begotten Son that whosoever believes in Him should not perish but have everlasting life. (John 3:16)

This is a very well known scripture. But John 3:36 is equally important:

> He who has the Son has life, but he who does not have the Son does not have life but the wrath of God abides on him.

I have heard this half-scripture quoted many times:

> Therefore, there is now no condemnation to them who are in Christ Jesus... (Romans 8:1 KJV)

But like all of God's promises, it is conditional:

> ...to those who walk every day not after the flesh but after the Spirit.

> My prayer for you is that you will overflow more and more with

love for others, and at the same time keep on growing in spiritual knowledge and insight. For I always want you to see the difference between right and wrong. (Philippians 1:9-10)

Our love for others must never be at the cost of disobedience to Jesus and His righteous commandments. True love is not indulgence. Love desires God's very best for others.

Remember it is a message to obey, not just to listen to. (James 1:22)

Back to Pergamum (Revelation 2:12), Jesus does not mess about with this church. Verse 16 says:

Change your mind and attitude or else I will come to you suddenly [Rapture] and fight against them [followers of Balaam] with the sword of my mouth.'

Next, the Church in Thyatira (Revelation 2:18). This Church is in idolatry. Again, this sounds like a really good church.

I am aware of all your good deeds. Your kindness to the poor, your gifts and service to them; also I know your love and faith and patience, and I can see your constant improvement in all these things. (Revelation 2:19)

This is a 'going-places' church, but there is one serious problem:

You are permitting that woman, Jezebel, who calls herself a prophetess to teach my servants that sex sin is not a serious matter. (Revelation 2:20)

There are a large number of false prophets and prophetesses operating in the spirit of Jezebel in the Church today, rebelling against God's established order for his creation, including mankind, and ignoring the commands of Jesus which remain unchanged. This is manifesting today in unprecedented evil throughout the world. Fornication, adultery, feminism, abortion and homosexuality, children being encouraged to choose their own identity, the breakdown of God's order in the family and in the Church (Isaiah 3:12). The list goes on and on.

These are just some of the horrible fruits of the spirit of Jezebel alive and well today. This is not some historical problem that Jesus is warning about, because He goes on to say in Revelation 2:25,

> Hold tightly to what you have until I come.

This is very obviously a 'today' problem and has only arisen in the past few years. The price of disobedience here is serious.

> Pay attention now to what I am saying. I will lay her upon a sickbed of intense affliction, along with all her immoral followers unless they turn again to me, repenting of their sin with her and I will strike her children dead.

These people are heading straight into the tribulation.

Next is Sardis (Revelation 3:1), where the wheat and tares are growing together (Matthew 13:24) Jesus gets straight to the point.

> I know your reputation as a live and active church, but you are dead. Your deeds are far from right in the sight of God. Go back to what you heard and believed at first. Hold to it firmly and return to me again. Unless you do, I will come suddenly upon you, unexpected as a thief, and punish you. [The rapture and tribulation.]

More on the Letters to the Churches (Revelation 2 & 3)

Matthew 13:30 explains what happens when wheat and tares grow together in the same fellowship. Jesus instructs the reapers at the harvest to gather the tares first and bind them in bundles to be burned. I believe this will be during the tribulation, where they may well have the scales removed from their eyes and become overcomers through the witness of the martyrs of Revelation 6:9 or the preaching of the 144,000 faithful Jewish missionaries.

Jesus follows this with,

> But gather the wheat into my barn.
>
> You do have a few in Sardis who have not soiled their garments with the world's filth; they shall walk with me in white. (Revelation 3:4)

Next is the Philadelphia Church (Revelation 3:7-13). This is not a big church, not strong but trying to obey and have not denied Jesus despite the persecution. This is the only church, apart from Smyrna, in which Jesus finds no fault and undertakes to protect and save them from the time of the Great Tribulation and temptation which is coming upon the world to test the faith of everyone alive; but He warns them,

> Look! I am coming soon! Hold tightly to the little strength you have so that no one will take away your crown.

Before we move onto the Laodicean Church let us summarise what we have learnt so far. As we saw at the start, Jesus emphasises to each and every church, 'Listen to what the Spirit is saying.'

The inference is that in most cases the church being addressed is not listening, even though we are told in John 14:26, 16:13 and 1 John 2:27 that we can trust the Holy Spirit to lead us into all Truth.

Indeed the Holy Spirit is the only teacher we can trust (1 John 2:27).

This leads us to the next question. How do we receive the Spirit of Truth? Luke 11:13 instructs us:

> How much more will your Heavenly Father give the Holy Spirit to those who ask Him.

But, and I emphasise the 'but', we need to be serious with our request. God is not interested in half-hearted and lukewarm requests. Cry out! Ask Jesus! 'Sanctify me in Truth! Your Word is Truth!' Pray and ask God, 'Surround me with your loving kindness and Truth.'

There are times when we need to separate ourselves from the world for a time and just wait on God for His answer.

> If you abide in My Word, you are truly My disciples and you will know the Truth and the Truth will set you free. (John 8:31-32)

Back to the letters to the churches...

The next point to consider is that Jesus promises a special blessing to each church but it is conditional to those who overcome.

Yes, it is addressed to every individual in every church.

Overcoming does not come entirely by Grace. Neither does Truth. Obedience and works play an important role in our spiritual growth.

What is it we must overcome? Anything and everything that could, or is, hindering our spiritual growth.

Love of pleasure, money, false Christs (Matthew 7:15, 7:19, 7:21, 2 John 9-10) and false teaching. Being caught up in New Age religion where inclusiveness and tolerance bring rebellion against Jesus's unchanging commandments.

Any form of anti-semitism, even sitting on the fence is totally unacceptable. We are given clear instructions regarding this precious nation which never again will be driven from their land.

> Take no rest, all you who pray, and give God no rest until He establishes Jerusalem and makes her respected and admired throughout the earth. (Isaiah 62:7)

Let the church never forget Jesus is returning at the end of the tribulation to rule the world for 1000 years from Jerusalem. This alone is one of the many reasons we should be longing and praying for His return (2 Timothy 4:8).

So much for global warming. The world is not coming to an end. We have God's word on it. Nevertheless, 2 John 1:8-9 are important verses,

> See to it that you win your full reward from the Lord. If you wander beyond the teaching of Christ, you leave God behind.

It is quite possible to be saved and born again as children of God, but miss out on the rapture into the Kingdom of Heaven when Jesus comes for His Bride.

The late Dr Neal Patterson's excellent book, *Created to Rule*, gives very sound teaching on this important truth:

> It is possible to be saved, yet fall short of the reward of the Millennium Kingdom. (Pg 57)

> To assume a package deal to all the rights to the Kingdom of Heaven, based solely on the fact of having been born again is both presumptuous and erroneous. The rewards are to be earned. Again, we stress we are not saved by works but we are

save for works and upon these works a believer will be rewarded. (Pg 72)

The question is: What happens to all those who have been born again but are not taken up at the rapture? Have they lost their salvation? Absolutely not, not at that stage (1 Corinthians 3:15)!

Those who are alive at that time and suddenly thrust into the tribulation to have their faith tested by fire will be given a second opportunity to become overcomers.

Those who have died during the church age and not taken up at the rapture will need to wait for the Great White Throne judgement at the end of the 1000 years millennium. If their names are entered in the Book of Life they will be saved and enter into the Kingdom of God.

To be an overcomer during the tribulation,

> They overcame him (satan) by the blood of the lamb, by the word of their testimony, for they loved not their lives even unto death. (Revelation 12:11)

Sadly there will be those who take the mark of the beast and will be thrown into hell. No wonder Jesus warns us in Luke 21:34-36,

> Watch out! Don't let my sudden coming catch you unawares. Don't let me find you living in careless ease, carousing and drinking and occupied with the problems of this life like all the rest of the world. Keep a constant watch and pray that if possible, you may arrive in My presence without having to experience these horrors.

It is not all by grace. We have to do our part also. We have to make the choice. Jesus first or the world's pleasures.

More on the Letters to the Churches (Revelation 2 & 3)

Now to the church in Laodicea (Revelation 3:14-22). I have deliberately left this letter until last. This message is from the One who stands firm, the faithful and true witness:

> I know you well. You are neither hot nor cold. I wish you were one or the other! Since you are merely lukewarm, I will vomit you out of my mouth. (Verse 15)

> You say, 'I am rich with everything I want. I don't need a thing!' And you don't realise that spiritually you are wretched and miserable and poor and blind and naked.' (Verse 17)

> My advice to you is to buy pure gold from Me. Gold purified by fire – only then will you be truly rich. And purchase from Me white garments. Clean and pure, so you won't be naked and ashamed, and get medicine from me to heal your eyes and give you back your sight. (Verse 18)

> I continually discipline and punish everyone I love; so I must punish you unless you turn from your indifference and become enthusiastic about the things of God. (Verse 19)

> Look, I am standing at the door and I am constantly knocking. If anyone hears me calling and opens the door, I will come in and fellowship with him and him with me. (Verse 20)

> I will let everyone who conquers [overcomes] sit beside me on My throne, just as I took my place with my Father on His throne when I had conquered. (Verse 21)

> Let those who can hear, listen to what the Spirit is saying to the churches. (Verse 22)

The Laodicean Church, which is representative of a great number of western style churches today, has fallen short spiritually in every which way possible and remains in total denial.

But – Jesus! Oh, the love of our Saviour!

We see Him locked out, knocking and trying to gain entry into His own church and although He warns them,

> I continually discipline and punish everyone I love; so I must punish you, unless you turn from your indifference and become enthusiastic about the things of God.

He then goes on to make the most incredible promises:

> If anyone [personal] hears me calling and opens the door, I will come in and fellowship with him and he with me. I will let everyone who conquers sit beside me on my throne, just as I took my place with my Father when I conquered. Let those who can hear, listen to what the Spirit is saying to the churches [plural].

In conclusion... The 7 year tribulation, followed by the 1000 year Millennium Kingdom, are both essential to God's great plan of redemption for Israel and indeed all of mankind.

The tribulation which is sent to test the faith of everyone alive grants further opportunities to become overcomers for Christ; albeit at the price of martyrdom.

The anointing of the 144,000 faithful Jewish servants (missionaries) will restore original worship and truth. Note their converts are all clothed in white linen with palm branches in their hands; whereas all the members of the Laodicean Church, as well as many others from some of the other churches, were naked and ashamed, lacking white garments as well as being deaf, blind and in a state of denial.

More on the Letters to the Churches (Revelation 2 & 3)

Denial is rife in the Church today. Thank God for these faithful Jews. It is they who will succeed in fulfilling the Great Commission and restore truth and obedience to the whole world.

Of real concern are the number of prominent church leaders today assuring their new converts of their entry into the Kingdom of Heaven based solely on their new birth. This false teaching, based on a few scriptures quoted out of context, ignores and disregards so much of Jesus's teaching, along with the Apostle's, which show clearly this is not correct.

One often quoted scripture is 1 Thessalonians 4:15-18. The believers being addressed here by the apostle Paul are not new converts, babies in the faith. These are all believers in Jesus and His commandments as in 2 John verses 9 to 10.

In his own words Jesus says in Luke 8:21,

> Believe in Me. Believe in my commandments...

and,

> My brethren are those who hear the word of God and obey it.

These are the ones clothed in white garments, not still naked and ashamed as were Adam and Eve after they disobeyed God, as indeed are all the adherents of the modern day Laodicean Church and many members of the four other churches in Revelation chapters 2 and 3.

We must never forget Jesus paid a terrible price on the cross of Calvary for our salvation and after Pentecost the Church was established through the blood of a multitude of martyrs.

Brother Andrew, founder of the Open Doors Ministry to the suffering church wrote years ago,

Do not believe the Christian Church will go out in a wave of glory but rather it will go down in apparent defeat.

There will be no revival before the Rapture (Luke 17:26-27 and Luke 18:8). Read 'Understanding the Times' in this book.

Dr Neal Patterson's book, *Created to Rule*, addresses this false teaching about immediate entry into the Kingdom of Heaven with clarity and sound scriptural evidence.

Along with Revelation chapters 2 and 3, which we have just delved into, the following scriptures show clearly that entrance into the Kingdom of Heaven is a reward for obedience and works, as against entry into the Kingdom of God which is by grace alone, and the necessity of one's name being written in the Lamb's Book of Life:

Matthew 13:10-17 (but all of chapter 13 is relevant)
Matthew 22, 24 & 25
Luke 21:34-36
Hebrews 3, 4 & 5
2 Peter 3:15-18
2 Timothy 2:19
2 Timothy 3:12-13
Jude 1:5 (but all of Jude is relevant)

To be 'cast into outer darkness' (Joel 2) does not mean to be 'cast into hell', neither does to 'have our work burnt by fire' (1 Corinthians 3:15) and to have 'one's faith tested by fire' (Revelation 3:18) mean a loss of salvation, but further opportunities to be overcomers during the tribulation; initially through the testimonies of the martyrs in Revelation 6:9 and also the witness of the 144,000 faithful Jewish witnesses (Revelation 7 & 13:10).

Those who accept the mark of the beast (Revelation 13) will

More on the Letters to the Churches (Revelation 2 & 3)

lose their salvation and along with the beast and false prophet, will be cast into a lake of fire and brimstone (Revelation 14:9-10 & Revelation 19:20).

Take time out to study all these scriptures. Ask the blessed Holy Spirit to lead you into Truth in this important message for today (1 John 2:27).

Let us never forget the Apostle Paul's words in 1 Thessalonians 2:4,

> For we speak as messengers of God, trusted by Him to tell the truth. We change His message not one bit to suit the taste of those who hear it, for we serve God alone who examines our heart's deepest thoughts.

Maranatha! Come quickly Lord Jesus.

Other Writings

Global Warming is Not the Issue

An issue which has received a great deal of undue publicity of late is that of global warming. Whether you believe or disbelieve the evidence being presented by those who are either for or against this concept, the truth is, it doesn't matter anyway. Global warming is not the biggest issue facing our planet and all life dwelling on it right now. In fact, it doesn't even rate.

An event of far greater importance, something which will impact hugely on every creature on earth, man and beast, in the near future, mostly likely within the next decade, is about to hit planet earth with full force. For those with eyes to see and ears to hear, there are warning signs in abundance.

What am I referring to? The wrath of God. Scripture clearly warns us of a seven-year period, referred to as the Tribulation, when the earth will be punished and cleansed of the evil which permeates it today. The disciples asked Jesus when this would happen.

> 'When will this happen?' the disciples asked him later, as he sat on the slopes of the Mount of Olives. 'What events will signal your return and the end of the world?' (Matthew 24:3)

> And when you hear of wars and insurrections beginning, don't panic. True, wars must come, but the end won't follow immediately. (Matthew 24:7)

Jesus listed a number of events:

> And when you hear of wars and insurrections beginning, don't panic. True, wars must come, but the end won't follow immediately – for nation shall rise against nation and kingdom against kingdom. (Luke 21:9-10)

> For nation shall rise against nation, and kingdom against kingdom: and there shall be earthquakes in divers places, and there shall be famines and troubles: these are the beginnings of sorrows. (Mark 13:8 KJV)

There have been more recorded earthquakes in the past 50 years than in all of previous history since the earth began.

> The world will be at ease, banquets and parties and weddings – just as it was in Noah's time before the sudden coming of the Flood, people would not believe what was going to happen until the Flood actually arrived and took them all away. So shall my coming be. (Matthew 24:37-39)

That the flood did occur has been well documented by geologists; the evidence still remains. It is interesting to recall conditions on the earth prior to the flood.

> Meanwhile, the crime rate was rising rapidly across the earth, and, as seen by God, the world was rotten to the core. As God observed how bad it was, and saw that all mankind was vicious and depraved, he said to Noah, 'I have decided to destroy all mankind; for the earth is filled with crime because of man. Yes, I will destroy mankind from the earth.' (Genesis 6:10-13)

According to the *Babylonian Talmud*, the book of Rabbi's interpretation of the scriptures 1000 years before Christ, there has only been one time in history when men were given in marriage to men and women given in marriage to women. Not Sodom and Gomorrah, not ancient Greece, Rome or Babylon, though homosexuality was rampant in all these cultures.

Homosexual marriages were solemnised during the days of Noah, and according to Jeffrey Satinover, author of *The Criminalization of Christianity*, that is what the Babylonian Talmud attributes as the final straw that led to the flood. Rabbi Aryeh Spero verified this to be true.

Paul wrote to Timothy 2000 years ago saying,

> You may as well know this too, Timothy, that in the last days it is going to be very difficult to be a Christian. For people will love only themselves and their money; they will be proud and boastful, sneering at God, disobedient to their parents, ungrateful to them, and thoroughly bad. They will be hard-headed and never give in to others; they will be constant liars and troublemakers and will think nothing of immorality. They will be rough and cruel, and sneer at those who try to be good. They will betray their friends; they will be hot-headed, puffed up with pride, and prefer good times to worshiping God. They will go to church, yes, but they won't really believe anything they hear. Don't be taken in by people like that. (2 Timothy 3:1-5)

> My people, what has become of you, children are your oppressors, women rule over you. Oh, my people, they who lead you cause you to go astray. Misleaders leading you down the garden path to destruction. (Isaiah 3:12-13)

No one can deny there is much evil in the world today. Even human slavery has reared its ugly head again. When I was a child, there was on average one murder a year. It was big news. Today violence is endemic. We blame the politicians and certainly they are not all innocent. Some of the legislation passed during the last decade is downright evil. Nevertheless, it is the church which must shoulder much of the blame for conditions which prevail in the world today. Many of our pulpits are filled with cowardly men and rebellious women who bring shame to the Christ they claim to serve and to his church.

A brave few are willing to stand against popular opinion and speak out in defence of the truth, but in too many instances their voices are drowned out by the clamour from within the church itself. One of the great tragedies of today is the fact that the church, in many cases, has abandoned its true role as God's voice to his people – both saved and unsaved. Instead of obeying God and rightly instructing the people with his unchanging Word, the church itself has been seduced into preaching 'man knows best' philosophies of the New Age movement.

Much of this New Age drivel, masquerading as Christ's teaching, which flows from many of our pulpits and national newspapers today bears no reality to the original text whatsoever. The meaning has been completely twisted.

Peter warned us this would happen:

> And remember why he is waiting. He is giving us time to get his message of salvation out to others. Our wise and beloved brother Paul has talked about these same things in many of his letters. Some of his comments are not easy to understand, and there are people who are deliberately stupid, and always demand some unusual interpretation – they have twisted his letters around to mean something quite different from what he meant, just as they do the other parts of the Scripture – and the result is disaster for them.

I am warning you ahead of time, dear brothers, so that you can watch out and not be carried away by the mistakes of these wicked men, lest you yourselves become mixed up too. (2 Peter 3:15-17)

Political correctness has been allowed to smother and, in many instances, completely drown the absolute truth and integrity of the scriptures. And not only has the baby (truth) been thrown out with the bathwater, it has been buried under a great pile of ecclesiastical garbage and sanctimonious crap. And yes, all in the guise of loving one another.

Inclusiveness and tolerance are the 'in' words today. These things are blatantly wrong, with the most dire consequences, and no one sounds a warning. No one speaks out. Nevertheless, God's Word endures. His truth stands firm like a great rock and nothing can shake it. He speaks no careless words, all he says is purest truth, like silver refined seven times.

But sad indeed are the consequences of the church ignoring him. Just look around you today. Babies are being murdered in the womb, thousands of them, and the pulpits are silent. 376,000 in New Zealand alone this past decade.

Sodomy is granted legal protection and the pulpits are silent. Muzzled.

Legislation has been passed to remove the rights of parents and the pulpits are silent.

Children are taught they evolved from apes and the pulpits are silent.

Same-sex marriages are being sanctified in the church of God and the pulpits are silent.

Tolerance and inclusiveness overrule the truth and the pulpits are silent.

Mother Earth is protected more than Father God is defended and the pulpits are silent.

The great prophetic truths of Scripture are not being taught. A great number of pulpits are filled by ministers and pastors who simply haven't got a clue about the future. Graduates of so-called Bible seminaries. Bible cemeteries more like it!

The entertainment industry celebrates debauchery and immorality in all its many forms and the pulpits are silent.

And perhaps the worst evil of all, man has exalted himself above his Creator to the point where man considers he knows best.

The problem is when you begin with a false premise, the conclusion is sheer nonsense or, at worst, anarchy.

All of the aforementioned things are blatantly wrong with the most dire consequences for those who persist in doing them, but no one sounds a warning. No one speaks out.

> The prophets prophesy falsely; the priests bear rule by their means; and my people love to have it so – but their doom is certain. (Jeremiah 5:31 KJV)

What is this doom, this time of Tribulation Jesus spoke of to his disciples? It is a seven-year period during which many cataclysmic events will occur on earth. So much so that a great number of people, probably two thirds of the world's population, will be killed, as well as much of the flora and fauna and everything in the ocean (Revelation 8:7, 9:18 and 16:3).

So much for global warming and endangered species, not to forget 'Save the whales.'

No wonder Isaiah said,

> You need fear nothing but the Lord of the Armies of Heaven. If you fear Him you need fear nothing else. He will be your safety. (Isaiah 8:13 KJV)

That is right. He will be your safety. No one needs to endure the horrors of the Tribulation which, by the way, does not signal the end of the world. At the end of the seven years, Christ will return exactly as the scriptures foretold and reign on earth for a thousand years.

But listen. Jesus did not come to condemn us but to save us.

> For God so loved the world that he gave his only begotten Son that whoever believes in him should not perish but have everlasting life. (John 3:16 KJV)

> Neither is there salvation in any other: for there is no other name under heaven given among men, whereby we must be saved. (Acts 4:12 KJV)

There is no other name under heaven whereby we might be saved. No one but Jesus can or has the authority to grant eternal life to anyone, and the only place we can go to be saved is the Cross of Calvary. There are no alternative routes to heaven. And no one can spare us from the horrors of the Tribulation but the resurrected Christ.

Did you know that 4000 prophecies in the Bible have already come true, right down to the last detail? That leaves about 1000 left to be fulfilled – those are the ones regarding the last days before the return of Christ, which are being ticked off the list right now.

Just watch the nation of Israel. If 4,000 out of 5,000 have already occurred exactly as the Bible predicted, you might want to pay attention to the rest.

John the Baptist began preaching out in the Judean wilderness. His constant theme was:

Sermons from the Bush

> Turn from your sins – turn to God – for the Kingdom of Heaven is at hand. (Matthew 3:1 KJV)

Thousands responded. From then on, Jesus began to preach:

> Turn from sin, and turn to God, for the Kingdom of Heaven is at hand.

Millions have responded.

The message for today is: Turn from sin, and from the ways of the world, and turn to God, for truly the Kingdom of Heaven is at hand.

It is not too late but be warned:

> For like a snare shall it come on all them that dwell on the face of the whole earth. (Luke 21:35 KJV)

> Keep a constant watch. And pray that if possible you may arrive in My presence without having to experience these horrors. (Luke 21:36)

There still remains a narrow window of opportunity to escape the Tribulation. When the snare is sprung, it will be too late. No, it is not the planet which needs saving – it is we, mankind, from our own blindness and rebellion against our Creator.

From: *Wairoa Star*, November 2009

The Bible: A Source of Guidance for the Future

In November 2009, I wrote explaining why the issue of global warming was not something we need to be concerned about. The world is not going to become uninhabitable in the near future, not for at least 1007 years anyway. How can we be certain of this? Very easily. We have God's word on it and in his own words, it is impossible for him to lie, or to be mistaken for that matter. The absolute truth is God is, and his Word is, rock-solid and infallible.

We may disagree with, argue against, and even deny these two facts, but it changes nothing. The Bible is the infallible word of God. Everything he says will happen exactly as foretold in his Word. There are 5000 specific prophecies in the Bible, 4000 of which have already been fulfilled exactly as they were written. To ignore or deny this is to deny reality. On December 25 we celebrate Christmas and the birth of Jesus. Between 500 and 700 years prior to his birth, there were a number of specific prophecies written relating to his birth, ministry, death on the cross, resurrection from death and coming again as ruler on the earth for 1000 years.

Quite apart from the prophecies of Isaiah and Micah relating to his birth, the Psalms alone include a vast body of Messianic prophecies relevant to Christ's suffering, death and resurrection and return to earth as king and ruler for one thousand years (soon to be fulfilled). We need to wake up and start listening to God, who speaks the truth through his infallible word and not to men and women who are easily deceived and often wrong. There is no question the birth of Jesus was an incredible event in the history of mankind. In fact, it split history in two; B.C. and A.D.

The words of the Angel of the Lord, who appeared to a group of terror-stricken shepherds say it all:

> The angel of the Lord came upon them, and the glory of the Lord shone round about them: and they were sore afraid. And the angel said unto them, Fear not: for, behold, I bring you good tidings of great joy, which shall be to all people. For unto you is born this day in the city of David a Saviour, which is Christ the Lord. (Luke 2:9-11 KJV)

> Don't be afraid, I bring you the most joyful news ever announced and it is for everyone. The Saviour, the Messiah, the Lord has been born tonight in Bethlehem. Don't be afraid. (Luke 2:10-11)

The most joyful news ever announced and it is for everyone. Why were they so scared? They were in the presence of God. So, will we be 'terror-stricken' when we have to stand before almighty God, having scorned the most incredible act of love the world has ever witnessed and rejected the most wonderful gift you will ever have offered to you? Truly the gift of salvation represents the most joyful news ever announced. To be saved and set free, born-again into an entirely new life defies all human logic and understanding, and yes, it is totally free of charge for everyone. But it has to be accepted. It is one thing to be offered a gift, but without acceptance, there can be no joy. What happens if we refuse so great an offer? In John 3:16 we read:

> And all who trust in Him – God's Son – to save them, have eternal life; Those who do not believe in and obey Him shall never see Heaven but the wrath of God remains upon them.

The Bible: A Source of Guidance for the Future

That God loves us is beyond question, but don't think for one minute that you can continue to reject his love without consequences. As I warned two years ago, the world is about to experience the wrath of God as foretold in the scriptures. In the near future, some startling events are going to occur.

Don't just take my word for it – read the Bible for yourself. Before the Tribulation occurs, the seven-year period when God scourges the world of every vestige of evil, Jesus is going to come down and remove those of his people who are ready (Matthew 25:1-13, 1 Corinthians 15:51-53, 1 Thessalonians 4:17, Revelation 3:10). It is not his intention that any one of us have to suffer the horrors of the Tribulation. It is not his intention any one of us has to suffer all eternity in hell, but there is no way we are acceptable in our present state, and there is no other name under heaven whereby we might be saved. No one but Jesus can, or has the authority to, grant eternal life to anyone and the only place we can go to be saved is the Cross of Calvary.

There are no alternative routes to heaven, and no one can spare us from the horrors of the Tribulation but the resurrected Christ. In the words of the angel of God,

> Behold I bring you the most joyful news ever announced and it is for everyone.

Are you willing to accept God's wonderful gift of salvation?

Coincidence or Stark Warning?

April 15th 2012 marks the one-hundredth anniversary of the most famous peace-time maritime disaster in history – this was also one of the deadliest.

To what am I referring? The sinking of the British ocean liner *Titanic* which still holds important lessons for us today.

On April 10th 1912, the 882-foot long British luxury liner, the largest passenger steamship of her day, set out on her maiden voyage from Southampton in southern England, bound for New York City. The *Titanic* had everything going for her. She was likened to a luxurious floating palace, one equipped with the most advanced engineering and safety features of her day.

Her captain was one of the most respected and experienced men in the White Star fleet, making this one last voyage before his planned honourable retirement.

It is said that an employee of the White Star line remarked at the Titanic's launch from its Northern Ireland shipyard – 'Not even God himself could sink this ship.' Evidently the same remark was made by a crew member at the start of her voyage nearly a year later.

The Captain, Edward J Smith, had previously stated in an interview that he couldn't 'imagine any condition that would cause the ship to founder. Modern shipping has gone beyond that.'

Indeed, the word unsinkable had been associated with the vessel, the White Star brochure stating that 'As far as it is possible to do so, she was designed to be unsinkable.'

Five days later, on a fine, clear night, about 400 miles off the coast of Newfoundland, disaster struck. In the calm moonless night there was not even any ocean swell that would have allowed the lookouts atop the ship to spot the looming iceberg that the *Titanic*, travelling at near full speed, was about to strike.

It is not as though there were no warnings. Earlier in the day radio messages were received from a number of ships in the area warning of icebergs.

Sitting stationary for the night about 10 miles away, the SS *California* radioed a last warning around 11:30 p.m. of more ice in the area, but *Titanic*'s radio operator Jack Phillips was in the middle of his job of relaying personal messages from the passengers to the relay station at Cape Race in Newfoundland. 'Shut up, shut up,' he sharply told the *California*, stating he already knew about the ice. In reality, he didn't understand the gravity of the situation and failed to pass the warning on.

The *Titanic* carried more than 2200 crew and passengers. The magnitude of the disaster seems unthinkable. More than 1500 passengers and crew lost their lives in the icy North Atlantic while only just over 700, mostly women and children, were saved.

More than two-thirds of those on board perished when the *Titanic* sank.

We too are warned of a looming disaster where two-thirds of the world's population are about to perish (e.g. in Revelation 8:7, 9:18 and 16:3). There are a great many other references in scripture besides these three, but you can be absolutely certain God's Word will come to pass, exactly as the scriptures warn, we have his assurance on it. 'I have spoken and I will do it,' declares the Lord.

In November 2009, I suggested that the Tribulation period would most likely begin in the next decade.

Today I would suggest that the Tribulation is imminent. It could begin at any time. Make no mistake, God will not be mocked.

He will not allow his commandments, which we are required to live by, to be ignored and disobeyed without consequence.

There is one way and one way only to escape the coming day of God's wrath, as the Tribulation is referred to. We must repent (turn away) from our disobedience of his commandments and come to the Cross of Calvary where Jesus paid the price for our forgiveness and salvation. There simply is no alternative.

> For God so loved the world, that he gave his only begotten Son, that whosoever believeth in him should not perish, but have everlasting life. (John 3:16 KJV)

> Whoever believes in the Son has Eternal life, whoever does not obey the Son shall not see life but the wrath of God remains on him. (John 3:36 KJV)

For those with eyes to see and ears to hear, there are warning signs aplenty that mankind is in big trouble. God gave us the Ten Commandments to live by in order to live safely and securely in his great love. Every single one us has broken some or most of the commandments. On that basis alone, he could have written us off. Instead, he sent Jesus to pay the price of our disobedience. We ignore Jesus' sacrifice on our behalf at our peril.

Confidence in the Bible

Billy Graham was thirty and already a well-known evangelist when he came to a crisis of faith. Could he believe the Bible to be the word of God? Some of his friends were raising doubts in his heart. In his autobiography, *Just As I Am*, it tells the story of what happened.

He took a walk in the moonlight in the San Bernardino Mountains in California. He dropped to his knees in the woods, opened his Bible and put it on a tree stump before him. He prayed,

> O God! There are many things in this book I do not understand. There are many problems with it for which I have no solution. There are many seeming contradictions. There are some areas in it that do not seem to correlate with modern science. I can't answer some of the philosophical and psychological questions Chuck and others are raising.

Finally, he was able to say,

> Father, I am going to accept this as Thy Word. By faith! I'm going to allow faith to go beyond my intellectual questions and doubts, and I will believe this to be Your inspired Word.

He says,

> When I got up from my knees at Forest Home that August night,

my eyes stung with tears. I sensed the presence and power of God as I had not sensed it in months. Not all my questions were answered, but a major bridge had been crossed. In my heart and mind, I knew a spiritual battle in my soul had been fought and won.

Lessons from Past Revivals
by Chris Strom

Why did the seven in the Hebrides, David Brainerd and the missionaries in Korea keep seeking God, month after month, squandering precious time that could have been spent doing so many visibly worthwhile things? What kept them going?

The answer: True humility. That is the key to Revival. Prayer alone is not enough. 2 Chronicles 7:14 puts first priority on the attitude with which we go to prayer. Humble ourselves, then pray.

If at heart we are fairly content with our lives and what we are accomplishing for God, we will soon stop the time-expensive exercise of seeking God. But if we are truly desperate for God to act, nothing can stop us seeking him. This is true humility: When man gives up his own small schemes and throws everything upon the answer that must come from God alone.

For Edward Miller, American missionary to Argentina, that point came after a disastrous evangelistic campaign. Not one person came to his 10 days of meetings. He decided, 'there was only one place for me: Home selling cars, or something!'

Missionaries said: 'You must be patient. We're sowing the seed. One day we'll have a crop.' But I wasn't getting patient. Where was the God I had seen as a child move into cities and sweep through them, where they had to close down the movies, dances and saloons because there was nobody to go to them? But he reasoned that such Revivals were for special saintly people. 'I didn't have anything special. As a preacher's kid you're either an angel or a devil, and I didn't choose to be an angel!' While deciding to quit, he felt challenged by God to fast and pray eight hours a day for a week, for Revival. 'Alright, God, I will. Then I'll go home in peace!'

I finished my fast and nothing happened except one thing, and it was frightening. I had laid everything down, now, that I knew. I had no other recourse left. I met God or, suddenly I realised, for me there was no God. I had come down to the final analysis of my life and suddenly I realised I couldn't get out of there in seven days or I'd go out an atheist.

His fast over, he continued to seek God every day, eight hours, 10 hours, sometimes all night. Some disapproved, questioning his sanity, saying that no one should receive a missionary's salary who spent so much time praying and not in normal missionary activities. Doubts, questions and fears marked the passing of the long hours. 'Where was God?' Two months passed. Then the enemy brought an almost successful attempt to halt the search. 'Set God a date. Surely by now you know you are mistaken!'

A date was set. 'God, if you don't manifest yourself then I will know I am mistaken; I will go out with tracts, returning to the conventional missionary unit.'

'The hour arrived and still God had done nothing. With unutterable bitterness of soul, with tears of frustration and defeat, I filled my pockets with tracts and slowly walked down the hall. God had not answered.' But...

Argentina, 1949. Edward Miller had just quit seeking God for revival. God had not answered after months of prayer and Edward was on his way to distribute tracts, when there was a knock at the door. It was a fellow pastor. Hours passed as Edward listened to his troubles. He had brought his unconverted son. A few words from Edward brought the boy under deep conviction and soon he accepted Christ. As the pastor went on his way rejoicing, an inner voice seemed to say, 'You see, son, when I wish, I can bring them in. Now return to prayer until I tell you it's time to leave.'

So back he went to wait on God. Some 10 days later, 'suddenly God was there. I met God. He spoke to me. He set me into praying for another six weeks.'

Then he felt God told him to call his people to special prayer meetings from 8 pm till midnight.

'If they are not prepared to stay the entire four hours, they must not come at all.' Could that be from God? Just before, a very sensible hour had been chosen for a prayer meeting and no one had come. Who then, would come to these? Yet when he announced it, three said they would.

The prayer meeting was a disaster. 'All three of them kneeled down, buried their heads in their arms, and that's the last I saw of them! We just waited it out.' At midnight he asked if God had spoken to them. They all said no, but one lady, Isobel, finally admitted that she had felt like getting up and hitting the table. 'Why didn't you do it?'

'Oh, no!'

Amazingly, all three came back the next night. 'We had another great prayer meeting! Four hours of silence! I asked them the same question. Again, Isobel felt she should hit the table, but it was "too stupid, too foolish", she said, and she wouldn't do it.'

After two more nights of the usual silence, he called them to the table. Everyone was to walk around the table and hit it. All did – except Isobel! So round and round they marched until finally she reached out and gently tapped the table.

'Immediately a rushing wind swept into the room from the south-east corner. In that act of obedience, the Spirit of God fell.' All three were filled with the Spirit and spoke in tongues. By the end week all church members except one had been filled with the Spirit. 'In weeks the little church doubled and re-doubled its membership. The people formed into little bands and went out to witness for the Lord; people were saved and healed.'

The revival quickly spread to other churches and towns. In one meeting, 'For hours great crying and groaning ascended. In terrible conviction, some wrestled for pardon; others shouted in mighty victory the praise of Zion and the Lamb.' Thus the Revival spread to Argentina.

So much had depended on such a tiny act of obedience! No wonder Edward Miller was now determined 'to walk the road of implicit obedience to what I felt was the word of the Lord.'

Reprinted from *Challenge Weekly*, October 1983

The Saint Must Walk Alone
by A.W. Tozer

Most of the world's great souls have been lonely. Loneliness seems to be one price the saint must pay for his saintliness.

In the morning of the world (or should we say, in that strange darkness that came soon after the dawn of man's creation,) that pious soul, Enoch, walked with God and was not, for God took him; and while it is not stated in so many words, a fair inference is that Enoch walked a path quite apart from his contemporaries.

Another lonely man was Noah who, alone of all the antediluvians, found grace in the sight of God; and every shred of evidence points to the aloneness of his life even while surrounded by his people.

Again, Abraham had Sarah and Lot, as well as many servants and herdsmen, but who can read his story and the apostolic comment upon it without sensing instantly that he was a man 'whose soul was alike a star and dwelt apart?' As far as we know not one word did God ever speak to him in the company of men. Face down he communed with his God, and the innate dignity of the man forbade that he assume this posture in the presence of others. How sweet and solemn was the scene that night of the sacrifice when he saw the lamps of fire moving between the pieces of offering. There, alone with a horror of great darkness upon him, he heard the voice of God and knew that he was a man marked for divine favour.

Moses also was a man apart. While yet attached to the court

of Pharaoh he took long walks alone, and during one of these walks, while far removed from the crowds, he saw an Egyptian and a Hebrew fighting and came to the rescue of his countryman. After the resultant break with Egypt he dwelt in almost complete seclusion in the desert. There, while he watched his sheep alone, the wonder of the burning bush appeared to him, and later on the peak of Sinai, he crouched alone to gaze in fascinated awe at the Presence, partly hidden, partly disclosed, within the cloud and fire.

The prophets of pre-Christian times differed widely from each other, but one mark they bore in common was their enforced loneliness.

They loved their people and glorified in the religion of the fathers, but their loyalty to the God of Abraham, Isaac and Jacob, and their zeal for the welfare of the nation of Israel drove them away from the crowd and into long periods of heaviness. 'I am become a stranger unto my brethren, and an alien unto my mother's children,' cried one and unwittingly spoke for all the rest.

Most revealing of all is the sight of that One of whom Moses and all the prophets did write, treading his lonely way to the Cross. His deep loneliness was unrelieved by the presence of the multitudes.

'Tis midnight, and on Olive's brow
The star is dimmed that lately shone;
'Tis midnight; in the garden now,
The suffering Saviour prays alone.
'Tis midnight, and from all removed
The Saviour wrestles lone with fears;
E'en the disciple whom He loved
Heeds not his Master's grief and tears.
– William B. Tappan

He died alone in the darkness hidden from the sight of mortal men and no one saw him when he arose triumphant and walked out of the tomb, though many saw him afterward and bore witness to what they saw. There are some things too sacred for any eye but God's to look upon. The curiosity, the clamour, the well-meant but blundering effort to help can only hinder the waiting soul and make unlikely, if not impossible, the communication of the secret message of God to the worshipping heart.

Sometimes we react by a kind of religious reflex and repeat dutifully the proper words and phrases even though they fail to express our real feelings and lack the authenticity of personal experience.

Right now is such a time. A certain conventional loyalty may lead some who hear this unfamiliar truth expressed for the first time to say brightly, 'Oh, I am never lonely.' Christ said, 'I will never leave you nor forsake you,' and 'Lo, I am with you always.'

How can I be lonely when Jesus is with me?

Now I do not want to reflect on the sincerity of any Christian soul, but this stock testimony is too neat to be real. It is obviously what the speaker thinks should be true rather than what he has proved to be true by the test of experience. This cheerful denial of loneliness proves only that the speaker has never walked with God without the support and encouragement afforded him by society.

The sense of companionship which he mistakenly attributes to the presence of Christ may, and probably does, arise from the presence of friendly people. Always remember; you cannot carry a cross in company. Though a man were surrounded by a vast crowd, his cross is his alone and his carrying of it marks him as a man apart.

Society has turned against him; otherwise he would have no cross.

No one is a friend to the man with a cross. 'They all forsook him, and fled.'

The pain of loneliness arises from the constitution of our nature.

God made us for each other. The desire for human companionship is completely natural and right. The loneliness of the Christian results from his walk with God in an ungodly world, a walk that must often take him away from the fellowship of good Christians as well as from that of the unregenerate world. His God-given instincts cry out for companionship with others of his kind, others who can understand his longings, his aspirations, his absorption in the love of Christ; and because within his circle of friends there are so few who share inner experiences, he is forced to walk alone.

The unsatisfied longings of the prophets for human understanding caused them to cry out in their complaint, and even our Lord himself suffered in the same way.

The man who has passed on into the divine Presence in actual inner experience will not find many who understand him. A certain amount of social fellowship will of course be his as he mingles with religious persons in the regular activities of the church, but true spiritual fellowship will be hard to find. But he should not expect things to be otherwise. After all he is a stranger and a pilgrim, and the journey he takes is not on his feet but in his heart. He walks with God in the garden of his own soul – and who but God can walk there with him? He is of another spirit from the multitudes that tread the courts of the Lord's house. He has seen that of which they have only heard, and he walks among them somewhat as Zacharias walked after his return from the alter when the people whispered, 'He has seen a vision.'

The truly spiritual man is indeed something of an oddity. He lives not for himself but to promote the interests of Another. He seeks to persuade people to give all to his Lord and asks no portion of share for himself. He delights not to be honoured but to

The Saint Must Walk Alone

see his Saviour glorified in the eyes of men. His joy is to see his Lord promoted and himself neglected. He finds few who care to talk about that which is the supreme object of his interest, so he is often silent and preoccupied in the midst of noisy religious shop-talk. For this he earns the reputation of being dull and over serious, so he is avoided and the gulf between him and society widens. He searches for friends upon whose garments he can detect the smell of myrrh and aloes and cassia out of the ivory palaces, and finding few or none, he, like Mary of old, keeps these things in his heart.

It is this very loneliness that throws him back upon God. 'When my father and my mother forsake me, then the Lord will take me up.' His inability to find human companionship drives him to seek in God what he can find nowhere else. He learns in inner solitude what he could not have learned in the crowd – that Christ is All in All, that he is made unto us wisdom, righteousness, sanctification and redemption, that in him we have and possess life's summum bonum.

Two things remain to be said. One, that the lonely man of whom we speak is not a haughty man, nor is he the holier-than-thou, austere saint so bitterly satirised in popular literature. He is likely to feel that he is the least of all men and is sure to blame himself for his very loneliness. He wants to share his feelings with others and to open his heart to some like-minded soul who will understand him, but the spiritual climate around him does not encourage it, so he remains silent and tells his grief's to God alone.

The second thing is that the lonely saint is not the withdrawn man who hardens himself against human suffering and spends his days contemplating the heavens. Just the opposite is true. His loneliness makes him sympathetic to the approach of the broken-hearted and the fallen and the sin-bruised. Because he is detached from the world, he is all the more able to help it. Meister Eckhart taught his followers that if they should find themselves in prayer and happen to remember that a poor widow needed food, they should break off the prayer instantly and go and care for the widow. 'God will not suffer you to lose anything by it,' he told them. 'You can take up again in prayer where you left off and the Lord will make it up to you.' This is typical of the great mystics and masters of the interior life from Paul to the present day.

The weakness of so many modern Christians is that they feel too much at home in the world. In their effort to achieve restful 'adjustment' to unregenerate society they have lost their pilgrim character and become an essential part of the very moral order against which they are sent to protest. The world recognises them and accepts them for what they are. And this is the saddest thing that can be said about them. They are not lonely, but neither are they saints.

The Church and the World
by Winkie Pratney

The church and the world walked far apart on the changing shores of time
And the world was singing a charts rock tune, but the Church a hymn sublime.
'Come, give me your hand,' called the laid-back world, 'and dance with me this day.'
But the love-cleansed Church hid her blood-bought hand and solemnly said, 'No way,
I will not give you my hand at all, and I will not walk with you
Your way is the way of Eternal Death and your words are all untrue.'
'Ah, walk with me! Just a little way,' said the world with insistent air.
'The space I am at is a pleasant place, and the night-life is manic there
You've been battling with me for far too long, and let's face it you've been so alone
Don't you think it high time that we called it a truce, and you found some place here for a home?
Your life is so narrow and thorny and tough, see how mine runs so easy and smooth
Why be so repressive and out of it? In the finest of circles I move...

My way, you see, is a fun, fast one, and my gate is so broad and
   so wide.
There is room enough for you and me to travel it side by side.'
Half shyly the Church approached the world, and gave him her
   hand of snow
And the fake world grasped it and drew her close, and
   whispered in accents low;
'Your dress is too simple to please my taste; I've got all kinds
   of things you can wear.
See these silks and chiffons and synthetic stones and this
   dazzling disco gear?'
The Church looked down at her plain white robes, and then at
   the glittering world
And blushed as she saw his superstar style and his smile
   contemptuous curled.
'I can change my dress,' she said to him. 'After all I am under
   grace.'
And her pure white garments were stripped away, and the
   World gave her wealth in their place.
'Now your house is passé,' said the proud grey World, 'let me
   build you a place like mine
With a barbeque pit for the parties we'll throw and a mirror-
   tiled bedroom so fine.'
So, the parties began and the dancing went on in a place that
   was once made for prayer
And the Church felt relief that the battle was over and that
   she at last had no care...
But an angel of mercy flew over the Church and whispered, 'I
   know your sin...'
Then the Church looked up and anxiously tried to gather her
   children in.

But some were down at the discotheque, and others were off
  at a play
And some were drinking in gay night bars, so she quietly went
  her way.
Then the sly world gallantly said to her, 'Your children mean
  no harm
Just having some fun,' he said as he smiled, so she took his
  proffered arm
And smiled, and went back to gathering flowers, as she
  chatted and walked with the world
While millions and millions of precious souls to the horrible
  pit were hurled.
'There are preachers you have that bother me,' said the world
  with contemptuous sneer.
'It seems they keep trying to frighten my kids with tales that I
  don't want them to hear.
They talk about 'sinning' and 'breaking God's heart' and this
  horror of 'endless night'
And the awful rude way they reject my suggestions is terribly
  impolite.
Now I have some men of a much better breed, contemporary,
  brilliant and fast
Who can show us all how to live as we like and go to Nirvana
  at last.
The infinite Spirit is within us all, and is peaceful, enlightened
  and kind –
Do you think it would take one child to itself and leave any
  other behind?
Go train up your speakers to fit with the times, adapt to the
  relevant way.
Everyone likes entertainment today, and it's only the good
  shows that pay.'

Sermons from the Bush

So, she called for those of the swift repartee, the gifted,
    flamboyant and learned
While plain good men who had preached the Cross were out
    of their pulpits turned.
Then the Church sat down in her ease and said, 'I am rich and
    in goods increased.
I have nothing I need and nothing to do but to laugh and to
    dance and to feast.'
And the sly world heard her and laughed within, and
    mockingly said aside –
'The Church has fallen, the beautiful Church, and her shame is
    her boast and her pride.'
And an angel drew near the mercy seat, and whispered in
    sighs her name
And the saints their anthems of rapture hushed, and covered
    their heads with shame
And a voice came down from the hush of Heaven, from Him
    who sat on the throne,
'I know your works and what you have said and I know that
    you have not known
You are poor and blind and naked and sick, with pride and
    ruin enthralled
The expectant Bride of a heavenly Groom, now the Hooker of
    all the world.
You have ceased to watch for your Saviour's return and have
    fallen from zeal and grace
So now, in tears, I must cast you out and BLOT OUT YOUR NAME
FROM THIS PLACE.'

Cry Our Beloved Country
A Prayer

Father God, we thank you for your great love and the promises you gave us all those years ago:

> If I shut up the heavens so that there is no rain, or if I command the locust swarms to eat up all the crops, or if I send an epidemic among you.
> Then if my people who are called by my name will humble themselves and pray and search for me ['Seek my face' – KJV] and turn from their wicked ways; then I will hear from heaven and forgive their sins, and will heal their land. (2 Chronicles 7:13-14)

Father, we who are called by your name, Christians, come before your throne of grace to cry for our beloved country.

This beautiful nation of Aotearoa, New Zealand, once called 'God's own country' has turned from you and become an evil and sinful nation. We are sinning against you in so many ways Lord.

In Genesis 1:31 we read,

> Then God looked over all that he made, and it was excellent in every way.

God loves his creation; every part of it is pleasing to him, especially mankind. But Lord we refuse to acknowledge you and the works of your hands.

Even our children are being taught the Evolution lie.
Forgive us Lord we pray.

And Father you commanded us: 'Go forth and multiply and fill the earth,' but we murder our babies – hundreds of thousands of them these past few decades.
Yet you made all the delicate, inner parts of my mother's womb (Psalm 139:13).
Please forgive us this horrible sin, Lord we pray.

In Psalm 50:14 you instructed us:

> What I want from you is your true thanks; I want your promises fulfilled [kept].

But in so many instances we have broken our marriage vows and infidelity and immorality are rife in our nation.
Father please forgive us this evil we ask.

And as if that were not enough, we have traded the natural for the unnatural.
Homosexuality is rampant and now our children are being encouraged in this horrible evil.
Forgive us Lord we pray.

We have filled our nation with false idols, sport, entertainment; even your church bows down to the false god of humanism.
Man knows best.
Forgive us Lord we pray.

Your prophet Isaiah warned us in Isaiah 3:12-13:

Sermons from the Bush

My people what has become of you? Children are your oppressors. Women rule over you. As for your leaders. Misleaders leading you down the garden path to destruction.

Forgive us Lord we pray.

We have refused to discipline. It started with our children and as a result has become endemic in every area of our society, and now we are paying the price.

Even your church has disobeyed and ignored your clear instructions in 1 Corinthians 14:34 and 1 Timothy 2:12.

And now the leadership and pulpits are often filled by women usurping the authority of men in spite of our Lord Jesus' clear warning about this in his letter to the church at Thyatira (Revelation 2:20-23).

Forgive us Lord we pray.

Father your prophet Obadiah warned us in verses 15 and 16:

As you have done to Israel so it will be done to you.

And yet we have ignored your clear instructions in Isaiah 62:7 regarding this precious nation. Our politicians have made serious errors when it comes to Israel.

Forgive us Lord we pray.

And now on top of all the other evils they are attempting to pass the law regarding euthanasia which you expressly forbid.

We have appointed leaders and approved legislation that calls evil good and good evil.

Forgive us Lord we pray.

Father, we spurn your love; love that saw you send us your only Son to show us not only the Way, the Truth and the Life, but to pay the price for our sinfulness and rebellion.

Enabling us to be forgiven, born again and made acceptable to you. Love does not come any greater than this. And yet we have scorned your love and our Saviour's suffering and sacrifice on our behalf.

Forgive us Lord we pray.

Let us never forget: those who have the Son Jesus have Eternal Life, those who reject his terrible sacrifice on our behalf shall not see heaven but your wrath abides, remains on them.

Open our eyes to see and our ears to hear, Lord we pray.

Father your Word instructs us:

> Not by might, nor by power but by my Spirit says the Lord. (Zechariah 4:6)

Father God, in Jesus' name we come before your throne of Grace and we humbly cry to you.

Send your Holy Spirit to this shameful and sinful nation.
Cause this nation to hear, Lord.
Cause this nation to fear, Lord.
Cause this nation to turn back to you.

Father in Jesus' name we bring our petition to you.
Please forgive us Lord.
Please heal us Lord.

Epilogue

There are far too many people today, even here in New Zealand and among my Maori and Pakeha friends, who believe in the power of the devil and a horde of false gods and evil spirits, yet reject the wonderful love of God and his Son Jesus whom he sent to save us and set us free from all these things.

Jesus did not come to condemn us. He came to pay the price to set us free from all these evils and our own disobedience and mistakes.

There is not a man or a woman alive who has not broken at least one or more of the Ten Commandments. This in itself separates us from our Heavenly Father who is totally without fault of any kind, yet such is his great love for each one of us that he sent Jesus, his Son, down here to earth to pay the price for us.

To forgive us, wash us clean, set us free so that we are made acceptable to God, and be granted eternal life with him in his never-ending Kingdom. Love does not come any greater than this.

The simple truth is, this Jesus, this same Jesus, whose name is so often taken in vain, used as a curse word, mocked and belittled by academia worldwide, hated by the devil and his horde of false religions. Jesus is rejected by countless millions today. Yet he alone is the only hope for mankind.

No question, the earth and all mankind are in big trouble. Left to our own devices, we are probably heading for self-destruction on a number of fronts, global warming being the least of our problems. A nuclear holocaust would be of much greater concern.

But Jesus, crucified on our behalf, who rose triumphant from the grave, was seen over a period of forty days by a great number of those who knew him. The same Jesus who split history in two (BC/AD), is coming back to earth in the very near future to take up his rightful role as King of all the nations to rule the world from Jerusalem for 1000 years.

You may disagree, even reject these things, but it changes nothing. God's Word is infallible. What he decrees will happen and nothing can change this fact.

It must be clearly understood, there is no other name under heaven whereby mankind might be saved. Jesus alone has the power to save because he alone paid the price for our salvation.

It is simple. It starts with being honest. We have all sinned one way or another, and so we cannot be accepted by God in our present state. We have to believe in Jesus and his Word. The Bible says he alone is the Way, the Truth and the Life. No one comes to the Father except through him.

We have to believe that Jesus paid the price for our salvation on the cross at Calvary. And finally, we have to put our belief into action. We have to call on his name, ask him to forgive us, save us, set us free and most importantly be born again by his Spirit. He came – that we might have life – and have it more abundantly.

I can tell you with absolute certainty, that if you take this step, you will never regret it.

About the Author

Born in 1938 in Featherston, Wairarapa, Ian Brickell has loved the bush since childhood and has been a lover of the Lord since 1957. Although his parents were not church members, his grandmother was a strong believer who claimed to be descended from one of the Wesley brothers, founders of the Methodist Church.

After leaving school, he worked in the Bank of New Zealand for four and a half years, before becoming a shepherd on a coastal station in the Wairarapa. It was there, whilst reading a Bible one night, that he came to the conclusion: *Jesus has to be real!* Up to this point he had had no church involvement.

Six years of possum trapping both strengthened his Christian walk and provided the deposit for a ballot farm in Hawkes Bay. Since then he has gradually purchased neighbouring farms.

He has been married to Carolyn for 53 years, and is the father of seven children, 24 grandchildren and three great-grandchildren.

Ian still actively farms in a remote mountain valley bordering the Urewera Ranges in Northern Hawkes Bay, one and a half hours from the nearest town, Wairoa. There he breeds fine horses, Welsh Black cattle and Perendale sheep.

His love of the bush has underpinned his 50-year involvement in Wairoa Search and Rescue in the Urewera National Park. He once led a group of 'Operation Raleigh Venturers' through a remote corner of Fiordland for three weeks. They were on what was designated 'an extreme trek', where they tramped over 100 kilometres of untracked wilderness.

Over the years, he has taken time out from his busy life to wait on God and receive inspiration from him. He has been a church elder, lay preacher and celebrant. This book is a compilation of the messages he has given and the sermons he has preached over many years.

Originally, he intended publishing it as a legacy for his family and friends, but is now making it available to the wider Christian church as well.

Bible Versions Quoted

Unless otherwise indicated, all Scripture quotations are taken from The Living Bible copyright © 1971. Used by permission of Tyndale House Publishers, Inc., Carol Stream, Illinois 60188. All rights reserved.

Scripture quotations marked (AMP) are taken from the Amplified Bible, Copyright © 1954, 1958, 1962, 1964, 1965, 1987 by The Lockman Foundation. Used by permission.

Scripture quotations marked (ASV) are taken from the American Standard Version (ASV). Public domain.

Scripture quotations marked (CSB) are taken from the Christian Standard Bible®, Copyright © 2017 by Holman Bible Publishers. Used by permission. Christian Standard Bible® and CSB® are federally registered trademarks of Holman Bible Publishers.

Scripture quotations marked (ESV) are taken from The Holy Bible, English Standard Version®, copyright © 2001 by Crossway Bibles, a publishing ministry of Good News Publishers. Used by permission. All rights reserved.

Scripture quotations marked (GNT) are taken from the Good News Translation in Today's English Version, Second Edition Copyright © 1992 by American Bible Society. Used by Permission.

Scripture quotations marked (Jerusalem Bible) are taken from The Jerusalem Bible © 1966 by Darton Longman & Todd Ltd and Doubleday and Company Ltd.

Scripture quotations marked (KJ21) are taken from the 21st Century King James Version®, copyright © 1994. Used by permission of Deuel Enterprises, Inc., Gary, SD 57237. All rights reserved.

Scripture quotations marked (KJV) are taken from The Authorized (King James) Version. Rights in the Authorized Version in the United Kingdom are vested in the Crown. Reproduced by permission of the Crown's patentee, Cambridge University Press.

Scripture quotations marked (NASB) are taken from the New American Standard Bible®, Copyright © 1960, 1962, 1963, 1968, 1971, 1972, 1973, 1975, 1977, 1995 by The Lockman Foundation. Used by permission. www.Lockman.org

Scripture quotations marked (NEB) are taken from the New English Bible, copyright © Cambridge University Press and Oxford University Press 1961, 1970. All rights reserved.

Scripture quotations marked (NIV) are taken from the Holy Bible, New International Version®, NIV®. Copyright © 1973, 1978, 1984, 2011 by Biblica, Inc.™ Used by permission of Zondervan. All rights reserved worldwide. www.zondervan.com

Scripture quotations marked (NKJV) are taken from the New King James Version®. Copyright © 1982 by Thomas Nelson, Inc. Used by permission. All rights reserved.

Scripture quotations marked (NLT) are taken from the Holy

Bible Versions Quoted

Bible, New Living Translation, copyright ©1996, 2004, 2015 by Tyndale House Foundation. Used by permission of Tyndale House Publishers, Inc., Carol Stream, Illinois 60188. All rights reserved.

Scripture quotations marked (NOG) are taken from the Names of God Bible, GOD'S WORD®, © 1995 God's Word to the Nations. Used by permission of Baker Publishing Group.

Scripture quotations marked (NRSV) are taken from the New Revised Standard Version Bible, copyright © 1989 National Council of the Churches of Christ in the United States of America. Used by permission. All rights reserved worldwide.

Scripture quotations marked (Phillips) are taken from the New Testament in Modern English by J.B Phillips copyright © 1960, 1972 J. B. Phillips. Administered by The Archbishops' Council of the Church of England. Used by Permission.

Scripture quotations marked (RSV) are taken from the Revised Standard Version of the Bible, copyright © 1946, 1952, and 1971 National Council of the Churches of Christ in the United States of America. Used by permission. All rights reserved worldwide.

www.ingramcontent.com/pod-product-compliance
Lightning Source LLC
Chambersburg PA
CBHW051416290426
44109CB00016B/1314